Pseudoscience and Mental Ability

Pseudoscience and Mental Ability

by Jeffrey M. Blum

The Origins and Fallacies
of the IQ Controversy

Monthly Review Press
New York and London

To the memory of Harry Braverman

Copyright © 1978 by Jeffrey M. Blum
All rights reserved

Library of Congress Cataloging in Publication Data
Blum, Jeffrey M   1949–
  Pseudoscience and mental ability.
  A revision of the author's thesis, University of
California, Berkeley.
  Includes bibliographical references and index.
  1. Intellect. 2. Intelligence tests. 3. Nature
and nurture. I. Title.
BF431.B6256 1978   153.9'3   77-81371
ISBN 0-85345-420-5

Monthly Review Press
62 West 14th Street, New York, N.Y. 10011
47 Red Lion Street, London WC1R 4PF

10 9 8 7 6 5 4 3 2 1

Manufactured in the United States of America

If you compare savage with civilized, or compare the successive stages of civilization with one another, you will find untruthfulness and credulity decreasing together; until you reach the modern man of science, who is at once exact in his statements and critical respecting evidence.

—Herbert Spencer,
The Study of Sociology (1873)

Contents

Preface

I began work on this project four years ago when it was a graduate tutorial paper in the sociology department of the University of California, Berkeley. My interest in the topic arose from several sources. Reviewing evidence on the validity of IQ and creativity tests made me realize that most academics and the general public placed far too much faith in these instruments. Leon Kamin's recent discoveries pertaining to the heritability of IQ scores showed that the case for genetic inheritance of ability was also greatly exaggerated. After reading the works of Francis Galton and some lucid histories of the eugenics movement I began to see the historical origins of present misconceptions. From there it was a kind of adventure putting the story together. The race-IQ controversy stimulated by Arthur Jensen and others aroused public interest in the history and abuses of testing and thus indirectly provided me with much encouragement. Also, the events of Watergate unfolding in the background provided inspiration by establishing an atmosphere conducive to the unveiling of scandal.

After completing the original version of the work, I began looking for a publisher and received a positive response from Harry Braverman at Monthly Review Press. He suggested revising a number of chapters and adding several new ones. In particular, Chapters 8, 9 and 12 were written at his request. My decision in the fall of 1976 to use this work for a dissertation brought about another set of revisions. I was fortunate in receiving invaluable assistance from my chairperson, Arlie Hochschild, as well as significant help from the others on my committee—Michael Rogin, Barbara Heyns, and Troy Duster.

While doing the research for this project I was supported as an NIMH trainee in social structure and personality in the program administered by John Clausen and Guy Swanson. Professor Swanson, in addition, provided important help and encouragement. It is a tribute to the liberality of the Berkeley sociology department that a project such as this was allowed to become a dissertation. The department at present maintains a level of intellectual freedom which most social science departments around the country unfortunately do not match. Within the Berkeley department reactions ranged from enthusiastic acceptance and support to strong ambivalence. Some "quantitative" sociologists tended to be unhappy about what they saw as an attack on testing and about the historical passages which portrayed the founders of modern statistical theory in an unfavorable light. Arthur Stinchcombe expressed these reservations when he read the first draft. Although reluctant to support anything critical of psychometrics from a historical perspective, he offered comments which helped me to sharpen the presentation of certain issues.

I am indebted to my father, Gerald S. Blum, for valuable editorial assistance. Also, a number of friends contributed to the project in a variety of ways. I would especially like to acknowledge the incisive comments and suggestions of Raymond Barglow, Jim Geiwitz, Theresa Gonzales, John Hurst, Jeffrey Johnson, Dan Katz, Jim Mulherin, Brian Murphy, Tom Nagy, and David Smith.

1. Introduction

Considerable confusion exists at present concerning mental ability, and particularly its relationship to heredity. The extent of relevant scientific knowledge is much exaggerated in the public mind. People believe that science has proven many things which science has no way of proving. They think that psychologists measure things which the psychologists cannot even conceptualize, let alone measure. It is thought that investigators have established beyond doubt that genetic differences play a major role in determining the intellectual and artistic capacities of individuals. Many people believe that IQ tests and creativity tests accurately assess these capacities, and that certain types of IQ tests can be used to compare the overall ability levels of different ethnic groups. It is even thought that the relative importance of heredity and environment can be gauged precisely, and that a key task for scientists is to decide whether or not the measured intellectual superiority of Caucasians over other groups has a biological basis.

All these ideas are fundamentally erroneous, yet they are widely held. Their popularity stems from many sources—consistency with folk wisdom, prevailing ideologies, prejudice, and the like—but a major factor contributing to their acceptance is their *apparent* scientific verification. This appearance is not simply a delusion conjured by the public. When one examines the history of psychometrics, or intelligence measurement, one finds a succession of recognized leading scientists boldly professing and claiming to have empirical verification for those ideas which the public now mistakenly accepts. Upon close inspection, however, it turns out that the supporting evidence and argumentation contain errors and ambiguities of such magnitude that no claim of scientific confirmation can possibly be warranted. Nevertheless, when viewed from a distance by people who are uncritical of the investigators, the display of voluminous studies attracts the attention of the popular media and acceptance by the general public. Thus, persuasion is effected by establishing a pretense of scientific discovery,[1] although the proponents are for the most part sincere and believe their work to be genuine.

This process of false persuasion by scientific pretense is called *pseudoscience,* and it is the central contention of this book that many popular beliefs about mental ability have been shaped largely by such a process. For pseudoscience to exist two different types of occurrences must be joined. First, there must be attempts at verification which are grossly inadequate. Second, the unwarranted conclusions drawn from such attempts must be successfully disseminated to and believed by a substantial audience.

The conclusions themselves may be demonstrably false or simply untested or untestable. But in every case the claim of scientific verification rests upon violations of the ordinary rules of logic and hypothesis-testing to such an extent that close inspection shows the claim to be clearly unjustified. It is not simply that subsequent evidence overturns established conclusions, but rather that the conclusions were never warranted in the first place.

It is difficult to specify a precise dividing line between legitimate scientific research which happens to have flaws, and research which is so deeply flawed that it becomes a possible component of pseudoscience. The issue clearly is complicated. All scientific work is guided by assumptions, and the defense of one's assumptions becomes a likely source of bias. Particularly when controversial topics are being researched, some amount of bias is inherent in the position of any investigator. The label "pseudoscience" becomes pertinent when the bias displayed by scientists reaches such extraordinary proportions that their relentless pursuit of verification leads them to commit major errors of reasoning. Simple tautological fallacies, a refusal to consider obvious alternative explanations, and the deliberate or unconscious falsification of data constitute some of the basic features of pseudoscience. One can debate whether work which has these flaws is qualitatively different from true science or merely different in degree of bias displayed. Exactly where science in general ceases to be science and becomes scientific pretense no one can say with authority. As one scientist wrote in defense of the pseudoscience concept, "The fact that black shades into white through many shades of gray does not mean that the distinction between black and white is difficult."[2]

While it is possible to identify particular writers and researchers who are clearly practitioners of pseudoscience, pseudoscience in its entirety is a collective product to which different people contribute in different ways. Those who devise the faulty arguments and evidence are the active originators; others who merely repeat and endorse the conclusions are simply carriers. Psychometric pseudoscience has been especially influential during the last sixty years, partly because it has secured acceptance within the field of academic psychology. Many authors of textbooks in that field have functioned unwittingly as carriers. Some have done so enthusiastically, giving full and unqualified endorsements to the erroneous conclusions of the originators. More commonly, however, the endorsements have been qualified and worded ambiguously. The ambiguous statements, though lacking any clear meaning, seem to have the effect of sustaining popular illusions about the extent of scientific knowledge.

The problem may be illustrated by listing six hypotheses which are erroneously viewed as scientifically proven facts. For each of the six I present an example of the kind of statements typically made in support of it. But then I attempt to clarify the hypothesis by giving it a specific meaning which can be evaluated as true, false, uncertain, or even unknowable, given present methodologies. Later in the book we can examine the evidence and arguments pertaining to each of the hypotheses.

Hypothesis #1: *That there are genetically determined differences in mental capacity*

This hypothesis receives a qualified endorsement from the country's most distinguished educational psychologist, Lee J. Cronbach:

> Children tend to be bright who have bright ancestors. Superior
> or inferior power to develop is passed along through heredity ...
> [but] hereditary potential must be stimulated and trained. ...
> Someone put it this way: "Heredity deals the cards, but environ-
> ment plays them."[3]

This view is echoed and elaborated in a major psychology textbook
which states:

> heredity does have an important influence on the development of
> the intelligence of the individual. One way to conceive of this he-
> reditary effect is to imagine the genetic factors as setting limits,
> or ranges, for intelligence which can be attained by people under
> appropriate circumstances. Intelligence scores can be significantly
> influenced by differences in the environment, but the upper limit
> in intelligence which the person can reach through more favorable
> experience is set by genetic mechanisms.[4]

Now consider the weaker interpretation of these statements, according
to which the statements are undeniably true, but also rather trivial:
human beings have a certain finite capacity to develop mental ability.
They depend upon their genes for this capacity, and indeed for their
very existence as human beings. If a person had been born with the
genes of a cat or a dog he would have a much lower mental capacity.
Moreover, there are genetic differences among people. In certain rare
cases—say about one out of every 200 people—persons are born with
known genetic abnormalities which definitely reduce their mental
capacity. It is also *possible* that genetic differences establish different
individual capacities for people generally.

No one can dispute this interpretation, but probably the authors
have something stronger in mind. What they seem to be saying is that
for people in general important differences in individuals' capacities
definitely do exist at birth, and these are caused by differences in their
hereditary genetic endowment. Moreover, the extent to which people
actually do develop mental ability or abilities depends in large degree
upon these differences in genetic potential.

The hypothesis of genetically determined differences in mental
capacity refers to this second interpretation. Generally it is viewed as
scientifically proven. Actually it is scientifically neither true nor false.

Its truth or falsity is both unknown and probably unknowable at present. The statement that science has proven it, or at least established its strong likelihood, is false.

Hypothesis #2: *That there is significant genetic determination of variations in mental ability*

This hypothesis is basically similar to the first, but slightly more modest in that it does not purport to have a way of estimating ultimate human capacities. It merely says that genes are important determiners of the variations observed. It too finds ambiguous support in introductory psychology textbooks, like, for example, the following:

> There is very strong evidence that "normal" variations in intelligence, as well as the more severe disorders such as phenylketonuria, are subject to hereditary influences. Intelligence is not inherited like money from a rich uncle, but IQ scores are strongly influenced by heredity.[5]

The ambiguity here is contained within the phrases, "subject to hereditary influences," and "strongly influenced by heredity." At least three different interpretations are possible. The first says that genetic differences must have *some* effect on variation in IQ scores, however minute or indirect this effect may be. This statement is undoubtedly true, but it is also uninteresting and has no policy implications whatever. Clearly it is not what the authors mean, since they use the word *strongly*. The second interpretation says that genetic differences are *in some way related to* a significant portion (say one-third or more) of the variance in IQ scores. This could be either true or false. Theoretically, it could be confirmed or refuted by evidence, but the current state of the evidence is so limited that no valid conclusions can be drawn. Further investigation may be able to resolve the question, but a number of inherent defects in the available experimental designs make it likely that even if more and better data were gathered, there would still be considerable uncertainty. Moreover, the second interpretation says nothing about the *kind of relationship* there is between IQ scores and genes. It could be direct and naturally occurring, or it could be an indirect result of some extraneous social process. For example, suppose that variations in IQ scores were strongly affected by racial discrimination such that persons with dark skins developed low scores. Conceivably, the effects of this discrimination could be counted as "hereditary influence" because skin color, the basis on which the discrimination took place, was shaped largely by genes. In other words, even if verified, the second interpretation would leave the basic question of nature versus nurture unresolved.

The really interesting question concerns the truth or falsity of the third interpretation, which says that genetic differences do not merely relate to variation in IQ scores, they *determine* it. There is a strong, direct, and naturally occurring relationship between genes and IQ scores. Thus we may use concepts like "intelligence genes," and genetic superiority or inferiority. The significant genetic determination hypothesis refers to this interpretation. Most people believe the hypothesis is true. It is currently a topic of some controversy. Considerable research is being done in an attempt to validate the second interpretation because most of the researchers mistakenly think their data will establish the validity of the third interpretation. But, alas, the interesting hypothesis in question admits to solution by no available methodology; thus whether or not it is true is presently unknown and unknowable. Claims that science has proven it, or is on the road to proving it, are false.

Hypothesis # 3: *That IQ tests measure mental capacity*

Fifty years ago test designers had no compunctions about saying that one's IQ score was a reliable indicator of one's capacity for intellectual or artistic achievement, and that to be a genius one had to have a very high IQ score. Nowadays, it is not usually stated so bluntly, but it is still implied in statements like the following one by Richard J. Herrnstein, a recent chairman of the Harvard psychology department.

> The major figures in the study of intelligence have called it "a capacity for abstract reasoning and problem solving," "the ability to educe relations," "general mental adaptability," "the capacity to act purposefully, and to think rationally and to deal effectively with the environment," and so on.[6]

Interpreted one way, this passage says that the major figures in the study of intelligence have realized that IQ tests do in fact measure mental adaptability and the capacity to think rationally and abstractly. Literally, however, the passage says only that certain persons have conceived of intelligence in this manner. This leaves open the possibility of another interpretation: that intelligence is a hypothetical construct which has been conceived of rather broadly; IQ tests do not necessarily measure all these things. The hypothesis that IQ tests measure mental capacity refers to the first interpretation. It gained acceptance at a time when available data did not permit any rigorous test. New evidence gathered during the last twenty years has discredited the hypothesis, so that we may now conclude that it is almost certainly false. At best it is a gross exaggeration of something else which is true—many persons with IQ scores below certain low levels appear to lack certain kinds of capacities.

Hypothesis #4: *That IQ tests measure abilities needed for success in high-level occupations*

Speaking on behalf of this claim, three respected sociologists write that what they "now mean by intelligence is something like the probability of acceptable performance (given the opportunity) in occupations varying in social status."[7] The stronger meaning of this statement makes it a very bold assertion indeed: in every occupation people with higher IQ scores are more likely to perform acceptably. The higher the status of an occupation, the higher IQ score one needs to have a good chance of doing well. In very high-status occupations only persons with very high IQ scores are likely to do well. This hypothesis has been discredited by several studies showing no correlation between IQ score and performance in a variety of high-level occupations. However, use of the qualifying words *something like* suggests that the statement may also have a weaker meaning, perhaps that for every occupation there is a threshold of minimum necessary IQ score, below which a person is not likely to perform acceptably. This threshold tends to be higher for high-status occupations than for low-status ones. Undoubtedly such thresholds exist for all jobs, although recent evidence suggests they are probably quite a bit lower than previously imagined. Since the thresholds have not been measured with any accuracy it is not known to what extent they parallel the status of occupations.

Hypothesis #5: *That blacks are intellectually inferior*

The topic of racial superiority and inferiority has become a delicate matter requiring tact. Many textbook writers simply omit all discussion of it. Not too long ago, however, one could find the author of a best-selling psychology text making the following statement: "Even under somewhat favorable circumstances the Negro intelligence mean tends to remain below that of Whites."[8] This passage was followed by a story about a town in Canada where escaped slaves were "treated with equality," but a hundred years later the average black IQ score was still fifteen points below the average white score.

The ambiguity here is contained in the word *intelligence*. On the one hand, it refers simply to score on IQ tests designed by whites. On the other hand, its popular connotation is much broader, being something like the all-around ability to adapt, to think rationally, to use abstractions, and so forth. The hypothesis of inferior black intelligence contends that blacks generally are less able to do these things than whites. However, this cannot reasonably be concluded from test scores because the tests generally are acknowledged to contain a variety of cultural biases favoring whites over blacks. On at least one test designed by blacks where the bias was intentionally reversed, blacks scored considerably higher than whites. Moreover, it is very doubtful that any tests measure abilities as broad as the popular meaning of the word *intelligence*. Thus the hypothesis of inferior black intelligence is certainly unconfirmed, and it is even difficult to imagine how it could be confirmed. Because making explicit arguments for it would justifiably open one to the charge of being a racist, most proponents have been content to use ambiguous language and let the matter rest at that.

Hypothesis #6: *That blacks are innately intellectually inferior*

This is the controversial assertion that blacks are genetically, biologically inferior to whites. It was considered unquestionably true in the United States until well after the First World War. Then it became associated with Nazi ideology, and partly for this reason it rapidly lost its respectability in the United States and Great Britain after 1940. For the last seven years it has been making a small comeback. Psychologists like Arthur Jensen have gone out on a limb to defend it and have bolstered its credibility somewhat, but in the process they have tarnished their own reputations. The strongest statement one will hear in support of it from "unimpeachable" scientists is that it may well be true. Consider the following from what purports to be the most recent, comprehensive, and objective treatment of the subject.

1. Observed average differences in the scores of members of different racial-ethnic groups on intellectual-ability tests probably reflect in part inadequacies and biases in the tests themselves, in part differences in environmental conditions among the groups, and in part genetic differences among the groups. It should be emphasized that these three factors are not necessarily independent, and may interact.

2. A rather wide range of positions concerning the relative weight to be given to these three factors can reasonably be taken on the basis of current evidence, and a sensible person's position might well differ for different abilities, for different groups, and for different tests.[9]

Literally this passage says that scientists are unable to answer the question, since "a rather wide range of positions ... can reasonably be taken on the basis of current evidence." However, the passage also projects a somewhat stronger meaning: although it is difficult to tell precisely how important genetic differences are compared with environmental differences and the effects of biases in the tests, the evidence shows that black genetic inferiority exists to at least *some substantial degree.* This latter meaning is clearly erroneous. The hypothesis is unverifiable for the same reasons that the second and fifth hypotheses cannot be verified. It is also much less plausible than is generally supposed.

Usually one associates pseudoscience with individual cranks working in isolation to promote their eccentric theories. Most instances of pseudoscience conform to this description and involve nothing more than the development of an idiosyncratic cult. When social circumstances are favorable, however, the perpetrators may acquire sufficient resources and respectability that they appear to the society generally as legitimate scientists rather than cranks.

The prevailing illusions about mental ability, heredity, and race stem from a kind of pseudoscience which has been for the most part highly respectable. Between 1900 and 1930 much of it occurred in a field known as eugenics; since 1917 it has flourished in the field of psychometrics, or mental measurement, particularly in relation to the IQ test. Then as now, the leading practitioners were housed in major universities, and for the last fifty years their work has received extensive financial support in grants from the federal government and major foundations. Nevertheless, the illusions perpetrated have been virtually as flagrant as might be expected from the work of an isolated crank.

If indeed the work is as fallacy-ridden as we suggest, one must wonder how respectable scientists could ever become involved in such a dubious enterprise. The answer lies in the fact that scientists do not make discoveries exactly as they please, but under constraints and within guidelines handed down by the history of their discipline. Every mature scientific field has an accepted *paradigm*—an overarching body of theory that specifies certain questions as worthy of study and suggests methods of investigation which can lead to appropriate answers.[10] But a paradigm can be *defective*. It can specify questions without having any available method of scientifically validating their answers. When a defective paradigm has been adopted by a community of scientists, individuals who subscribe to it continuously face a dilemma of whether to admit failure and give up or to bend the rules in order to arrive at conclusions by means normally prohibited in scientific inquiry. In short, they must either distort or fail. Those who decide to admit failure and give up do not become eminent. The field's leaders are those who manage to swallow the necessary corruption of scientific practices and then to delude themselves, their benefactors, and the public.

This in essence is what happened during the key formative period of eugenics and psychometrics (1900-1925). The leading eugenicists and mental testers devised a number of false solutions to major theoretical problems. Although their work was criticized, social conditions were sufficiently auspicious for them that they retained important academic posts, attracted extensive funding, and recruited a sizable number of disciples, assistants, and successors. Their work, while almost worthless as science, did perform important ideological services for the ruling elite, and this was sufficient to ensure the field's survival and growth. As the field developed, this pseudoscience increased in complexity and became more and more a product of the cooperative efforts of many individuals. Tacit norms of communication emerged, allowing key words and concepts to be used in ways conducive to its spread. Thus much of the deception has come to be embedded in the common usage of terms like *intelligence, heritability* and *culture-fair*. Although critics repeatedly have pointed to the major fallacies and uncertainties, proponents have either ignored these issues or have mentioned them in passing without acknowledging their true significance. Persistent criticism has not yet managed to cripple the pseudoscience totally, but has at least given it an aura of slight disreputability. This in turn has made most textbook writers want to maintain some distance between themselves and the false ideas they convey. Recourse to ambiguous phraseology has become a favorite device for accomplishing this. Hence the statements described previously.

Contemporary pseudoscience in psychometrics can be understood only by knowing how the discipline developed its concepts, vocabulary, and experimental procedures. For this reason we begin by reviewing the history of eugenics and intelligence testing. Chapter 2 examines the origin of the eugenics paradigm in the writings of its two seminal theorists, Francis Galton and Herbert Spencer. Chapter 3 focuses on the eugenics movement and the social conditions which led to the adoption of the eugenics paradigm by scientists. Chapter 4 looks at early empirical studies attempting to prove the inheritance of mental ability. Chapter 5 examines the transition from eugenics to psychometrics— how mental testing grew out of the concerns of eugenicists, and how the subsequent decline of eugenics affected mental testing.

Part II assesses contemporary arguments and evidence that pertain to the six hypotheses discussed above. This is done in three separate chapters, one on the validity of IQ tests, one on the question of heritability, and one on IQ scores and race. This section also examines two departures within psychometrics which have occurred during the last twenty years. The first is the restorationists, a group of scientists who have been attempting through their own rhetorical persuasiveness to revive some previously discredited portions of the old pseudoscience of eugenics. The second is creativity tests, an enterprise which, despite the noble intentions of its proponents, has furnished fertile ground for the extension of pseudoscience.

The third and final part of this book seeks to interpret the historical record and to deal with some of the social issues underlying the testing controversy. Its first chapter presents a theory of pseudoscience and discusses it in relation to the two cases of eugenics-psychometrics in Western countries and Lysenkoism in the Soviet Union. The second chapter analyzes the related issues of social class, meritocratic ideology, and inequalities in schooling. The concluding chapter attempts to alter the image of mental ability by pointing to evidence drawn from studies of persons with notable accomplishments.

The Rise of
Eugenics and Psychometrics

2. Galton, Spencer, and the Eugenics Paradigm

The defective paradigm that has molded the field of mental testing and individual differences took shape during the last thirty years of the nineteenth century. It developed as a part of the general effort to apply concepts of biological evolution to problems of human societies. Usually known as Social Darwinism, this effort found its most prolific and influential spokesman in the British philosopher, Herbert Spencer. The theory that humans differ from one another in amount of general intelligence was first formulated by Spencer. Previously the concept of intelligence differences had been used by Charles Darwin as a way of discussing contrasts in the behavior of various animal species. Spencer simply imported the concept into psychology by assuming that humans differed from each other in the complexity of their nervous systems, just as birds and mammals differed from bugs and fishes.

Although Spencer usually wrote his ideas down in the form of rigid, scientific laws, he rarely attempted to test them empirically. The vision of a science of individual differences devoted to proving Social Darwinist ideas mathematically emanated from Sir Francis Galton, a cousin of Darwin and founder of the eugenics movement. Galton fully elaborated a theory of mental ability and proposed ways of testing it which formed the basis of many subsequent attempts by his followers to prove the theory true. Galton and Spencer shared many similar ideas, but it was Galton and his disciples in the eugenics movement who gathered data and elevated the ideas from the realm of ideology into the realm of pseudoscience. For this reason, the paradigm in question is called the *eugenics paradigm.*

At its core is the overarching, general theory that social conditions are determined by the hereditary, biological qualities of the people involved. This theory was applied principally to five kinds of conditions: (1) outstanding accomplishment; eminence; genius; (2) social problems in general; pauperism, crime, insanity, alcoholism, etc.; (3) economic inequality; the existence of social classes; (4) racial and ethnic domination; white supremacy in particular; (5) unequal performance in schools; good and poor students. Once one gets the general gist of the theory, anticipating its various usages becomes easy: the poor are poor because they have poorly developed nervous systems; the rich are rich because they are highly intelligent; recognized geniuses become eminent because they have tremendous natural ability; crime, unemployment, insanity, and alcoholism are all caused by congenital feeble-mindedness; blacks were made into slaves because they were less intelligent than whites; certain students do better in school because they have greater mental capacity than others; and so forth.

The attempt to build a science around propositions such as these began with the publication of Galton's *Hereditary Genius, an Inquiry into its Laws and Consequences* in 1869.[1] As the general theory is enunciated more clearly in this work than anywhere else, it is worthwhile to examine a few notable quotations.

Galton began by stating his intention:

> I propose to show in this book that a man's natural abilities are derived by inheritance, under exactly the same limitations as are the form and physical features of the whole organic world. Consequently, as it is easy, notwithstanding those limitations, to obtain by careful selection a permanent breed of dogs or horses gifted with peculiar powers of running, or of doing anything else, so it would be quite practicable to produce a highly-gifted race of men by judicious marriages during several consecutive generations.[2]

Galton arrived at this bold conclusion by examining the pedigrees of famous people. He discovered that close relatives of eminent people had a much better than average chance of being eminent themselves, and from this he concluded that talent and genius were both hereditary. Galton reasoned that character and abilities were probably inherited in much the same way as height and eye color. The person's environment was simply like a kind of screen onto which innate qualities were projected. To be successful required *natural ability*—a combination of intelligence, motivation, and mental power, all inherited. Specific interests and aptitudes, as well as general ability, were transmitted biologically. Hence, one could be a born musician or have an innate taste for science.

Galton equated eminence with outstanding natural ability, and wrote,

> I feel convinced that no man can achieve a very high reputation without being gifted with very high abilities; and I trust I have shown reason to believe that few who possess these very high abilities can fail in achieving eminence.[3]

Equating the two enabled him to estimate the amount of innate talent any given race or nation possessed according to how many eminent persons it produced. On this basis he concluded that the ancient Greeks were far superior to modern Europeans, and that blacks were an inferior race. He attributed the Dark Ages to the improper breeding practices of the Catholic Church. Supposedly the Church had prolonged that culturally barren period by encouraging celibacy which kept the "abler classes" from reproducing themselves, and "brutalized the breed of our forefathers" by "selecting the rudest portion of the community to be, alone, the parents of future generations."[4]

Galton's *Hereditary Genius* was influential from the start. Prior to its publication people generally had believed that, except for a few geniuses and a few idiots, all persons were equally endowed, and achievement mainly depended upon hard work.[5] Galton, on the other hand, insisted that hereditary endowment was the major determinant of any kind of success or achievement. Included among the early converts was Charles Darwin. Previously he had espoused the traditional view, but after reading *Hereditary Genius* he wrote his cousin that he had never "read anything more interesting and original."[6] Two years later Darwin himself was writing that heredity shaped different levels of intelligence among humans.[7]

Galton's theory was vigorously attacked by liberal sociologist Lester Ward. Ward's passionate concern was to promote universal public education, and he strongly objected to any theory that implied that schooling would be wasted on the lower classes.[8] He agreed with Galton that genius was hereditary, but he rejected the attempt to equate genius and eminence. He insisted that the lower classes spawned numerous "potential geniuses" born with sufficient natural ability to become great, but were thwarted by their environments which offered too little opportunity for education. Charles Cooley, another sociologist, used the metaphor of a river to argue that the number of eminent people was not a good measure of the natural ability possessed by a race:

> We know that a race has once produced a large amount of natural genius in a short time, just as we know that the river has a large volume in some places. We see, also, that the number of eminent men seems to dwindle and disappear; but we have good reason to think that social conditions can cause genius to remain hidden, just as we have good reason to think that a river may find its way through an underground channel. Must we not conclude, in the one case as in the other, that what is not seen does not cease to be, that genius is present though fame is not?[9]

Ward and Cooley did not reject Galton's theory completely; they modified it to give the environment more of a role. They were willing to accept hereditary determinants of behavior as long as these did not rule out the possibility of environmental determinants along with them.

Galton was ambitious. He shunned the easy compromise position that both heredity and environment were important, and sought to prove that heredity was overwhelmingly more important. He coined the phrase, *nature and nurture,* saying that the latter was only a minor contributing factor to life outcomes. Thus began the nature-nurture controversy, which has attracted considerable attention off and on for the last hundred years.

Galton's theory and the controversy which arose from it defined two major research questions. One was to identify and measure the hereditary traits which caused success and failure. Since it was not agreed that high natural ability and eminence were equivalent, Galton and his followers needed to find some independent measure of natural ability which could then be used to predict greatness. The second problem was to prove that the measured abilities were indeed hereditary. This meant showing that they were determined by genetic endowment and were not greatly affected by variations in environment or experience.

As things turned out, both questions were elusive, and efforts to answer them generated a vast flow of pseudoscience. Galton's major attempts to prove his theory will be examined in Chapter 4, but here it is worth noting that the widespread acceptance of that theory by IQ testers guided the development of IQ testing in several important ways. Galton hypothesized that natural ability had a normal distribution throughout the population; tests were subsequently designed to display a normal distribution of scores.[10] Galton's theory lent credibility to the assumption that performance in school was a valid indicator of mental capacity. Because natural ability always manifests itself, and great accomplishment was not possible without high natural ability, schools could be regarded as places of fair and open competition in which students with high or low ability demonstrated their level of innate talent by compiling excellent or mediocre academic records, respectively. Galton went so far as to use the results of a mathematics prize competition at Cambridge to calculate precise ratios and distribution of natural ability among the entrants.[11]

He also originated the practice of setting up absurdly simplistic environmentalist explanations as "straw men." For example, he reasoned that if social obstacles affected a person's chances of becoming eminent, America would have more eminent people per capita than England, because America's class barriers were less rigid and defined. The fact that England had more famous persons supposedly proved that the English were a superior breed and social obstacles were unimportant.[12] Like the straw man in *The Wizard of Oz,* this one seemingly has no brain. There were many good environmentalist explanations of why America had fewer eminent persons—e.g., economic underdevelopment, shortage of time span to develop cultural institutions, and the complete absence of universities—but Galton ignored these and attributed a ridiculous position to his hypothetical opponents in order to "prove" them wrong. This practice, along with the normal distribution and the view of school as proving ground, is encountered repeatedly in the development of eugenics and psychometrics.

Although Galton devised mental tests and launched the concept of individual differences in ability, subsequent researchers chose to emphasize Spencer's concept of intelligence rather than Galton's natural ability construct. Probably this was because Galton's concept was too comprehensive. It included motivation as well as capacity. Saying that both were shaped by heredity left too little room for learning and environment to affect performance. As a kind of expedient compromise with learning theorists and proponents of education, psychologists decided that only intelligence or mental capacity would be viewed as inherited, and that motivation would be seen as something acquired. The problem thus became to measure the hereditary trait, intelligence.

Spencer defined intelligence as the biologically given capacity of organisms to adapt to their environments. One gets a good idea of how he conceptualized it by reading his explanation of why Caucasians predominated over other races. He wrote that those grades of humans,

> having well-developed nervous systems will display a relatively marked premeditation—an habitual representation of more various possibilities of cause, and conduct, and consequence—a greater tendency to suspense of judgments and an easier modification of judgments that have been formed. Those having nervous systems less developed, and with fewer and simpler sets of connexions among their plexuses, will show less of hesitation—will be prone to premature conclusions that are difficult to change. Unlikenesses of this kind appear when we contrast the larger brained races with the smaller brained races—when from the comparatively-judicial intellect of the civilized man we pass to the intellect of the uncivilized man, sudden in its inferences, incapable of balancing evidence, and adhering obstinately to first impressions. And we may observe a difference similar in kind but smaller in degree between the modes of thought of men and women; for the women are the more quick to draw conclusions, and retain more pertinaciously the beliefs once formed.[13]

Having a well-developed nervous system was synonymous with having high intelligence, and in this regard white males clearly were superior to women and blacks. They were, in Darwinian terms, more highly evolved. It should not be thought, however, that Spencer had any great respect for the intelligence of the average white male; people in general he held in low esteem.

> We have but to observe human action as it meets us at every turn, to see that the average intelligence, incapable of guiding conduct even in simple matters, where but a very moderate reach of reason

would suffice, must fail in apprehending with due clearness the natural sanctions of ethical principles. The unthinking ineptitude with which even the routine of life is carried on by the mass of men, shows clearly that they have nothing like the insight required for self-guidance in the absence of an authoritative code of conduct. Take a day's experience, and observe the lack of thought indicated from hour to hour.[14]

Observations like these convinced Spencer that differences among humans could best be understood by using Darwin's conception of evolution to describe differences among diverse members of the animal kingdom. But why measure differences in intelligence among humans? Spencer might have answered—to prove once and for all that most humans are subhuman!

Spencer's theory posited a necessary inverse relation between intellectual capacity and fertility. As recent observers have pointed out:

Equating an increase in intelligence with greater growth of the nervous system, and an increase in fertility with greater growth of the reproductive system, Spencer proposed that the nervous and reproductive systems of individuals compete for the same fund of "phosphorous," "neurine," and other nutrient elements. His political economy of cellular relationships was like two parties *competing* for the same (scarce) sum of wealth; an acquisition on the part of one party would imply a loss to the other. Because of this inverse relation, an increase in the intellectual status of the race can only take place at the expense of its ability to propagate at previous rates.[15]

Within any given race the least intelligent individuals were likely to be the most fertile. If all persons lived long enough to reproduce, then the relatively intelligent would dwindle in proportion, and social progress would be replaced by decay. Spencer suggested that humans might even lose their competitive advantage over other species. Fortunately, however, many people starved to death at an early age. Since the poorest people were almost always the least intelligent, plagues, starvation, and inadequate shelter kept their fertility in check and preserved the desirable qualities of human beings. Any attempt to ameliorate these conditions by social reform thus could have disastrous consequences for humanity as a whole. This was the main conclusion Spencer reached by using the concept, "intelligence."

It is often erroneously claimed that IQ tests have no specific theoretical basis, and that they are simply a pragmatic attempt to assess individual differences which have been discovered empirically. Actually, efforts to measure intelligence *do* stem from a theory—Spencer's—but it is a theory which most psychometricians would prefer not to remember.

The eugenics paradigm turned out to be defective because the two major research questions which defined it were dictated by the desire to validate Social Darwinism without having a method of scientifically doing this. On the one hand, Social Darwinist theories were probably false in their entirety. On the other hand, the wish to validate them preceded by at least a century the development of methods which could make scientific validation possible, if the theories were true. To use Thomas Kuhn's metaphor of routine science as puzzle-solving, we might say that Galton and Spencer handed their disciples a puzzle whose pieces did not fit together.

The first research question was how to measure intelligence—accepted as the crucial hereditary trait in question. Spencer's original theory that intelligence levels were indicated by brain size proved to be erroneous. Repeated efforts failed to discover any reliable correlation between brain size and measures of performance.[16] It was also found that certain Asiatic races tended to have brains larger than those of most whites. Researchers' inability to identify physical traits which could be equated with intelligence created a void subsequently filled by the use of IQ tests. Researchers next sought to measure capacity for performance in general (that is, intelligence) by measuring a particular kind of performance. IQ tests were asked to predict a great deal—not only marks in school, but economic success or failure, excellence as a scientist or artist, life-adjustment, and various other things. The widely disparate nature of the different behaviors involved made it impossible for the tests to closely simulate any one of the activities. This greatly decreased the likelihood that tests would have any significant validity for most of the things they sought to predict.

Proving that intelligence was hereditary constituted the second question. If intelligence had been a simple, measurable, physical trait, probably this would have been possible. Testers could point to the stability of the trait over time, its immunity to change when the environment was altered, and these coupled with some measure of relationship between close relatives on the trait would provide convincing evidence that the trait was largely hereditary. However, the decision to measure intelligence with performance tests meant that researchers would have to prove that a specific kind of performance was inherited. To do this they would have to take people with identical environments and differing genetic endowments, and measure differences in performance between the two. But this was a logical impossibility because a person's own performance is a crucial part of his or her environment. Thus, people performing differently cannot possibly have identical environments.

This is a bare outline of why the eugenics paradigm was defective. The process will become clearer when we examine actual empirical studies in Chapters 4 and 5. First, though, we must ask why the paradigm was adopted in the first place.

3. Social Darwinism and the Eugenics Movement

Francis Galton devoted most of his career to promoting eugenics as a science. His empirical investigations began with those which preceded publication of his first book in 1869 and continued until shortly before his death in 1911. He did not, however, acquire many coworkers and disciples until after eugenics had become an active movement for social reform in England and America around the turn of the century. At that time a science of eugenics seemed like a worthwhile project, partly because several decades of Social Darwinist influence had already conditioned people to accept the major assumptions of the eugenics paradigm. As Richard Hofstadter puts it, "popular credulity about the scope and variety of hereditary traits had been almost boundless."[1]

Particularly in the United States, Herbert Spencer enjoyed tremendous popularity. Charles Cooley estimated that between 1870 and 1890 most Americans who had undertaken to study sociology were drawn to the subject chiefly through Spencer's writings.[2] Educated people during this period viewed Spencer as "a great man, a grand intellect," and "a giant figure in the history of thought."[3]

Spencer's popularity, on one level, is attributable to his role as an ideologue whose theories justified the more grotesque features of capitalist development. On another level, his notion of biological pre-destination may be viewed as an outgrowth of traditional religious doctrines. Nicholas Pastore points out that in the nineteenth century it had been common to justify social institutions as products of divine will. Economic success and failure were thought to have been pre-ordained by God. General acceptance of Darwin's controversial theory, however, undermined traditional religious beliefs and created a need for new legitimating explanations. Into this void stepped Spencer, Galton, and other theorists who took the older religious idea of predestination and adorned it with a new, scientific vocabulary. No longer were eco-nomic success and failure preordained by God; they were predestined by differences in the complexity of individuals' nervous systems.[4] Thus, eugenics, being an offshoot of Social Darwinism, would occa-sionally be referred to as "scientific Calvinism."

Although Spencer was most influential in the United States and England, the first major scientific community associated with the idea of biological predestination developed in Italy. During the 1870s Cesare Lombroso, professor of legal medicine at the University of Turin, established the field known as criminal anthropology. Lombroso and his colleagues invoked the eugenics paradigm to explain crime. Criminality was assumed to be hereditary, and different sorts of crimi-nals—murderers, rapists, and thieves, for example—were each thought to have distinguishing physical traits which differentiated them from other kinds of criminals as well as from normal human beings. In general, lawbreakers were conceived to have facial and cranial features re-sembling those of wild animals and non-European races. Numerous studies were carried out to establish the validity of these theories, and although the results were mostly negative, and investigators gradually came to stress the role of environment and society in determining crime, biodeterminist pseudoscience was sufficiently strong that the original theories became influential worldwide.

Around the turn of the century, the advent of powerful eugenics movements in England and America caused the international center of hereditarian pseudoscience to shift to those two countries. Regardless of how popular Spencer's philosophy became, it was never likely to inspire much scientific investigation. As for policy, its major recom-mendation was simply that the government *abstain* from intervening in the economy, for which no precise science, merely a general sense of agreement with the philosophy, was needed. Eugenics, on the other hand, called for active government intervention to alter society's breeding patterns. For laws to be passed and sterilizations enforced, officials needed to know in more than a general way what laws were best and which people should be sterilized. Thus the activist, reformist nature of eugenics made it a source of pseudoscience where earlier versions of Social Darwinism had produced only treatises unaccompanied by data.

Spencer's laissez-faire Darwinian individualism gave way to the Darwinian collectivism of eugenics and race theories when social conditions altered the public's attitude toward government regulation. In the United States this trend came to be known as the Progressive Movement, an odd assortment of predominantly middle-class agitation for reform during the period 1900 to 1917. The American eugenics movement arose simultaneously with the Progressive Movement, and the two had many members in common.[5] In both England and America eugenics had liberal as well as conservative proponents. Eugenicists agreed upon the need for societal planning to achieve better breeding. They joined in rejecting Spencer's conclusion that progress occurred only through natural selection while accepting his premise that social events were determined by the biological heredity of persons. The previous, widespread acceptance of this premise made it likely that as soon as complacency and individualism were replaced by reformist sentiment, regulation of breeding practices would be one of the reforms sought. Conservatives viewed eugenics as a substitute for economic reform; liberal eugenicists saw it as a necessary supplement.

Eugenics became popular in the United States because its ideas seemed plausible and correct, and its reforms seemed urgently necessary. The plausibility of the claim that better breeding could cure most social ills stemmed from its compatibility with existing prejudices and past intellectual trends. Most important was the continuity with earlier versions of Social Darwinism. Also important was the racism espoused by both liberal and conservative eugenicists. The Civil War and the abolitionist movement had inspired a brief flourish of idealism dedicated to the proposition that all men were created equal, but after the failure of reconstruction in the South, Americans settled back into a wholehearted acceptance of racial prejudice.

Thomas Gossett points out that

> what is noticeable is that American thought of the period 1880–1920 generally lacks any perception of the Negro as a human being

with potentialities for improvement. Most of the people who wrote about Negroes were firmly in the grip of the idea that intelligence and temperament are racially determined and unalterable. They concluded, therefore, that the failures of Reconstruction, the low educational status of the Negro, the high statistics of crime, disease, and poverty, were simply the inevitable results of his heredity. The defenders of the Negro were thus cast in the role of sickly humanitarians who refused to face facts.[6]

Eugenicists and Progressives jointly promoted laws which sanctioned the emerging caste system of racial segregation.[7] The popularity of these laws among most whites contributed indirectly to the popularity of eugenics. Theodore Roosevelt aided the movement when he repeatedly warned Anglo-Saxon mothers to have more children so as to avoid the danger of "race-suicide." America was sufficiently racist that Galton's favoring the eventual elimination of blacks did not appear to undermine eugenics. Galton wrote that he regretted that "there exists a sentiment, for the most part quite unreasonable, against the gradual extinction of an inferior race."[8]

Eugenics also derived credibility from the prevalence of nativist sentiment. Many eugenicists argued for the innate superiority of native-born white Americans and those of Anglo-Saxon stock. Anti-immigrant ideas were supported by the fact that most immigrants were lower class, a fact which was interpreted as proving their innate inferiority. Eugenicists could point to the influx of many immigrants from central and southern Europe whose rustic habits and poor English created the impression of a decline in "the nation's average intelligence."[9] Nativism undermined working-class unity. It made native-born white craft-union leaders wary of unskilled immigrant laborers, and discouraged native-born white craft workers from following radical labor leaders, most of whom were recent immigrants. Because business managers found this prospect congenial, they encouraged nativist sentiment, and thus accorded it considerable respectability.

The sudden emergence of modern genetics provided the immediate stimulus for formation of eugenics movements. The rediscovery of Gregor Mendel's writings on genetics in 1900, together with August Weismann's studies of evolution during the previous fifteen years, formed the basis of the new science. Galton first launched the movement in England amidst the excitement created by the rediscovery of Mendel. However, it was Weismann's conclusive refutation of the

Lamarckian hypothesis of the inheritance of acquired characteristics which seemed to provide the crucial evidence in favor of eugenics. Previously most people had agreed with Lamarck that acquired characteristics could be passed on by heredity: Darwin and Spencer were among these, as were almost all liberal intellectuals. Lester Ward, immersed in the biological reductionism of the period, had refused to abandon the Lamarckian hypothesis because he felt that by doing so he would be conceding that education had no value for the future of mankind, but solely for those presently receiving it. He proposed to "retain the illusion until science has decided the matter definitely."[10]

By 1900 the matter had been decided experimentally. Numerous attempts were made to demonstrate the inheritance of acquired characteristics in the laboratory, but all failed. The weight of evidence clearly supported Weismann's contrary hypothesis. In the context of the times this was a dramatic victory for eugenics and an apparent catastrophe for advocates of social reform. If the hereditary qualities which constituted human nature could not be altered by changes in the environment, then clearly the most useful sort of reform would be that which altered society's breeding practices. So thought the many persons who joined Galton in a eugenics crusade for human betterment.

Earlier Galton had prophesied that the spread of a eugenics creed would be fostered by scientific advances in the study of heredity. The rise of modern genetics constituted such an advance and it had this effect. So Galton's prophecy proved correct, despite the fact that he persistently refused to accept Mendel's work, preferring as he did the more traditional belief that hereditary traits were transmitted through the blood corpuscles.

Around the world, eugenics movements and the young science of genetics cross-fertilized one another. The science acquired enthusiasm and a sense of importance from the movements, and the movements derived respectability and an aura of tested validity from the science. By 1910 eugenics campaigns were underway not only in England and the United States, but also in Scotland, Ireland, Germany, Austria, Scandinavia, France, Italy, Japan, and across South America.[11] Prior to 1930 eugenics was most influential in Great Britain and the United States. Between 1930 and 1945 its greatest impact was felt in Germany and the adjacent territories.

The fact that many people believed eugenics could solve major social problems is accounted for by the compatibility of this belief with prevailing ideological trends. The sense of urgency which translated this belief into an actual eugenics *movement* stemmed from the worsening of social problems at the end of the nineteenth century. Particularly in the United States, massive immigration and rapid industrialization had within a few decades created cities with poor sanitation, high crime rates, and clearly visible concentrations of poverty. Attempts of social workers and institutions to deal with these problems only made them more apparent. Unprecedented levels of class conflict between workers and capitalists likewise contributed to the feeling that reform was urgently needed. Different groups favored different sorts of reforms, but among the respectable, white, Protestant middle class, eugenics was a favored cause.

Much of the appeal of eugenics rested on the belief that scientific breeding could provide an effective means of reducing crime, poverty, and labor unrest. Increasingly, the supporters of eugenics emphasized their creed's importance as social control. The president of the American Association for the Advancement of Science foreshadowed this trend in 1893 when he proposed to end all crime and drunkenness "by expressing in positive or creative terms the scientific breeding of man."[12] One might say that eugenicists, intoxicated by the rapid progress in genetics, saw no limits to what their enterprise could accomplish.

One index of the popularity attained by the American eugenics movement is the estimate that between 1910 and 1914 the general magazines carried more articles on eugenics than on the three questions of slums, tenements, and living standards, combined.[13] The movement's respectability is attested to by the definition of eugenics put forward in the 1910 edition of the *Encyclopedia Britannica:*

> Eugenics—the modern name given to the science which deals with the influences which improve the inborn qualities of a race, but more particularly with those which develop them to the utmost advantage, and which generally serves to disseminate knowledge and encourage action in the direction of perpetuating a higher racial standard.[14]

In England, Galton received many honors for his work: the royal medal in 1886, the Darwin medal in 1902, honorary degrees from

Oxford and Cambridge in 1904 and 1905, and finally in 1909, knighthood.[15] Having the dimensions of a fad and the reputation of a science, eugenics naturally exerted considerable influence on government. In the United States, by 1931 thirty states had passed compulsory sterilization laws, despite the strong opposition of the Roman Catholic Church.[16]

Eugenics quickly developed a strong presence in American universities as well. Because faculties were generally drawn from the social strata most sympathetic to eugenics, they typically included a significant number of the movement's proponents. One historian examined the backgrounds of 144 leading eugenicists and found that roughly two-thirds had occupations of "Educator, Scientist, Professor, or Physician."[17] A 1928 survey of heads of biology departments dramatically illustrated the fact that most scientists thought highly of eugenics. When asked, "Do you believe it advisable at the present time to establish graduate work in eugenics?" 106 replied "yes" and only 41 said "no." When asked if they felt eugenics courses should be required of all sociology students, 73 percent said "yes," and only 8 percent disagreed.[18]

A number of important leaders in the field of psychology were either eugenicists or strong sympathizers of the movement. As these people frequently acknowledged their intellectual debt to Galton, they were sometimes known as "the Galton school." Included among them was William McDougall, unquestionably the country's leading social psychologist until his influence was undermined by the spread of behaviorism in the 1920s. His textbook, *An Introduction to Social Psychology,* was published in over twenty editions, more than any other psychological text of the period. Even more important was Edward L. Thorndike, the country's leading educational psychologist until around 1940. Thorndike, who authored fifty books and received over $300,000 in grants from the Carnegie Foundation, did much to shape the curriculum and teaching methods of American public schools.[19] Also important were Lewis Terman and the other psychologists who did most to popularize and promote IQ tests.

To become a leading academic required then, as it does now, some combination of intellectual ability and the ability to attract funds. Charles B. Davenport, America's foremost eugenicist, had the former to some extent and the latter in great abundance. Initially Davenport was a respected biology professor who experimented with plant and animal breeding. Several years of lobbying for funds paid off in 1904 when the newly incorporated Carnegie Institution agreed to support a biological experiment station on Long Island with Davenport as head. This greatly enhanced Davenport's prestige, so that when his interests turned toward eugenics three years later, he was able to secure funds for that as well. In 1910 Mrs. E.H. Harriman, wife of the railroad magnate, was persuaded to support a Eugenics Record Office near the original experiment station. Over the next eight years she contributed something in excess of $500,000 to the office, which became a kind of national headquarters for the eugenics movement. In 1918 the Carnegie Institution assumed financial responsibility for both operations and merged the two under Davenport's leadership.[20]

It would be too simplistic to attribute the Carnegie Institution's interest in eugenics to the fact that Andrew Carnegie was for many years an ardent disciple of Herbert Spencer. However, the fact that the rich generally favored the eugenics movement made it possible to obtain philanthropy on a large scale. This in turn enabled some scientists to further their careers by embracing eugenics. Charles Davenport, for example, was widely viewed as America's leading geneticist between 1910 and 1925. In England, Galton was a major philanthropist of the movement as well as its founder. He donated money to establish a eugenics laboratory, and in his will he endowed a professorship which came to be occupied by Karl Pearson, Galton's disciple and handpicked successor. Pearson thus became the leader of the English biometrical school.[21]

From all the above one can see why in the early twentieth century serious attempts were made to establish a science of eugenics. That these attempts produced a considerable flow of pseudoscience is due to the defectiveness of the eugenics paradigm on the one hand, and to the context of popular enthusiasm on the other. Eugenics, since its inception, had been a kind of political crusade with religious overtones. "There are three stages to be passed through," Galton wrote about eugenics:

> Firstly it must be made familiar as an academic question until its exact importance has been understood and accepted as a fact; secondly it must be recognized as a subject whose practical development deserves serious consideration; and thirdly it must be introduced into the national consciousness as a new religion.[22]

According to Karl Pearson, his biographer, Galton preached eugenics orthodoxy with a kind of evangelical zeal.[23] Many of the followers behaved in ways which revealed that they were committed not merely to building a science, but to launching a crusade to save humanity. One eugenicist, described as fairly typical, exclaimed that "the laboratory" was "the new Mount Sinai," and spoke of "the Ten Commandments of Science."[24]

Psychologists and biologists who believed in the efficacy of eugenics as a science also supported its goals of social reform. The rapid progress of Mendelian geneticists studying plants and small animals imbued sympathetic scientists with a faith that the contentions of eugenicists would soon be proven unequivocally. So in the meantime, if the evidence seemed a bit ambiguous, it was better to pretend that what would soon be known was already known than to risk sabotaging through excessive caution the very movement to which the science was dedicated.

4. Early Attempts to Prove the Inheritance of Mental Ability: Galton, Pearson, and Davenport

The attempt to construct a science of eugenics created a paradoxical situation in which leading scientists repeatedly committed major errors. Galton, Pearson, and Davenport tried to build a science, but could not because their theories were incorrect and the kinds of data needed to test them were unavailable. So the three unwittingly devoted their careers to generating and maintaining the illusion of a science.

Although they gathered data and made some real discoveries, their work must be classified as pseudoscience because their major conclusions were not really supported by evidence. Being unable to confirm their theories scientifically, they produced a parody of hypothesis testing in which (a) clearly biased data were collected repeatedly in a sloppy manner, (b) excessively bold inferences were drawn from very ambiguous evidence, and were supported by either (c) persistent refusal to consider plausible alternative hypotheses, or (d) the use of straw-man theories to dismiss alternative hypotheses prematurely and unfairly. In some cases the phrase "bold inference" is a tremendous understatement, as clear logical fallacies can be detected; conclusions sometimes were based on elementary errors in reasoning. The appearance of bona fide science was often maintained by taking some genuine scientific advance, like Mendel's theory or certain statistical concepts, and stating it repeatedly in conjuction with the erroneous theory being promoted. Although this gave no real support to the theory, it seemed to justify faith in the investigator. Thus, what was legitimate scientific progress in another context, functioned as a kind of *scientific icon* when used as a part of pseudoscience.

Prior to the development of IQ tests, there was little apparent progress in regard to the first major question of the eugenics paradigm—how to measure intelligence. Because the serious attempts to measure innate ability and intelligence had failed to show positive results, most investigators contented themselves with using rough estimates of ability given by teachers and relatives. In *Hereditary Genius* Galton had used eminence as his measure of natural ability. The major drawback of this was that it produced an obvious tautology, since Galton was trying to *prove* that natural ability caused eminence. Assisted by his critics, Galton recognized this drawback and devoted much of his later career to finding ways of measuring innate abilities. Hence he came to be known as "the father of the mental test."

In 1884 Galton opened his Anthropometric Laboratory in London. The purpose was to get extensive data on individual differences in a wide range of sensory capacities. People who came to it paid threepence to have measurements taken and recorded in a file which ultimately collected information on over 9,000 people. An account of the laboratory listed the data as "height, weight, span, breathing power, strength of pull and squeeze, quickness of blow, hearing, seeing, color sense, and other personal data."[1] Galton had reasoned that if mental abilities were inherited in the same way as physical characteristics, then perhaps they could be measured by similar methods. Using scales, balloons, tuning forks, and color charts, he sought to detect the artist's eye, musician's ear, and orator's lungs.

Unfortunately, he failed. He could not find any clear relationship between simple sensory acuities and the more global phenomenon of mental ability. Likewise, J. McKeen Cattell, who studied with Galton, attempted similar kinds of measurement in the United States, and elaborate statistical analysis of his data failed to show any dependable relationships with course grades of college freshmen.[2] Galton's only major conclusion from his own studies was that women on the average were inferior to men in every respect.[3] But the basis for this conclusion is obscure, and subsequent investigators have rejected the finding.

The failure of Galton's and Cattell's biometric measurement could have been interpreted as evidence against the theory that mental ability was determined biologically. But at that time allegiance to the theory was sufficiently strong that negative results seemed to indicate only that different kinds of measures of innate ability were needed. IQ tests, invented some twenty years after the opening of Galton's laboratory, eventually came to be seen as the needed measures.

The main result of early biometric experiments was to establish the principle that mental ability is best studied by using standardized tests in a controlled, laboratory situation. In retrospect it appears that this much-lauded accomplishment may have been a fatal error. A review of evidence pertaining to sixty years of mental testing suggests the ironic possibility that reputation, Galton's first crude measure of ability, might in fact be a better measure of mental ability than all the more sophisticated psychometric approaches developed subsequently.

Lacking measures of hereditary intelligence, investigators at first had difficulty developing a pseudoscience of white superiority. Early statements of black inferiority were so simplistic that they fail even to qualify as pseudoscience. Instead they resemble the garden variety of racial prejudice. In a chapter entitled, "The Comparative Worth of Different Races,"[4] Galton proclaimed blacks to be the lowest of all races. He presented three kinds of evidence to support this contention: few blacks were considered eminent by Englishmen; slave owners in the United States frequently spoke of their slaves as childish and stupid; and white travelers in Africa rarely considered themselves inferior to village chiefs. On the basis of this evidence, Galton estimated the natural ability of blacks to average about two grades below the average of Anglo-Saxons on a distribution scale which included sixteen grades. For some reason this estimate closely resembled the average black-white difference found later using IQ tests.[5]

The second major aspect of the eugenics paradigm—proving that intelligence was hereditary—attracted the most attention and produced the most outrageous results.

To this end, Galton, in *Hereditary Genius,* examined the pedigrees of famous people. He found that people with famous relatives were far

more likely to become eminent themselves than those randomly selected. On the basis of a sample with "no less than 300 families containing between them nearly 1,000 eminent men," he claimed to have
discovered that the chances of kinsmen of illustrious men rising to
eminence were:

> one in six for fathers
> one in seven for brothers
> one in four for sons
> one in twenty-five for grandfathers
> one in forty for uncles and nephews
> one in one hundred for first cousins.[6]

Galton noticed that outstanding painters and musicians of the Renais-
sance frequently had close relatives who were painters or musicians. He
emphasized that it was only the close relatives who were likely to be
eminent, because artistic eminence rarely "passes through more than
two degrees of kinship." From an examination of 196 notable clergy-
men he concluded that "a pious disposition is decidedly hereditary."[7]

Despite indications that Galton may have chosen a biased sample,[8]
we can agree with the thrust of his data. Children of eminent parents
have a better than average chance of becoming eminent themselves;
children of clergy, painters, and musicians have a good chance of growing up to be clergy, painters, and musicians respectively. But does this
support Galton's contention that abilities are hereditary? It does *only*
if one assumes that differences in ability are determined biologically
and genetically. One's family completely determines one's genetic
endowment (assuming one lives with one's biological parents), but it
also largely shapes one's environment and experiences. Galton's data are
consistent with environmentalist as well as hereditarian explanations.
For example, artistic or musical parents may train their child in art or
music beginning at a very early age. If not, they can at least provide
role-models and bolster the child's self-confidence. Artistically talented
families can be expected to inculcate values conducive to artistic
achievement. Awareness of the child's famous parents may affect
others' expectations of the child in ways that encourage achievement.
Or the child, believing that ability is inherited, may make a special
effort to develop his or her talents.

Most of Galton's eminent families were wealthy. Hence, leisure time
and affluence probably are factors increasing the likelihood of emi-

nence. Finally, the parents' eminence may improve the family's social standing, thereby providing access to positions of responsibility, from which fame is more easily attainable than otherwise. This last point is particularly relevant to Galton's samples of judges, politicians, commanders, and ministers.

Galton argued that environment was unimportant because people with natural ability would surmount any obstacles placed in front of them, and people without natural ability could not succeed with any amount of encouragement. However, Galton also recognized that pedigree studies could not prove his case, and that he would have to find some other means of demonstrating that environment and experience were not important determinants of performance and reputation.[9]

Demonstrating that "nature" was vastly more important than "nurture" proved to be a sticky problem for Galton and those who followed him. His first technique was to set up simpleminded environmentalist theories and refute them. Then he began to assume that any talent which displayed itself early in life was genetically determined. In *English Men of Science* (1874), Galton's second book, he attempted to show that a taste for science was innate by listing the ages at which future scientists first became interested in objects of scientific study. If a young child displayed any noticeable interest in nature or mechanical things, this was interpreted as an instinctual craving for science. Using such criteria, Galton concluded that in his sample of ninety-one scientists, the taste for science was "decidedly innate" in fifty-six cases, "decidedly not" in eleven, and doubtful in the remaining twenty-four.[10] Of course, we would now say that Galton's reasoning was fallacious on two counts. His criterion of innateness was so loose that most children would qualify as having an innate taste for science. Even in the few cases where early interest reached unusual levels and was accompanied by demonstrations of ability, this could have been due instead to childhood experiences and learning. Nevertheless, Galton's reasoning is used today by people who interpret the existence of child prodigies as evidence that genius is inborn.

Finally, in *Inquiries into the Human Faculty* (1883), Galton proposed to resolve the nature-nurture issue by studying identical, or monozygotic, twins. Previously he had surveyed people who either were twins or close relatives of twins, and had received about eighty replies. Regarding the physical similarity of monozygotic twins, he received some very impressive confirming evidence. Regarding in-heritance of character and abilities, however, the evidence was sparse and anecdotal. But that did not keep him from interpreting the results boldly:

> We may, therefore, broadly conclude that the only circumstance, within the range of those by which persons of similar conditions of life are affected, that is capable of producing a marked effect on the character of adults, is illness or some accident which causes physical infirmity.[11]

Although the evidence was almost worthless and the conclusions glar-ingly incorrect, Galton nonetheless established a direction which mental testers would follow for another century.

After 1900 Galton became important primarily as a spokesman and philanthropist for the eugenics movement. For the actual development of pseudoscience the torch was passed to Karl Pearson. Galton's be-quest to Pearson was fourfold: first was leadership of the eugenics movement in England; second was Pearson's job at London University. Third was a mathematical orientation toward problems of eugenics. Believing that quantitative measurement was the mark of a full-grown science, Galton had devised the theory of correlation coefficients.[12] Pearson gave the theory its present mathematical foundation, and thus created the commonly used measure known as *Pearson's r*.[13]

Fourth was an utterly erroneous belief in the existence of universal laws of organic transmission. From Galton, Pearson acquired the notion that all traits, physical and mental, were inherited in the same way and to the same degree, and that by careful quantitative observation one could discover the proportion of each trait passed on from parents to offspring. Pearson's stubborn adherence to this theory proved to be his undoing as a scientist and provided a springboard for numerous in-stances of pseudoscience.

Pearson's 1904 study, "On the Laws of Inheritance in Man," was a classic example destined to be replicated many times. In it he used teachers' rankings based on a seven-point scale of intellectual capacity and found positive correlations of .52 between brothers, .51 between sisters, and .52 between brothers and sisters. He observed that these correlations were of roughly the same magnitude as ones obtained with physical characteristics like health, hair color, and cephalic index.

On this basis he concluded that mental characteristics were inherited in the same way and to the same extent as physical features.[14]

Throughout his career, Pearson continued to find correlations around .50 for a wide variety of characteristics. This appears to have been due at least partly to biased data collection.[15] When one investigator found a correlation of .61 between the IQ scores of siblings, Pearson reworked her data and succeeded in lowering it to around .50.[16] Correlations significantly lower than .50 typically were attributed to measurement error. Pearson thought he was proving the validity of Galton's laws of organic transmission. Popular acceptance of Pearson's ideas made him increasingly bold, to the point of estimating that heredity accounted for nine-tenths of human mental capacity.[17]

Pearson had thus embarked on a wild expedition in the field of numerology. His studies are no longer taken seriously because virtually everyone acknowledges that correlation implies only association, not causation. Least of all does a similar level of correlation mean that the sources of the two correlations are the same. Heredity could have produced the physical similarities, environment the mental ones, and coincidence (aided by biased data collection) the fact that the two correlations were similar. Ironically, the inventor of the correlation coefficient repeatedly made the most flagrant errors associated with it.

Pearson's use of the correlational method on a variety of topics usually led to the conclusion that the characteristic in question was hereditary. He came close to performing a *reductio ad absurdum* of his own life's work when he attacked the Fight Against Tuberculosis movement in Great Britain for its environmentalist stand. That tuberculosis could be caused by a tubercule bacillus, or that the incidence of the disease could be greatly reduced by better sanitary conditions, he viewed as patently absurd. For he found the correlation between parents and children with regard to tubercular infection to be .50, "precisely that which we find for other characters where the relationship is due to heredity."[18] Environmental factors like sanitary conditions could not be important causally because a .50 correlation was what one would expect if heredity alone were operating. The decline in the frequency of tuberculosis observed during the last several centuries had to be due to the increased resistance of racial stock caused by the process of natural selection.

Pearson's way of dealing with environmentalist interpretations of his own data was simply to dismiss them as irrelevant. For example, in a painstaking statistical study of the inferiority of Jewish immigrants, he concluded that while their average mental ability was somewhat lower than that of native-born Englishmen, the clearest difference was that Jewish children were innately dirtier than Gentile ones. When it was objected that immigrant Jewish children might be dirtier because most of them lived in slums, Pearson replied that the reason most of them lived in slums was that they were innately dirty.[19]

Pearson believed he was well on the way to proving the validity of Galton's laws of organic transmission when Gregor Mendel's genetic theory began attracting adherents. Unfortunately, the two theories seemed to contradict each other. Whereas Galton claimed that a proportion of each trait was passed on from generation to generation, Mendel seemed to imply that traits were passed on in all-or-none fashion, and that even after a trait had disappeared from a strain it could reappear in subsequent generations. Possibly because Galton and Pearson felt that accepting a distinction between genotype and phenotype would make it much more difficult to demonstrate the inheritance of traits, they rejected Mendel's theory. This produced a major split in the eugenics movement.

In America, the rising leader of the movement was Charles Davenport, a biologist who accepted Mendel's theory. Partly because he was articulate and understood Mendelian principles, and partly because he was able to command considerable financial resources, Davenport was widely respected by geneticists and eugenicists alike. His major work, *Heredity in Relation to Eugenics* (1911), was "considered by many the era's most important treatise on eugenics," and it "came to be recognized as the period's most important human genetics text as well."[20] The following year Davenport was elected to the National Academy of Sciences.

Davenport was a Mendelian and a Galtonian simultaneously, but where the two diverged he was a Galtonian trying to appear Mendelian. He believed in Mendel's theory of heredity, but attempted to use it to prove Galton's contention that mental abilities were inherited. Mendel had worked only with the observable, physical characteristics of plants. Because he could produce several generations within a short period and measure their characteristics precisely, he was able to demonstrate that certain attributes like the color of flowers appeared in the offspring in predictable ratios. By producing these ratios in large numbers of progeny Mendel could demonstrate that the color of flowers was inherited, and that a particular color was either dominant or recessive. Having studied people rather than plants, Galton never was able to predict or obtain precise ratios. He could merely demonstrate approximate similarities between parents and offspring, which he interpreted as evidence of biological inheritance.

At first Davenport had worked mostly with plants and lower animals, but as his fame and influence grew he became more exclusively concerned with problems of human heredity. *Heredity in Relation to Eugenics* began with a description of eugenics and a statement of its importance. In Chapter 2, entitled "The Method of Eugenics," he presented basic Mendelian principles and illustrated them with a discussion of eye color in humans. The critical Chapter 3, entitled "The Inheritance of Family Traits," comprised most of the book. It began by using Mendelian methods to demonstrate the inheritance of eye color. From there he proceeded to discuss such mental characteristics as musical ability, artistic ability, mechanical skill, and memory, gathering data from the pedigree studies of eugenicists, the surveys of eugenics fieldworkers and old family albums. Most of the data collection was so slipshod that even if these abilities had been simple Mendelian traits, the predicted ratios could not have been obtained. What resulted was a travesty of Mendelian genetics. For his "proof" of innateness Davenport followed Galton's line of reasoning that an early demonstration of ability proved it was innate:

> Like musical ability, artistic talent shows itself so early as to demonstrate its innateness. Thus extraordinary talent was recognized in Francesco Mazzuoli (though ill taught) at 16, in Paul Potter at 15, in Jacob Ruysdael at 14, in Titian Vecelli at 13.[21]

Davenport's role as the leading figure of human genetics, or "pure eugenics," as it was often called, placed him in a contradictory position. The important problems for which people wanted answers were those posed by Galton (i.e., inheritance of human character and abilities), but the reputable methods, which people trusted and admired, were the methods used by Mendel (i.e., obtaining precise, predictable ratios). Ideally, Davenport would have wanted to obtain Galton's results with Mendel's methods, but this usually did not work. Only rarely and by coincidence or biased data collection would he obtain anything close to a Mendelian ratio. To achieve Galton's results he had to use Galton's methods while still paying homage to Mendelism as the real, scientific basis of human heredity. This placed him in the difficult position of having to reconcile Mendelian precision with Galtonian imprecision, something he sought to do in two ways. Without claiming to have discovered that a trait was Mendelian, he would, nonetheless, state his conclusion authoritatively as a prediction, thereby implying that he had. For example, about artistic ability he wrote:

> When one parent is artistic and the other neither himself artistic nor of artistic ancestry then probably none of the children will have high artistic talent. But if the unartistic parent have artistic ancestry there will be artistic children.[22]

This gave the impression that artistic ability was a Mendelian recessive trait. It sounded a lot like, "When both parents have brown iris either all the children will have brown iris or else about a quarter will lack brown pigment and so will be blue-eyed."[23]

Davenport's other ploy was to emphasize that human genetics was an infant science, and that the imprecision involved in some of the analyses represented a transitional stage en route to a fully developed Mendelian science. For example, he noted that the "popular classification of traits is often crude, lagging far behind scientific knowledge," and that "unit characters can rarely be recognized by inspection." But then he proceeded to reason:

> Even without a complete analysis of a trait into its units we may still make practically important studies by using the principle that when both parents have low grades of a trait complex the children will have low grades of that complex . . . [Galton's method].

> Despite the difficulties in analysis of units of heredity and despite the complications in characters it is possible to see clearly the method of inheritance of a great number of human traits and to predict that many more will become analyzed in the near future.[24]

Not all the investigators were as patient, however. Rather than accept Davenport's loose way of drawing conclusions from the data, some preferred to bury their imprecision in the actual collection of data, and thereby obtain the desired Mendelian ratios. One such researcher was eventually described as "a tireless worker and full of ideas, but over-apt to find the 3:1 ratio in everything he touched."[25]

It has been said that under Davenport's guidance, American eugenicists "used Mendel's concepts to advance Sir Francis Galton's social philosophy."[26] To this one must add that they used the concepts as a scientific icon, whose presence bolstered their faith that Galtonian ideas would be proven by advances in science. Combining Mendelian genetics and Galtonian eugenics in the same widely read text may have enhanced the prestige of the latter, but since the predicted Mendelian ratios usually were not found for human character traits and abilities, it could not be said that Galton's conclusions were supported by Mendelian genetics.

The obvious deficiencies of Davenport's approach did not escape the discerning eye of Karl Pearson and the English biometrical school. These people felt that they already had quantitative precision, and they deplored its absence in the American movement. David Heron, a colleague of Pearson, criticized the American studies of mental defects, arguing,

> that the material has been collected in an unsatisfactory manner, that the data have been tabled in a most slipshod fashion, and that the Mendelian conclusions drawn have no justification whatever.[27]

The Americans, on the other hand, felt that British biometricians were unscientific because they continued to accept Galton's outdated theory of inheritance through the blood corpuscles. What good were statistics if the theory they were proving was completely wrong? Because each could see the deficiencies of the other's approach, a bitter rivalry developed between the English biometricians and the American Mendelians, despite the fact that both groups were very successfully gaining public acceptance of Galton's ideas in their native countries.[28] At the time the debate appeared to be: Which school is truly scientific, Davenport's or Pearson's? In reality it was: Which important scientific advance— Mendelism or statistics—should be used to inspire faith in the creed of the eugenics movement?

Following the American entrance into the First World War, a reconciliation between the two schools was brought about. Based on some earlier scientific work done in America, the Americans accepted that most traits were not carried by single genes, but were "multiple gene" traits which could not be expected to display simple Mendelian ratios.[29] Hence, the way to study these "metrical" characteristics was by using statistics. In return, the British agreed that Mendel's theory of heredity was a definite advance over Galton's. With this reconciliation the eugenicists were able to exorcise some of their more glaring absurdities. Now it was possible to believe in both Mendelian genetics and statistics. Instead of arguing about which scientific icon to use, eugenicists found they could use both. But the two were merely icons and nothing more. Neither method had come close to proving the inheritance of mental ability. Pearson's use of correlations meant that his data were in some ways more impressive than Galton's, but his grandiose errors in reasoning totally negated any increase in precision which might have been accomplished by the use of correlations. Davenport was no more successful than Pearson. To believe that differences in mental ability were inherited required the same leap of faith that it did when Galton first wrote. Because of the Social Darwinist legacy and the emergence of a powerful eugenics movement, many people were willing to make that leap. And for similar reasons they found themselves willing to believe the small group of psychologists who stepped forward and claimed to have discovered a way of measuring the all-around, innate, adaptive capacity of the human nervous system.

5. The Transition from Eugenics to Psychometrics

The invention of IQ tests constituted a modest advance for a science of educational psychology. The test could predict fairly well how children would do in school. At the same time, the advent of IQ tests constituted a tremendous, revolutionary advance for the development of Galtonian pseudoscience. Eugenicists envisioned in the tests a way of solving the hitherto unsolvable problems of the eugenics paradigm. They rapidly embraced the notions that IQ tests measured innate intelligence, the basis of all achievement in life, and that data from these tests proved intelligence to be hereditary. Now that measures of innate mental capacity could be obtained by giving one or more hour tests of vocabulary, puzzles, and arithmetic, it became possible to compare the capacities of people and groups, and to demonstrate with an appearance of scientific precision unprecedented in the field that whites were superior to blacks, as rich people were to poor people, and native-born white Americans were to immigrant foreigners.

Standardized testing as such was probably a necessary accompaniment of the growth and rationalization of educational systems. IQ testing, on the other hand, was largely superfluous. Intelligence tests did little scientifically that could not have been done as well by exclusive reliance on achievement tests and teachers' assessments. The tremendous interest in IQ tests stemmed not from their utility as predictors of achievement, but from the fact that they seemed to provide the breakthrough which would make possible a science of eugenics. But this hope, like others before it, was illusory. The best that could be done was to raise the caliber of pseudoscience by replacing older, threadbare fallacies with newer and more elaborate ones.

The first intelligence tests were developed in Paris shortly before 1905 by French psychologist Alfred Binet. The French government had given Binet the task of devising ways to identify children likely to fail in grammar school. He and his colleagues possessed a large laboratory full of apparatus, and there they devised a variety of tests, using essentially trial-and-error methods to see what worked. They began by considering the kinds of anthropometric measures used by Galton and Cattell. Binet noted the negative results of their studies and suggested that intellectual performance depended upon something other than simple sensory acuities.[1] He examined an extensive collection of photographs to determine whether facial features revealed probable success or failure in school. Again the results were negative. Binet even called in a Parisian palmist to read the lines in the hands of a hundred boys, but palmistry could not provide the necessary explanation.[2] What Binet and his colleagues eventually found was that if children were asked to perform simple tasks *like those they performed in school,* then performance on these tests could predict with some accuracy how children would do in school. Tasks appropriate for children ages three through twelve were compiled, and these comprised the Binet-Simon intelligence scale published in 1908.

Binet called his product an "intelligence test," but his conception of intelligence differed greatly from that of Galton and Spencer. To eugenicists and Social Darwinists, that term denoted a fixed, hereditary trait of individuals which was responsible for success or failure in any sphere of life. For Binet intelligence was a way of describing behavior at a particular time in a particular setting. Scores on his tests were seen as measures of how children had adapted to schooling—whether they were more advanced or less advanced than most others their age. Binet insisted that intelligence was not fixed biologically, and he advocated a system of mental orthopedics to improve the performance of children with low scores.[3] He also made no claims about what the tests could measure after graduation. He clearly did not view scores as indices of mental capacity.

The conception of intelligence shifted and the claims made about tests became correspondingly more exaggerated when the Binet-Simon scale was translated and imported into the United States. The major importers and promoters of Binet's tests were either eugenicists or eugenics sympathizers. The three well-known American translations of the Binet-Simon test were those authored by H. H. Goddard, Frederick Kuhlmann, and Lewis Terman. All three had studied with G. Stanley Hall at Clark University, where Hall had professed a theory of inherited mental ability similar to Galton's. Goddard introduced the tests first, in 1908, and became a leading hereditarian spokesman almost immediately. His work at the Vineland, N.J., training school for the retarded gave him expert credentials in the area of feeble-mindedness and earned him a place on the Eugenics Record Office's committee on heredity of the feeble-minded. In 1912 Goddard wrote *The Kallikak Family,* a popular book which purported to demonstrate the all-powerful influence of good and bad heredity. Terman authored the influential Stanford-Binet revision which became the prototype of most subsequent IQ tests. He was a leading member of the Human Betterment Foundation, which promoted widespread use of sterilization in California.[4] He wrote that "of the founders of modern psychology, my greatest admiration is for Galton."[5] Terman's admiration led him to publish a study in which he estimated Galton's IQ score[6] at "around 200."[7]

The administration of IQ tests to nearly 2 million army recruits in 1917 catapulted the tests into public prominence. Robert M. Yerkes, the psychologist who convinced army officials to use IQ tests, was at the time both president of the American Psychological Association and a member of the Eugenics Record Office's committee on the inheritance of mental traits. For construction of the army tests he recruited Terman, Goddard, and several other psychometricians. Edward L. Thorndike and R. S. Woodworth pioneered in using data from twins to estimate the heritability of IQ scores. Both had studied under J. McKeen Cattell, who in turn had been Galton's research assistant. Thorndike, like Yerkes, had a place on the committee on inheritance of mental traits. An index of psychologists' respect for eugenics is the fact that Hall, Cattell, Yerkes, Terman, Thorndike, and Woodworth all became presidents of the American Psychological Association.[8] In England as well, IQ testing was quickly adopted by eugenics—most notably by the social psychologist William McDougall; by his outstanding student, Cyril Burt; and by Karl Pearson.

British and American psychometricians in effect grafted Galton's theory onto Binet's instrument. By so doing they transformed IQ testing into a major locus of pseudoscience. They successfully made it appear that the tests measured intelligence as defined by Galton and Spencer, when actually the evidence never justified such a conclusion. The mental testers' arguments seemed convincing mainly because many people were predisposed to believe the conclusions regardless of evidence.

One can understand the relationship of IQ tests to the eugenics paradigm by imagining a very large and heavy railroad train built with rectangular wheels. Such a train would be very difficult to move, as indeed the major problems of the eugenics paradigm were very difficult to solve. The early IQ testers were like engineers assigned to build an engine which could pull the train. They knew that all previous efforts had failed. Neither Galton nor Cattell nor the criminal anthropologists had been able to measure the important hereditary traits. At last news came of a man in France who had invented an engine more powerful than any before it. Binet's tests correlated with performance in school, whereas Galton's and Cattell's did not. So the new engine was acquired and placed at the front of the train. But, alas, this train was so immovable that no engine could pull it. Even Binet's tests could not measure Galtonian natural ability. Fortunately for the engineers, however, the train was poised at the top of a long downhill slope, and the force exerted by the new locomotive was sufficient to start the train on a downward path, whereupon it picked up speed. As long as the tracks continued downhill, the train continued to move and the engine appeared to be pulling it. As long as social conditions predisposed people to uncritically accept the claims that IQ tests measured innate mental capacity, the tests appeared to vindicate the eugenics paradigm. But when the slope changed and the train slowed to a halt, it became clear in retrospect that the locomotive had never really pulled the train. In a similar way, it is now clear that despite earlier appearances, IQ tests never could measure innate capacity.

We can understand the process by which investigators came to have so much faith in the Binet tests if we use another metaphor—that of a man lost in the desert, dying of thirst. Under what conditions could such a man be expected to see a mirage? He would be most likely to imagine water was present if: first, he believed that water was out there somewhere to be found; second, he had developed a strong need to find water; and, third, he encountered some real phenomenon, the appearance of which superficially resembled that of water—say, for example, the shadow of a mountain in the distance.

First, there can be no doubt that prior to 1930 psychologists generally accepted the Galton-Spencer conception of different intelligence levels. By 1900 Spencer had passed out of vogue, so he was rarely given credit for originating the concept. However, his influence can readily be detected in a survey of twenty definitions of intelligence put forward between 1909 and 1927. Eleven psychologists defined it as the capacity or ability to adapt or adjust; several of these stressed that adaptation resulted in competitive success. Five defined intelligence as the capacity or ability to learn; three called it either a general efficiency of mind or the ability to engage in abstract thinking. Five of the twenty stressed that intelligence was innate and physiologically determined; none said it was learned or the result of experience.[9] Lewis Terman, the leading proponent of IQ tests and one of the psychologists participating in the survey, endorsed Galton's theory explicitly:

> Intelligence is chiefly a matter of native endowment. It depends upon physical and chemical properties of the cerebral cortex which, like other physical traits, are subject to the laws of heredity. In fact, the mathematical coefficient of family resemblances in mental traits, particularly intelligence, has been found to be almost exactly the same as for such physical traits as height, weight, cephalic index, etc. . . . The attempts to explain familiar resemblances on any other hypothesis than that of heredity have not been successful. All the available facts that science has to offer support the Galtonian theory that mental abilities are chiefly a matter of original endowment.[10]

Terman agreed that his tests did not measure native intelligence precisely, but he insisted that "nearly all the psychologists believe that native ability counts very heavily" in determining scores.[11] He conceded that home environment could affect a child's score, but only very little.[12]

The pressing concerns of the eugenics movement made discovery of measures of hereditary potential seem like an urgent necessity. Terman, like others, believed that something had to be done quickly. "It has been figured," he noted,

> that if the present differential birth rate continues, 1,000 Harvard graduates will at the end of 200 years have but 50 descendants, while in the same period 1,000 South Italians will have multiplied to 100,000.

> The differential birth rate is doubtless a social rather than a biological phenomenon, and it is one that threatens the very existence of civilization.[13]

The "science" of eugenics had developed unevenly. Galton and Pearson had very successfully devised statistical techniques to handle numerical data, but the anthropometric measurements had failed to yield any convincing representation of intelligence. Poised on the verge of quantification, investigators found they needed something to quantify. Tests like Binet's seemed to provide the best measure of Spencerian intelligence levels, given that investigators *had* to find a measure.

The social context had helped to make Terman and other researchers naively credulous. Guided by their credulity, they amassed extensive data which was only vaguely consistent with their theory, but was nonetheless sufficient to be interpreted as clear proof by gullible investigators. Much of the evidence is summarized in Terman's *The Intelligence of School Children* (1919). In his second chapter, Terman stated the main conclusion:

> The facts which will be presented point fairly definitely to the conclusion that the differences which have been found to exist among children in physical traits are paralleled by equal differences in mental traits, particularly intelligence. It will be shown that these innate differences in intelligence are chiefly responsible for the problem of the school laggard.[14]

The book presented two kinds of evidence to support claims about the validity of IQ tests. First, there were a variety of correlations between children's scores and their school grades, also between scores and teachers' estimates of intelligence. These correlations were obtained for first graders, fifth graders, and high school students, and they generally ranged between .40 and .60.[15] Among adults Terman found correlations of roughly the same magnitude between IQ scores and occupational status.

Because contemporary claims of test validity rest on this and similar evidence, critical discussion of it is reserved for the next chapter. Here we may speculate that belief in IQ tests rested not only on this evidence, but also on the fact that comparison of different ethnic groups produced results which confirmed the expectations and prejudices of respectable white, middle-class Americans. The 1917 army data firmly established that blacks on the average scored a full standard deviation (about 15 IQ points) below whites. Subsequent analysis of the data showed that Polish, Italian, and Russian immigrants scored almost as low as blacks, and that persons of the Nordic race were on the average clearly superior to southern and eastern Europeans.[16] Henry Goddard had earlier tested immigrants at the receiving station in New York harbor, and was able to conclude that 83 percent of the Jews, 80 percent of the Hungarians, 79 percent of the Italians, and 87 percent of the Russians were "feeble-minded."[17] As the superiority of rich over poor, white over black, and Nordic over Slav was basically what Galton had prophesied, it seemed reasonable to his disciples that the tests did indeed measure natural ability.

Terman's claim that differences in intelligence were innate and physiological rested on an elaborate analogy with physical traits. He gathered and presented data in a way which made IQ scores appear to be shaped by the same process as height. Test scores were reported in units of "mental age," which was a kind of mental stature. (The Intelligence Quotient—IQ—was calculated as mental age divided by chronological age.) Like a child's height, his mental age grew steadily until he was around sixteen, and then growth slowed down or stopped. Thereupon it remained constant through most of adulthood. Like measurements of height, IQ scores approximated the bell-shaped curve of the normal distribution when examined in large numbers. But most important, a child's IQ score remained roughly constant as he passed through school. This was to be expected since children who were taller in one year usually would also be taller two or three years hence. The approximate constancy of the IQ score gave the impression that it could not be altered by the environment, and that it was therefore shaped almost exclusively by heredity. Finally, there were Pearson's correlations, showing that resemblance between siblings and between parents and children was almost the same for IQ as for height. All this taken together, Terman reasoned, constituted overwhelming evidence that the mental trait, intelligence, was determined in the same way and to the same extent as the physical trait, height.

In retrospect it appears that this similarity was a kind of mirage. The normal distribution in and of itself meant nothing. Walter Lippmann pointed out that Terman could have expected an even more perfect normal distribution if instead of using test scores he had tabulated the results from flips of a coin.[18] The stoppage of mental growth around age sixteen was an illusion generated by the selection of test items appropriate for school children. For example, if a group of mathematicians were tested annually on their understanding of complex mathematical concepts, one would probably find that mental growth continued well past age thirty. However, if the same group were tested on their abilities to add, subtract, and multiply quickly, one could well discover that growth had stopped at age sixteen. The illusion also stemmed from the use of unrepresentative samples of teenagers and adults. Terman classified anyone older than fourteen as an adult. He administered the tests to "a motley crew made up of 150 hoboes, 30 businessmen, 159 adolescent delinquents, and 50 high school students." Because the teenagers and the grown men received comparable scores on the tests, he concluded that the "average adult" score fell in the range of fifteen to seventeen years.[19]

The much-touted constancy of IQ scores turned out to be a fallacious argument in favor of hereditary intelligence for several reasons. First there is the simple, logical point that constancy of a trait does not mean that the trait is shaped by heredity. It could as well be shaped by the environment, but in such a way that it does not vary much over time. Secondly, the approximate constancy of IQ scores was again largely a product of the manner in which test items were selected. If scores on a given question did not correlate highly with scores on other items, then the question was intentionally deleted from the test. This in effect guaranteed that people who were superior to others on test items having a certain level of difficulty would also be superior on items at the next level up, and it maximized the likelihood of their maintaining superiority over time. Third, constancy had been discovered only for children already in school. Subsequent invention of preschool IQ tests showed that children's scores were by no means stable prior to age seven. While children's IQ scores at age nine correlated .85 with their scores at age twelve, the correlation between ages two and five was only .30, between four and seven only .50.[20] Stable IQ scores appeared only after a year or more of formal schooling. This suggested that they might be a product of the school experience rather than of heredity. Finally, studies appeared which showed that dramatic increases in test scores could be produced by changes in the environment.[21] By 1950 Terman's reasoning that stable test scores proved intelligence to be hereditary was no longer taken seriously.

Terman's belief that he had substantiated Galton's theory was an illusion which he projected onto his own data. But the data themselves were not entirely illusory. They reflected the real social phenomena of brightness and dullness in school, and the relation of schooling to the economy. Children relatively advanced or slow in scholastic achievement tended to remain that way as they grew older. Those who did better in school and stayed in school longer were likely to get more prestigious jobs and make more money than persons who did poorly and dropped out early. Moreover, children whose parents had been good students were more likely to be good students themselves. The parent-child correlation in IQ scores reflected this tendency. As these phenomena taken together loosely resembled Galton's and Spencer's image of society as a hereditary meritocracy, it became possible to envision in data which reflected these phenomena proof of the Galton-Spencer theory. Hence the mirage.

Walter Lippman criticized Terman and other psychometricians for seeking to become celebrities by dispensing with scientific caution:

> If only it could be proved, or at least believed, that intelligence is fixed by heredity, and that the tester can measure it, what a future to dream about! The unconscious temptation is too strong for the ordinary critical defence of the scientific methods. With the help of a subtle statistical illusion, intricate logical fallacies and a few smuggled obiter dicta, self-deception as the preliminary to public deception is almost automatic. . . .

> The claim that Mr. Terman or anyone else is measuring hereditary intelligence has no more scientific foundation than a hundred other fads, vitamins and glands and amateur psychoanalysis and correspondence courses in will power, and it will pass with them into that

limbo where phrenology and palmistry and characterology and the other Babu sciences are to be found. In all of these there was some admixture of primitive truth which the conscientious scientist retains long after the wave of popular credulity has spent itself.[22]

Lippmann was too optimistic, however. Terman, Thorndike, and other intelligence testers occupied key positions in leading university departments of psychology and education. Their work was extensively supported by the government and foundations. They trained many school psychologists and administrators. Future teachers read their textbooks in college. Moreover, their views were congenial to school authorities concerned with setting up a tracking system which would encourage acceptance of inequality and social class divisions. Testing quickly became a major industry. Between 1921 and 1936 over 5,000 articles on mental measurement appeared in print. By 1940 virtually every major school system had a full program of IQ and achievement testing.[23]

On the other hand, after 1925, several different trends began to undermine hereditarian pseudoscience. Ironically, the very success of its proponents created the precondition for its downfall. Investigators conducted a number of relatively unbiased studies which provided ample evidence to undermine Terman's original claims. For example, William Bagley reanalyzed the First World War army data and showed convincingly that average IQ scores were higher in regions where people stayed in school longer.[24] The fact that blacks in some northern states outscored whites in some southern states persuaded even most eugenicists that educational opportunity affected IQ test results. Studies like this, together with the evidence that undermined claims about the constancy of IQ scores, made it impossible to assume any longer that tests measured native intelligence.

Hereditarians responded to these setbacks by devising ways of estimating the proportion of variance in IQ scores determined by heredity. Edward Thorndike inaugurated the new era of hereditability estimates in 1940 when, after reviewing evidence on twins and adopted children, he concluded that intelligence was determined, "80 percent by heredity, 17 percent by training, and 3 percent by accident."[25]

The rapid decline of the eugenics movement after 1929 resulted in a general lessening of interest in Galton's theory. The eugenicists' interpretation that poverty was caused by hereditary feeble-mindedness quickly lost its credibility when previously respectable middle-class citizens suddenly became impoverished. The eugenics movement, already weakened by the great depression, had its reputation tarnished further by the atrocities of its proponents in Nazi Germany. As Allan Chase points out, the early Nazi attempts to achieve racial purification were influenced and to some extent inspired by the model sterilization laws of the United States.[26] While some American eugenics leaders had attacked the Nazi conception of "race-hygiene," most felt that Hitler's implementation of the Eugenic Sterilization Law on a grand scale meant the Nazis were "proceeding toward a policy that will accord with the best thoughts of eugenists in all civilized countries."[27] As England and America moved toward war with Germany, and Hitler's actions came to be viewed as less defensible, the number of persons who wanted to be considered eugenicists declined. The Carnegie Institution stopped funding the Eugenics Record Office in 1939;[28] after that the movement was never more than a shadow of its former self.

Developments in genetics and anthropology undermined the academic respectability of eugenics. Mendelian geneticists discovered that their science could progress most rapidly by concentrating on the physical characteristics of plants and lower animals. After Davenport, most geneticists disavowed any interest in the key questions of eugenics. Others attacked the crude racial theories and obvious class biases of eugenicists.[29] Anthropologists led by Franz Boas persistently attacked theories of white racial superiority. Boas had written forcefully on the subject as early as 1911.[30] Over the next thirty years his influence mounted steadily such that by 1945 racial theories were no longer considered scientifically respectable. Most psychologists decided that the hypothesis of black genetic inferiority should be abandoned.

In psychology the ascendance of behaviorism and its later offshoots distracted attention away from the eugenics paradigm, and eventually produced a renunciation of the mental traits concept.[31] Psychologists' interest in IQ tests, and their acceptance of the Galton-Spencer theory of intelligence, originally had stemmed from an interest in eugenics. But the tests had a utility beyond their service to the eugenics movement. They furnished a convenient means of organizing and justifying hierarchies and inequality. So while the eugenics movement declined, IQ tests continued to be used in corporations and schools. Psychologists' commitment shifted accordingly from the theory which underlay the tests to the tests themselves. This led to rejection of earlier attempts to define intelligence, and reliance on the simple, operational definition: intelligence is what IQ tests measure.

A small core of hereditarians remained committed to the eugenics paradigm. They continued to define intelligence as "an innate, general, cognitive, ability factor."[32] They persisted in efforts to show that what the tests measured was primarily inborn, hereditary talent. Most psychologists, on the other hand, opted for the easy compromise which Galton had originally rejected—a vague statement that both heredity and environment were important determinants of intelligence, and that nobody could measure which was more important. After the Second World War a number of studies attempted to predict scientific creativity and performance in high level occupations by using IQ tests. Data from these studies has made possible a more serious assessment of the tests' validity, but a continuing tradition of pseudoscience has discouraged investigators from making such an assessment.

The Modern Form of the Psychometric Illusion

The term "psychometric illusion" refers to the array of false notions generated by efforts to construct a science based upon the eugenics paradigm. Basically, the illusion is threefold, and consists of the following: (1) that it is possible to design tests which measure mental capacity; (2) that by comparing test results one can determine the differential capacities of various races, social classes, and ethnic groups; and (3) that one can discover the extent to which capacity is shaped by heredity as opposed to environment.

The early form of this illusion took shape during the period 1900 to 1925. It associated mental capacity with a single trait, intelligence, and proposed to measure capacity with a single kind of test. Geniuses were defined as those having very high IQ scores. Standard IQ test results were used to conclude that blacks generally were less intelligent than whites, and most investigators agreed that test scores were shaped almost entirely by heredity.

After 1925 evidence became available to support several objections to the early format. It was learned that scientific creativity and performance in high-level occupations did not correlate with IQ test results. It was demonstrated that changes in environment could greatly affect test scores, and it was argued that standard IQ tests had a cultural bias which discriminated against blacks and lower-class people. The modern form of psychometric illusion evolved in response to these objections. It has been an attempt to sustain the basic illusion in the face of arguments and evidence which have made its earlier form clearly untenable. The modern version sees mental capacity as resulting from two separate traits, intelligence and creativity, both of which can be measured with tests. It contends that IQ scores are shaped by a combination of genetic and environmental factors, and that heritability estimates provide an approximate index of the relative importance of heredity and environment. Finally, it says that there are "culture-fair" IQ tests which enable investigators to get a true, unbiased assessment of racial differences in intelligence. Like its predecessor, the modern form has been developed by a process of pseudoscience, comprised of fallacies, exaggerations, and false claims.

6. The Validity of IQ Tests: Do They Measure Mental Capacity?

Two issues are at stake in any discussion of the validity of IQ tests. One is the validity of the "general intelligence" concept; the other is the validity of IQ tests as measures of that concept. Psychometricians agree that no precise definition of intelligence is possible. They claim that intelligence is a worthwhile scientific concept because it can be measured. If, however, the evidence indicates that no existing test can measure anything as broad as general intelligence, then the concept should be abandoned as an object of research. A concept which cannot be measured or defined is inherently unscientific.

One also cannot measure anything which cannot be identified. *Some* way of defining intelligence is needed before one can say that tests measure it. Most psychometricians have settled upon a way which is maximally conducive to the development of pseudoscience. Part of the definition is stated explicitly; part is implicitly assumed. The explicit definition of intelligence is that which IQ tests measure, or more recently, "the repertoire of skills and knowledge sampled by IQ tests."[1] The implicit assumption is that tests measure a person's capacity for intellectual achievement and professional success. This is the everyday, common-sense usage of the term. It need not be said explicitly by contemporary mental testers because their predecessors popularized this part of the definition so successfully that everyone now knows vaguely what intelligence means. Current proponents of IQ testing need only stress that their tests measure intelligence.

Using an operational definition has discouraged investigators from questioning the validity of the general intelligence construct. Because intelligence was defined as what the tests measured, the one question— is intelligence general or specific—could be quickly converted into the other—does test performance depend upon a single, general ability, or upon several specific ones? Analysis of test results consistently showed a moderate level of intercorrelation among scores on different parts of the tests. In other words, performance depended upon a single, general test-taking ability, known as the "g-factor," as well as upon a number of more specific abilities. This was interpreted as clear evidence in favor of the general intelligence concept. The question of whether abilities exhibited in the testing situation were the same as abilities used in real intellectual achievement was bypassed.

Psychometricians then proceeded to assess the validity of IQ tests in a very one-sided manner. They reasoned that since factor analysis had shown differences in general intelligence to exist, and since it was important to measure such differences, existing IQ tests could not be rejected until demonstrably better measures were invented. Data which seemed to support assertions of the tests' validity were hailed as proof that the tests measured intelligence. Data which contradicted these assertions were interpreted not as evidence against the tests, but as evidence that the activity in question required something besides intelligence. In this way mental testers managed to construct a durable form of pseudoscience which could absorb contradictory findings without being significantly impeded.

The thinly veiled fallacy in all this was that factor analysis of test results never really validated the general intelligence concept. All it showed was that some sort of general test-taking ability existed. It said nothing about whether differences in this ability were specific to the test situation or whether they applied generally to all tasks which required abstract thinking. The only way to validate the construct scientifically would have been to discover consistent high correlations between IQ scores and reliable ratings of performance in a wide variety of artistic, scientific, and professional activities. Such data were never obtained. A number of attempts produced negative results.

There has never been strong evidence that IQ tests measured general intelligence. Claims that they did rested on two kinds of correlations: one between IQ scores and performance in school, the other between IQ scores and occupational status.[2] Lewis Terman and associates first discovered the correlations. Many subsequent studies have produced figures similar to the original ones.[3] The data certainly are valid. The key question is what can be inferred from them.

Grades in school are determined primarily by performance on examinations, most of which are somewhat similar to IQ tests. Correlations between IQ scores and scholastic achievement would support use of the term general intelligence *only* if ability in school provided a good index of ability in subsequent intellectual endeavors. The early psychometricians believed very strongly in Galton's conception of the school as proving ground, and they successfully advocated the idea for many years before bothering to test it. Those who performed poorly in school and on tests were thought to have low capacities in any situation. Henry Goddard went so far as to interpret Huckleberry Finn's dislike of school as proof that the boy lacked intelligence.[4] But the belief was based only on faith, and the data eventually gathered contradicted it.

The claim that IQ tests measured capacity for competence in different level occupations also rested on tenuous grounds. Correlations between IQ scores and occupational status could have been interpreted several ways. But psychometricians immediately gravitated toward the meritocracy interpretation which attributed the correlation to differing intelligence demands of different status occupations. They assumed that only people with high IQ test results could perform adequately in high status jobs, and that those with low scores could be competent only in low status ones. They were so sure that this interpretation was correct that they proceeded to rank the intelligence demands of one hundred occupations. Terman described how the Barr Scale of occupational intelligence was constructed:

Mr. F.E. Barr drew up a list of 100 representative occupations, each definitely and concretely described, and had 30 judges rate them on a scale of 0 to 100 according to the grade of intelligence which each was believed to demand. The ratings were then distributed and P. E. values were computed for all the occupations. The P. E. values express in the case of each occupation the number of units of intelligence [as measured by IQ tests] which, according to the composite opinion of these 30 judges, the occupation demands for ordinary success.[5]

Terman was confident that combining the ratings of thirty judges would produce a close approximation of each occupation's actual intelligence requirements:

It has been found that different judges agree fairly closely in rating the intellectual demands of occupations by this scale. It can not be claimed that the Barr Scale values correspond exactly to the facts, but they unquestionably approximate the facts more closely than would the judgments of any one individual.[6]

Not surprisingly, the Barr Scale values closely paralleled ratings of occupational status. For the forty-seven occupations whose titles matched, the correlation between Barr Scale scores and NORC ratings of occupational prestige was +.91.[7] A mere glance at Barr's list makes the same point. The occupation which supposedly required the highest IQ scores was inventive genius; second was surgeon; third was research leader like Binet or Pasteur; fourth, writer; fifth, high national official; sixth, musician; seventh, great merchant who owns and operates a million dollar business; eighth, university professor; and so on. At the bottom of the list were hobo and garbage collector.[8]

In reality the Barr Scale was nothing more than elaborate testimony of psychologists' faith in the meritocracy conception. But the exact quantitative estimates made it look like actual data. The close agreement of the thirty judges' ratings made the ratings appear correct. Actually it showed only that the thirty judges had similar preconceptions about the importance of IQ tests and similar hierarchies of occupational prestige. Nevertheless, many social scientists have taken the Barr Scale seriously. Three very respected sociologists, for example, recently cited the scale as evidence, and then testified to their own faith that IQ tests measure the capacity for competence in different status occupations:

Our argument tends to imply that a correlation between IQ and occupational achievement was more or less built into IQ tests, by virtue of the psychologists' implicit acceptance of the social standards of the general populace. Had the first IQ tests been designed in a hunting culture, "general intelligence" might well have turned out to involve visual acuity and running speed rather than vocabulary and symbol manipulation. As it was, the concept of intelligence arose in a society where high status accrued to occupations involving the latter in large measure so what we now mean by intelligence is something like the probability of acceptable performance (given the opportunity) in occupations varying in social status.[9]

To demonstrate that having very high IQ scores made people geniuses, Terman again called upon the faithful to testify in a manner which superficially resembled scientific evidence. The early proponents of IQ tests judiciously neglected to administer them to eminent artists and scientists who were living; instead they had themselves estimate the IQ's of 300 geniuses who were deceased. Raters used the same methods by which Terman earlier had estimated Galton's IQ score to be around 200. Naturally, the figures were very high. Catherine Cox authored *The Early Mental Traits of Three Hundred Geniuses*, in which subjects' IQ scores were rated for them at ages seventeen and twenty-six. Averages for the entire group at these ages were 155 and 165, respectively. Philosophers and scientists scored highest with means of 180 and 175 at age twenty-six. Soldiers were lowest with a mean score of 140.[10] The five raters had been instructed to give estimates only slightly above 100 when they had no information about the subject's background. So the original estimates averaged only 135 and 145, but Cox corrected for this by revising them upward:

> The result of the correction indicates that the true IQ's of the subjects of this study average above 160. It further indicates that many of the true IQ's are above 180, while but few of them are below 140.[11]

This process of estimating IQ scores retrospectively was christened "historiometry," and defended as an exact science.[12] It was anything but an exact science. The raters all believed that IQ scores were a measure of capacity for intellectual accomplishment, so they interpreted any significant achievement as *prima facie* evidence of very high score. The fact that most subjects had begun their life's work as young adults guaranteed that their scores would be high. In addition, much of the information upon which estimates were based came from biographies, in many cases glorifying the person's character and achievements. Often, an otherwise undistinguished paper written when the person was a teenager might become "a notable treatise" when viewed retrospectively in light of his subsequent fame. All 300 geniuses had lived between 1450 and 1850 A.D. when age-grading was much less rigid than it is today.[13] It was not uncommon for a child's academic education to begin at age three or four. So, many subjects displayed evidence of precocity. Because the raters believed in the constancy of IQ scores, they interpreted precocity as evidence of a high score during adulthood. Schools frequently placed young children in the same classes with older ones. Hence, a biographer could often report that his subject was "in with others twice his age, who viewed him as their equal."

Despite its obvious flaws, the Cox study has been well received by members of the academic community. Textbooks and secondary sources generally have reported the findings uncritically, giving the impression that they are proven facts rather then pseudoscientific statements. The public, already accustomed to believing that geniuses are mysterious, alien beings, has had little difficulty accepting the proposition that all geniuses have IQ scores far above the normal range. As long as no data were available to contradict the proposition, it seemed like a reputable scientific finding.

If viewed in a jaundiced manner, the Barr Scale and Cox study look very much like false advertising. Similar methods could be used with as much justification to demonstrate that mental capacity depends primarily on amount of alcohol consumed. The liquor industry, for example, could hire five of its spokesmen to estimate the drinking habits of 300 deceased geniuses. Sincerely believing that genius flows from the bottle, the spokesmen would comb through biographies and historical records for any evidence of alcohol consumption. Such evidence would then be exaggerated and interpreted as proof that the artists and scientists in question were habitual drunkards. When no evidence was found, subjects would be classified as average drinkers. But since these estimates were based on lack of information, they could safely be revised upward, given the shared faith in the magical, stimulating properties of alcohol.

The liquor industry might then hire thirty psychologists to demonstrate that occupational success requires regular intoxication. The psychologists could begin by correlating amount of money spent on liquor with socioeconomic status. Probably they would find a moderate-sized positive correlation in the range of .40 to .60.[14] They could then construct something like the Barr Scale assessing the liquor demands of various occupations. How much liquor must one consume to achieve ordinary success in a given occupation? First on the list would be an inventive genius, second a surgeon, third a research leader, and so forth. The fact that all thirty judges were experts in the field of human abilities, and all thirty agreed about the importance of liquor might be taken as strong evidence that only heavy drinkers could succeed in high-level occupations.

In addition to mounting an advertising campaign for IQ tests, Terman and his colleagues conducted a major longitudinal study of "gifted" persons, which could have revealed much about the tests' validity, had the results of the study not been interpreted so onesidedly. One thousand California school children with IQ scores above 140 had their life accomplishments monitored as they grew up to become middle-aged adults.[15] Despite expectations that most would show evidence of genius, very few did. The gifted sample produced a large number of well-adjusted middle- and upper-middle-class people. Many of the men became doctors, scientists, teachers, and engineers; most of the women became housewives. Close to 90 percent entered college, and 70 percent graduated. By 1950 when the 800 men had an average age of forty years, they had produced among them sixty-seven books.[16] Terman did not try to assess whether the gifted persons were more productive, creative, or brilliant than others in their occupations. The mere fact that many of them went to college and entered professions was sufficient for him.

Nearly all these numbers are from 10 to 20 to 30 times as large as would be found for 800 men of corresponding age picked at random in the general population, and are sufficient answer to those who belittle the significance of IQ differences.[17]

Understanding the significance of IQ test scores requires more than an awareness that people with very high scores differ from those picked at random. One must know *why* they differ. One must examine the sources of the correlation between IQ scores and occupational status. Specifically, one must take advantage of data gathered during the last thirty years to test the meritocracy interpretation accepted uncritically by Terman and his followers. This interpretation runs as follows: People differ markedly in their levels of general intelligence. Those with higher IQ scores do better in school because they are more intelligent, and they do better at work for the same reason. Society values scarce talent, and places its more intelligent members in the important, high-status jobs. The higher the status of an occupation, the more intelligence is required to perform competently in it. This is why IQ scores correlate not only with school grades, but also with occupational status.

There are, however, at last two other explanations of the IQ-job status correlation. The first may be called the *educational credential* interpretation, and runs as follows. IQ tests do not measure general intelligence or mental capacity; they only measure how a child has adapted to schooling. People with higher IQ scores tend to do better in school and, partly for this reason, to stay in school longer. Hence they acquire the higher degrees (e.g., Ph.D., M.D., M.B.A., etc.) which allow them to enter professions and managerial jobs. Many people with lower IQ scores could perform competently in these occupations, but they are rarely given the opportunity. They are denied access to graduate and professional schools, so they receive neither the necessary training nor credentials. The second can be termed the *social class* interpretation. According to it, social class background is an important determinant of future occupational status. Children of wealthy parents tend disproportionately to have the motivation and financial resources needed to enter graduate and professional schools. They often have family connections which aid their careers. They also tend to have childhood home environments which encourage them to do well in school and develop relatively high IQ scores. IQ scores correlate with occupational status not because tests measure abilities needed for success, but because both IQ scores and status are related to social class background.

To evaluate the validity of IQ tests and the efficacy of a general intelligence concept, we must ask whether the meritocracy theory is correct, or whether data are accounted for better by some combination of the other two interpretations. The meritocracy theory makes three predictions which the other interpretations do not make. The accuracy or inaccuracy of these predictions may serve as a basis for accepting or discarding the meritocracy conception. They are: (1) People with higher grades in school also will perform better in occupations, since differences in general intelligence underlie both sorts of performance. (2) Among those with similar class backgrounds and equivalent educational levels, those with higher IQ scores will get better jobs and make more money than those with lower scores. (3) Within a variety of professions, people with higher IQ scores will perform better than those with lower scores.

Available evidence in each case does not support the meritocracy interpretation. All three predictions appear to be wrong. The evidence is most unequivocal in regard to the first prediction. Donald P. Hoyt has summarized the results of about forty separate studies correlating college grade point average with different measures of occupational performance.[18] Twelve studies examined the performance of teachers, and all except a few found no relationship between college grades and measures of teaching success. The few exceptions reported very low correlations. Seven studies of success in business mostly used income as the measure, and only one found any relationship between it and college grades. Of the five studies of engineers, only one reported a significant positive correlation, and even this was probably due to use of a seriously flawed measure. The same professors who had graded the engineers when they were students also estimated their professional competence. Eight studies of medical doctors found performance unrelated to undergraduate grade point average. Medical school grades related somewhat to the early success of physicians, but only during the first few years of practice. Five studies of scientists showed a low positive correlation between college grades and subsequent research contribution. The two largest studies showed correlations close to zero, and in at least one of the other three, the relationship seemed to stem from differential access to research opportunities.[19] Hoyt concluded that college grades "have no more than very modest relationships to measures of research performance."[20] Other studies not summarized by Hoyt also support that conclusion.[21]

The lack of correlation between college grades and professional competence appears not to depend upon how performance is measured. Peer ratings, supervisor's ratings, direct measures of productivity, and monetary income all point in the same direction—college grades predict occupational achievement very little, and in most cases not at all. The lack of relationship cannot be attributed to a restriction of range in college grade point average. Most of those studied graduated prior to 1960 when it was still possible to enter graduate and professional schools with mediocre grades. So studies frequently showed a range of straight "A" to "C–" averages. Finally, as far as eminence is concerned, school grades appear to have virtually no predictive value. A study of college graduates in *Who's Who in America* showed the majority to have grade point averages in the range of "B" to "C+".[22]

Galton's and Terman's conception of schools-as-proving-grounds has been contradicted further by studies of extracurricular achievements in high school. A study of 7,262 college freshmen found no relationship between their course grades and nonacademic accomplishments in high school.[23] Students listed achievements in areas ranging from science projects to dramatic ability, musical talent, and social leadership. Accomplishments were rated and correlated with high school grade point average. Despite the large size of the sample, hardly any of the correlations were statistically significant.[24] The seventy-seven correlations produced medians of +.03 for men and +.06 for women. Similar results appeared when standardized academic achievement tests were used instead of course grades. The authors then replicated this study with a sample of 18,000 students, and confirmed the reliability of the self-reported extracurricular achievements.[25]

After reviewing these and several other studies, the psychologist and test designer Michael Wallach concluded that,

> high school grades and test scores tend to intercorrelate, and both tend to predict college grades. Neither test scores nor grades, on the other hand, predict which students have excelled in nonclassroom projects in the sciences and humanities in high school or in college, but achievements in some field while in high school tend to give a good basis for predicting that the person will continue to manifest accomplishment in that field while in college.[26]

Thus extracurricular intellectual abilities[27] appear to be real in the sense that they have some stability over time, but they are uncorrelated with, and probably quite different from, the abilities measured by scholastic aptitude tests and ratings of classroom performance.

Several attempts[28] have been made to test the second prediction that IQ scores will manifest in income and occupational status, even when its association with social class background and effect upon level of schooling completed are somehow discounted. The studies have used a variety of statistical techniques, most of which do not yield quantitative results immediately intelligible to the lay reader. Fortunately, however, the results have been in substantial agreement concerning the way in which IQ scores manifest in earnings and status. Here I will quote the two pertinent conclusions of Samuel Bowles and Valerie Nelson, although it should be borne in mind that the first is reached by all the above cited studies, whereas the second is contradicted by some and appears to depend upon the age at which IQ tests are taken.

   (1) The direct effect of childhood IQ upon income and occupational status is considerably less than on years of schooling; the total effect of early IQ upon income and occupational status operates in large part indirectly via the effect of childhood IQ upon years of schooling.

   (2) The effect of socio-economic background on each of the three adult status variables—schooling, income, and occupational status—is greater than the effect of childhood IQ.[29]

Some investigators report that IQ scores have no direct impact on income, while others say that they have some, but the amount is small. The most popularly accessible of the studies, Bowles's and Gintis' "IQ in the U.S. Class Structure," generate figures which dramatically illustrate the weakness of the meritocracy interpretation. Their basic findings are essentially in line with those of the Bowles and Nelson study, although the specific figures should not be taken literally because the methodology employed is considered faulty.[30]

Taken as a whole, the studies clearly do not support any conception of IQ test results as a measure of general adeptness which would enable one to function effectively and rise in the occupational hierarchy. Of the three alternative explanations for the IQ-job status correlation, the one which receives most support is the educational credential interpretation. However, limitations on the quality of data and the applicability of statistical techniques preclude the possibility of any precise, definitive answer concerning the relative explanatory power of the different interpretations.

The third prediction—that IQ scores will correlate with performance in high-status occupations—has consistently failed to find support among the relevant data. In part this may be due to a problem of restricted range. The IQ scores of learned professionals typically have ranged from about average to very high. When tested in the army during the Second World War, lawyers' IQ scores ranged from 96 to 157; engineers' scores were between 100 and 151; chemists' ranged from 102 to 153.[31] People with scores well below 100 generally have lacked the necessary certification to enter most professions.[32] Nevertheless, if IQ tests measured capacity for intellectual achievement, one would expect to find at least a moderately strong relationship between the score and occupational performance, even given the restricted range. The fact that four studies have found essentially zero relationship and none have found otherwise must be taken as evidence against the prediction.

Strong doubts about the IQ test results being a measure of genius were generated first by Ann Roe slightly over twenty years ago. She administered IQ tests to sixty-four eminent scientists and reported that while some had scored very high, there were "a number of subjects for whom none of the test material would give the slightest clue that the subject was a scientist of renown."[33] Two years later Meer and Stein obtained supervisors' ratings of the creativity of sixty-four chemists working in an industrial setting. When they correlated these ratings with IQ scores, they initially found a small but significant positive relationship between the two. However, upon closer inspection they learned that the relationship applied only to chemists who lacked the Ph.D. degree and worked in sections where there were numerous obstacles to doing research. Under these conditions only the more "intelligent" were allowed to conduct experiments. So Meer and Stein concluded that IQ scores were not an important indicator of the research performance of chemists, provided they were given the opportunity to do research.[34] Harmon's study of 493 scientists who had applied for AEC fellowships found virtually no relationship between test scores and a variety of measures of scientific accomplishment. Average correlations with rated accomplishment were +.10 for the verbal test taken in the senior year of college and +.06 for the quantitative test.[35]

The most comprehensive study of IQ scores and creative achievement was reported by Donald MacKinnon about fifteen years ago. The Terman Concept Mastery Test (1956) was administered to groups of mathematicians, creative writers, architects, research scientists, and electronic engineers. Test scores were correlated with reliable ratings of creative accomplishment for each group. Among mathematicians there was a low positive correlation between test scores and rated achievement, but among the other occupations there was essentially zero relationship between the two variables. MacKinnon stressed that this was not due simply to restriction of range, and that the test scores had varied widely.[36] He also reported that when a group of outstanding architects were compared with undistinguished architects of the same age, there was no difference in the average IQ scores of the two groups.[37]

A study of research scientists by H.G. Gough produced similar findings. Correlations of on-the-job creativity were −.07 with the Terman Concept Mastery Test, +.13 with the Minnesota Engineering Analogies Test, and +.07 with the General Information Survey. None of the three correlations was statistically significant.[38]

The fact that the studies have reached similar conclusions lends credence to their findings. Nevertheless, all should be interpreted cautiously. People who enter high-level professions have already undergone a fairly strenuous selection procedure. Those with the lower IQ scores may have been selected because they excelled in certain other qualities. So it is possible that a genuine effect of IQ scores on performance would be masked by the fact that the people with higher scores were inferior in other respects. Overall, the third prediction certainly is not supported, but neither is it emphatically disproved. It is merely discredited insofar as the available data permit any test of it. In this area further research is warranted.

An appropriately cautious conclusion from present data is Frank Barron's statement,

> that for certain intrinsically creative activities a specifiable minimum IQ is probably necessary to engage in the activity at all, but beyond the minimum, which is often surprisingly low, creativity has little correlation with scores on IQ tests.[39]

Whether this minimum is around average for the population (i.e., IQ score in range of 95 to 105) or somewhere in the dull-normal range (i.e., IQ score between 80 and 90) has not been established. Certainly adults classified as retarded would have little chance of succeeding in professions which require higher education. A common interpretation is that intelligence and creativity are separate abilities, so IQ tests would not be expected to predict creative accomplishment. This, however, assumes that IQ tests measure intelligence, an assumption which must seriously be called into question, given the failure of predictions generated by the meritocracy hypothesis. The fact that IQ scores correlate very highly with performance on standardized achievement tests, moderately well with course grades determined partly by tests, and hardly at all with performance in occupations not requiring tests, seems to suggest that IQ scores are primarily a measure of test-taking ability.[40] Rather than confuse matters by using loaded and ambiguous terms like *intelligence,* it is better to say simply that the test-oriented skills which determine IQ scores differ markedly from the abilities which underlie other sorts of intellectual achievement.

It is, of course, possible that IQ tests have greater predictive validity in the lower ranges than in the upper ones. While the difference between 110 and 150 seems to reflect mainly variation in test-taking ability, the difference between 60 and 100 may reflect general brightness and dullness to a somewhat greater extent. This interpretation is not supported by data, but neither has it been conclusively disproven. The most pertinent evidence is Edwin Ghiselli's correlations of IQ scores with ratings of job proficiency and trainability for a large number of low- and middle-status occupations. These average +.23 and +.42 respectively.[41] However, the data are ambiguous in several respects. David McClelland has pointed out that the correlations seem to be higher in jobs where having upper-class manners and dress conceivably could contribute to one's proficiency rating.[42] Thus, the correlations may merely reflect a tendency of employers to discriminate against people from lower class backgrounds, who would on the average have lower IQ scores. The correlations with "trainability" are particularly suspect because Ghiselli did not control for level of education attained. In many occupations it is common practice to promote, and therefore to train, the people who have had the most education. Supervisors would tend to rate these people as quite trainable for this reason. Because adult IQ score correlates +.70 with level of education attained,[43] these more "trainable" employees could be expected to have relatively high IQ scores. On the one hand, the .23 and .42 correlations are not very high to begin with, and they may stem mainly from a relationship between supervisors' attitudes and employees' class background and educational levels. The .23 figure accounts for only 5 percent of the variance in rated competence, and even this 5 percent may not reflect actual performance. On the other hand, most of the occupations are not high-status ones, and they are not thought to require much intelligence. From Ghiselli's data one can conclude only that for most occupations the observed differences in IQ scores are not very important determinants of performance.

The suggestion that IQ scores are a measure of test-taking ability seems contrary to common sense. We are accustomed to hearing that the abilities measured by tests are basic ones used in any kind of intellectual endeavor. On one level this is true. At the same time, however, the test situation differs greatly from the behavioral process involved in complex cognitive tasks. As one researcher has stated,

> Intelligence tests measure how quickly people can solve relatively unimportant problems making as few errors as possible, rather than measuring how people grapple with relatively important problems, making as many productive errors as necessary with no time factor.[44]

While it is true that mathematicians multiply and divide when they are solving problems of advanced calculus, this does not mean that speed and accuracy in doing arithmetic constitutes a valid measure of mathematical ability. Even if there is a low or moderate level correlation between the two, this does not mean that the one can be used as a measure of the other. After all, temperature correlates with time of day, and weight with height, but this does not justify determining the weather with a clock or measuring pounds with a yardstick.

Principally what is needed is an abandonment of the general intelligence concept. The concept of intelligence has no clear definition, and there are no good measures of it. In everyday language it subsumes many different behaviors, and is used as a highly subjective, all-around assessment. If it is to be examined scientifically at all, it should be treated as a labelling device and perceptual category rather than an attribute of people or behavior. IQ tests have a very limited use as clinical diagnostic devices for understanding learning disorders. Differential performance on parts of the tests can help to determine whether brain damage is present. Overall score can sometimes help teachers understand the sources of learning difficulties. This is the same use for which

Binet originally designed the tests. The problem has been that ever since Goddard and Terman grafted the Galton-Spencer theory onto the tests, they have been misused so consistently and so widely that they have appeared primarily as articles of pseudoscience.

Some of the more reputable psychometricians have sought gradually and unceremoniously to discard the concept of intelligence. They have done so principally by substituting for it terms like *scholastic aptitude* and *cognitive skills*. However, an almost universal reluctance to acknowledge the impact of pseudoscience has allowed a large number of psychometricians to remain committed to both the tests and the concept. Their influence has been sufficiently strong that the norms of the field continue to discourage any serious assessment of the tests' validity. Even the better textbooks make statements like, "the IQ is also an effective predictor of performance in many occupations and other activities of adult life,"[45] without examining pertinent evidence. These omissions are the lingering results of an unbroken attachment to pseudoscience.

Knowing more about what IQ tests measure should diminish but not completely eliminate our interest in knowing whether IQ scores are shaped by heredity. The tests do measure certain kinds of abilities, and if these could be proven to be hereditary, then perhaps similar methods could someday be used to prove that other abilities were hereditary.

7. The Hereditability Question: To What Extent Are Test Scores Determined by Heredity?

The discrediting of Pearson's, Davenport's, and Terman's arguments that IQ test results were hereditary confronted the early psychometricians with an agonizing choice. They could either abandon their efforts to construct a science of eugenics and become essentially technicians who designed tests for tracking children in the public schools, or they could undertake the difficult task of devising new ways of showing that IQ ability was hereditary. Most psychometricians chose the first alternative and downplayed the question of heredity; but an influential minority remained committed to the eugenics paradigm and made important methodological advances which increased the complexity and persuasiveness of Galtonian pseudoscience.

Contemporary claims that IQ scores are determined genetically rest on four kinds of evidence.[1] The two most popular and seemingly most definitive kinds of data come from studies of separated monozygotic twins, and studies of adopted children. The twins have the same genes and have been raised in different families, so the similarity or dissimilarity of their IQ scores presumably tells much about the relative importance of heredity and environment. Adopted children's test scores are compared with the scores of their natural, biological parents, as well as with those of their adoptive parents. Depending upon which set of parents the children most resemble, the studies seem to provide a way of calculating whether nature or nurture is more important. The third kind of evidence is referred to generally as kinship correlations. It involves estimating the degree of resemblance in the IQ scores of different sorts of relatives. For example, the similarity of monozygotic twins' scores is compared with the similarity of fraternal or dizygotic twins' scores. Finally, there are breeding studies which show that certain strains of laboratory rats tend to perform better or worse than average rats running a particular kind of maze.

Since the discovery of irrefutable evidence that variations in a person's environment can affect his or her score on IQ tests, it has not seemed plausible that IQ results could be shaped entirely by genes. Hereditarians have retreated to arguing that test scores are determined *mostly* by heredity. This tactical retreat has created a need for a quantitative index of the relative importance of heredity and environment. Psychometricians and behavior geneticists have sought to fill the need by borrowing the concept of *heritability* used by plant and animal breeders. The heritability of a trait can be calculated for a particular population existing under given environmental conditions. It may range anywhere from 0 to 1.00, the former denoting no influence due to heredity, the latter indicating a pervasive influence. Based upon studies of humans, a number of psychometricians have concluded that for Caucasians in the United States and some European countries, IQ scores have a heritability around .80. They have interpreted heritability coefficients as showing "the proportion of the variance attributable to various genetic and environmental components." Hence the .80 figure means that 80 percent of the variation in IQ scores "can be said to be due to genetic variation," and only 20 percent to environmental differences.[2]

The discovery and dissemination of this finding may be viewed as pseudoscience for two reasons. The .80 figure is a cumulative result of exaggerations, methodological errors, and systematic biases, all serving to elevate heritability coefficients far above what would be found by less highly flawed scientific procedures. But also, the very concept of heritability has been misunderstood. A coefficient of .80 does not mean that 80 percent of the trait's phenotypic (or observed) variation is determined by heredity and 20 percent by environment. It means that for 20 percent of the phenotypic variation genetic differences play no role, whereas for the remaining 80 percent they do play *some* role, possibly in conjunction with environmental differences. The crucial importance of this distinction will be illustrated later in the chapter.

This second point is in some ways more important than the first. Since heritability coefficients do not provide a true measure of genetic determination, even the most reliable could not resolve the nature-nurture controversy. Hence, the problem of proving IQ scores to be largely hereditary is unsolvable within the framework of available methodologies. Investigators do not simply need more and better data; they need to ask different questions altogether. The apparent solution of the heredity vs. environment question by heritability estimates has been a kind of mirage stemming from a strong need to solve an old and persistently unsolvable problem.

Debate over the precise heritability of IQ scores is inappropriate at the present time because the available data are such that no accurate estimates can be drawn from them, and furthermore, all known experimental designs have inherent ambiguities sufficiently great that it seems very unlikely that any precise estimate could be obtained in the foreseeable future. On the other hand, the heritability debate is of considerable interest to the historian of pseudoscience. Because the widely accepted .80 figure has been based upon numerous deceptions and misinterpretations extending over a fifty year period, any serious attempt to refute it necessarily involves gathering extensive evidence of the manner in which false claims have been promoted. The first such attempt is found in Leon Kamin's recently published book, *The Science and Politics of IQ* (1974). Kamin's work constitutes a major breakthrough both for environmentalists wishing to argue that IQ scores are not hereditary, and for people attempting to understand the dynamics of pseudoscience. Here we will briefly describe some of his findings and interpret their significance. Those interested in the heritability question should read Kamin's book along with the critical reviews by hereditarians.[3]

Kamin's review of the data assaults all major sources of evidence for the heritability of IQ scores—the separated twin studies, the studies of adopted children, and the kinship correlations. For some of the evidence, the critique is completely devastating; for most of what remains, it manages to cast very serious doubts upon the validity of the

conclusions. Like other critics,[4] Kamin discusses the ambiguities involved in comparing different kinship correlations. For example, the
higher correlation found when comparing monozygotic twins' IQ
scores may reflect some genetic determination of IQ, but it may also
stem from the fact that monozygotic twins have more similar environments than ordinary siblings because people treat them more alike.
Evidence for the latter interpretation is included in the book.[5]

Studies of separated twin pairs seemingly could provide less ambiguous evidence, but Kamin shows that all four twin studies are plagued
with major difficulties. The separated twins' environments are almost
never random, for the simple reason that adoption agencies usually
follow a policy of placing twins in similar kinds of homes. In many
cases the pairs have been raised by relatives; occasionally they have not
been separated prior to age six. In one of the studies, unconscious
experimenter bias appears possibly to have inflated the twins' correlations. In two others, use of tests poorly standardized for age has resulted in an apparent confounding of variables. Much of the twins'
similarity may be due to the fact that they are the same age, and test
scoring procedures tend to favor people with certain ages and discriminate against those with others. Worst of all is the work of Sir Cyril Burt,
winner of the American Psychological Association's Edward Lee Thorndike Award. For many years Burt was thought to have provided the
strongest evidence for the genetic determination of IQ scores. The
reason for his seemingly definitive results is exposed by Kamin:

> We must recognize that Burt's data base, by his deliberate choice,
> was of a very unorthodox type. The "empirical" correlations were
> instead based on Burt's "adjusted assessments." The purpose of
> adjusting raw test scores was to remove most of the "disturbing
> effects of environment." The Burt data were thus subjected to a
> deliberate and systematic bias, justified by Burt's faith that he
> could intuitively detect the genotypic value behind the raw test
> score.[6]

Since Kamin's critique it has been discovered that Burt's alleged research collaborators may not have existed, or at least may not have
collaborated with him.[7] This has raised the suspicion of deliberate
fraud in most of Burt's work. Although unproven, the charge of fraud

has sufficient weight to suggest that Burt can no longer be taken seriously as a source of evidence.

Conclusions drawn from studies of adopted children also become clouded by doubt when the data are examined closely. The apparently greater similarity with biological parents than foster parents may be attributable to defects in the studies which reported it. Adoption agencies frequently have tried to place infants in homes with the same socioeconomic status level as that of their natural parents. Children born to parents with low or high IQ scores would tend to receive foster parents with similar ones for this reason. So the foster home environments selected in this manner could very plausibly produce correlations with the biological parents' IQ scores. Correlations with the adoptive parents' test scores appear to have been lowered by a restriction of range due to the fact that impoverished and culturally deprived families were not allowed to adopt children.

Kamin examines the role of secondary sources in generating the illusion of conclusive evidence. Over time there has been a selective reporting of studies in favor of those which produce positive results. For example, the two studies of adopted children whose data clearly contradict a genetic interpretation have been dropped from contemporary reference lists while the other three studies have been cited repeatedly, attracting considerable attention. The irregularities and uncertainties contained in the original investigations are almost invariably overlooked when the studies are summarized in textbooks and reviews of the literature. For example, the environments of separated twins are usually described as random, despite extensive evidence that this is not the case. Seemingly impressive evidence that genetic models can predict observed kinship correlations is often presented without explanation. It turns out, however, that the "models" were constructed after the data were observed, by inserting rather arbitrary values into the equations so as to produce figures closely resembling the observed ones.[8]

There is no reason to believe that Kamin has exposed *all* the errors underlying heritability estimates, or even a representative sample. However, his critique is sufficiently broad to document a process of *cumulative* pseudoscience. The fact that one investigator can suddenly reveal so many previously unknown errors and uncertainties indicates that the norms of the field have been such as to discourage critical methodological inquiry and encourage slight exaggerations and oversimplifications. This makes possible a cumulative process of deception in which the total effect of false persuasion exceeds the sum of the infractions committed by the culpable people. When the original researchers overlook or downplay serious ambiguities, and subsequent popularizers report the findings briefly and enthusiastically, the overall effect on the public may be equivalent to that produced by deliberate fraud, despite the fact that neither the researchers nor the popularizers have done anything worse than exercise inadequate caution and critical judgment.

Most of the errors Kamin cites involve a refusal to acknowledge uncertainties inherent in the data. This suggests that an inability to secure an adequate data base—adoption agencies do not place children randomly, separated twins do not have random environments, the IQ scores of foster parents do not range as widely as those of biological parents, and so forth—may lie at the root of the field's having norms conducive to pseudoscience. If rigorous critical inquiry were continuously present, then it is likely that no credible estimates of heritability could be issued. However, commitment to the eugenics paradigm in the face of opposition to it requires that there be heritability estimates, and to preserve the credibility of these estimates investigators simply avoid being too critical of the data.

The major defect with Kamin's work is that he unfortunately chooses to defend the hypothesis of zero heritability. He does not say that IQ scores have zero heritability; he merely adopts the stance of a defense lawyer in asserting that the hypothesis has not been proven false:

> To assert that there is *no* genetic determination of I.Q. would be a strong, and scientifically meaningless, statement. We cannot prove the null hypothesis [that heritability is zero], nor should we be asked to do so. The question is whether there exist data of merit and validity that require us to reject the null hypothesis. There should be no mistake here. The burden of proof falls upon those who wish to assert the implausible proposition that the way in which a child answers questions devised by a mental tester is determined by an unseen genotype.[9]

After reviewing the evidence he exclaims: "The hypothesis of zero heritability stands unscathed."[10] Most likely his case is strong enough to produce a hung jury, with votes depending upon the jurors' preconceived biases. He does manage to cast doubt upon all the evidence, but whether there are insufficient grounds for rejecting the null hypothesis depends upon how one gauges the doubts. The magnitude of effects produced by the various errors often cannot be calculated. For example, the similarity or dissimilarity of environments cannot be accurately assessed because the ways in which environment affects IQ test results are understood only very crudely. In one study of separated twins, the difference between the twins' IQ scores was about three times as great when they were tested by different investigators as when they were tested by the same person. This suggests that correlations may have been inflated by unconscious experimenter bias, but the discrepancy can also be attributed to peculiarities of the five pairs tested by different investigators. In two other studies an age-IQ score confound (that is, a tendency for scores to be higher at certain ages than others due to poor standardization procedures) may have been responsible for some of the twins' similarity, but Kamin has no reliable way of estimating the effect of such a confound, and the method he uses may greatly overestimate its significance.[11]

In short, Kamin clearly demonstrates that existing heritability estimates are tremendously inflated by an uncritical reliance on faulty data, and that if valid estimates could be derived, they would be much lower than the figures currently discussed. He shows how the .80 figure is largely a product of pseudoscience, and why no valid estimates can be derived from available evidence. Whether he, in addition, completely invalidates all evidence for any significant heritability is problematical.

Kamin's decision to focus on the question of zero heritability is unfortunate for another reason as well. It subtly reinforces the illusion that heritability is a yardstick measuring the relative importance of heredity and environment. Complete victory for environmentalist theories should not be equated with zero heritability. Such theories, which assert that virtually everyone is born with the biological capacity to become a genius, are equally consistent with a low heritability of IQ scores—say in the range of .10 to .30—as they are with no heritability. Also, it is quite unlikely that any behavioral characteristic would have absolutely no heritability.

Why this is so can be understood by considering the case of the maze-bright and maze-dull rats. When it was learned that rats could be bred to make more or fewer errors running a T-shaped maze, this finding was hailed as proof that intelligence was at least partly inherited. Later it was discovered that on mazes with better lighting, the "bright" rats did worse than the "dull" rats. So probably what was being shaped by heredity was not differences in intelligence, but differences in sensitivity to nonvisual cues.[12] This in no way contradicts the conclusion that maze performance has a significant heritability. Performance clearly depends upon a genetic characteristic, even though the characteristic is reliance on sense of smell rather than overall mental capacity. As long as *some* genetic differences relate *somehow* to differences in a given behavior, it may be said that the behavior is significantly heritable. The relationship may be quite arbitrary. Consider the hypothetical laboratory in which researchers have bred two strains of rats differing only in fur color. Researchers like the white rats better than the black ones, and reward them more after successful completion of learning tasks. Consequently the white rats regularly do better on a variety of tests. They tend to be test-bright whereas the black rats tend to be test-dull. Does test-brightness have a significant heritability? Indeed, it does—at least for this population of rats existing under these conditions.

As two critics of the heritability concept have stated, "a genetic characteristic may function as a signal to initiate an array of social processes."[13] It thus becomes important to distinguish between genes as *determiners* of a trait, and genes as *markers* which influence how a person will be affected by the social processes which determine a trait. It is quite plausible that normal genetic differences do not limit mental capacity in any important way. It is very implausible that of all the possible genetic differences, none would play *any* role in the social processes which determine scores on IQ tests.

With this in mind it is easy to understand the fallacy exposed by David Layzer. He notes that while heritability analysis is used to divide a population's IQ score variance into separate genetic and environmental components,

> the variance splits up into separate genetic and non-genetic parts only if each measurement can be expressed as the sum of *statistically independent* genetic and non-genetic contributions—that is, only if the relevant genetic and non-genetic factors contribute additively and independently to the character in question.[14]

Since this is almost certainly not the case for IQ scores among humans, the separation into discrete components is not justified. Another way of stating the problem is that if heritability is calculated for human behavioral traits, the estimates will probably greatly exaggerate the extent to which traits are controlled by heredity, because heritability coefficients confound the effects of genes-as-determiners with those of genes-as-markers.

This basic objection has been expressed since at least 1943, shortly after all the discussion about heritability of IQ scores began.[15] Hereditarians, however, have had difficulty comprehending it. Two current proponents of the eugenics paradigm have referred to this issue as a "technical obfuscation," and as "technical minutiae."[16] If it is in any sense a small point, then it is like a pinprick in a filled balloon, for it completely negates the use of heritability as a measure of genetic determination. The validity and significance of the point becomes clear if we keep in mind what is meant by variation in IQ scores.

Three things in particular should be remembered:

(1) Performance on IQ tests depends upon how well one concentrates while taking the test, and upon how much of the relevant information one has learned previously. Much of the knowledge called for on IQ tests is similar to knowledge acquired in school, so a child's IQ score may be viewed as an approximate indicator of how well he or she is learning in school.

(2) The phenomenon of a stable IQ score first appears in the child around age seven, after he or she has been in school for a year or two. This parallels the fact that the same children tend to be bright or dull in school as they pass from one grade to the next. IQ scores are more stable than teachers' marks because the tests have been designed to maximize stability, and different teachers respond differently to the same pupils. An adult's IQ score closely resembles the score which developed while the person was in school.

(3) Children with high IQ scores usually behave differently in the classroom than children with low scores, and for this reason they are treated differently. Test-bright children tend to concentrate on tests, pay attention in class, and give back correct answers. So they are viewed and treated as bright by teachers, and usually feel confident about performing in school. Test-dull children do not concentrate or pay attention as much, and they do not perform as well. So they are

viewed and treated as dull, and usually lack self-confidence. Interaction between teachers and pupils is reciprocal: it is easier for the teacher to reward a child's performance if the child performs well, and it is easier for the child to perform well if his performance is rewarded.

So far we have said nothing about the causes of variation in IQ scores; we have only briefly described part of the behavioral process associated with it. The process will be described more fully in Chapter 12, but here it is pertinent to note the possibility of genotype-environment correlation. If one assumes that the test-bright children have superior genes, then one may also note that they have superior environments—they are treated in a manner conducive to maintaining a high IQ score. "Environment" does not mean simply which house one lives in, or which school one attends; it refers to the totality of a person's experience. After all, psychologists do not expect two rats to behave identically because they have been raised in the same cage; psychologists are concerned with the specific reinforcement contingencies confronting each rat. Probably there would be less confusion if the word *experience* were used instead of environment, but since this is not likely to happen, it is important to remember that any sophisticated environmentalist theory will use the term broadly to mean something like the entire array of stimuli and reinforcement contingencies confronting a person. In this sense, two children raised in the same family and attending the same school will have very different environments if one performs much better than the other on tests.

Let us now propose hereditarian and environmentalist theories to account for variation in IQ scores. The hereditarian theory is easy to understand. It says that the variation is largely predetermined by genetic differences. Some children are born with superior genes, predisposing them to be bright, others with defective genes, causing them to be dull. Behavioral processes observed in the classroom merely involve students and teachers adapting to the fact that genetic differences have caused students to learn at different rates. The environmentalist theory asserts that the behavioral processes are a major cause of the variation in test scores. It asserts that nearly all children are born with genotypes which would allow them to be either bright or dull, and that children are selected to be one or the other by their environments. How does the selection occur? In the classroom, it is most likely brought about by an uneven distribution of rewards and punishments.[17] Children who do well are rewarded and find it worth their while to pay attention, learn, and concentrate on tests. Children who do not do well are rewarded less, and consequently find that time spent in class can be more gratifying if they daydream, doodle on desk tops, or talk with other children—anything but concentrate on learning tasks. In short, they *disengage* their minds from the tasks, success or failure on which largely determines IQ test results. Over time this practice of disengagement becomes habitual and difficult to change. So children with low IQ scores learn slowly and retain low scores. According to this theory, schools do more than provide opportunities for learning; they inadvertently induct children into upward and downward cycles of motivation and accomplishment. They inadvertently train some students to be bright and others to be dull.[18] How is it decided which students receive which kind of training? Probably the most important thing is the students' initial performance, which in turn depends upon the kind of preparation for schooling provided by the home environment. However, it may also depend upon a number of genetic factors.

We want to know which of the two theories is more correct, so we turn to heritability estimates as a way of resolving the issue. Suppose we somehow learn that the heritability of IQ scores in the United States and Western Europe is .50. Probably this estimate is much too high, but it is a good hypothetical figure because it seems to imply that the two theories are equally valid. Fifty percent of the variance is clearly not genetic in origin and can be attributed to environment or experience. But what about the remaining 50 percent? Can it be attributed to genetic factors?

The answer depends upon the *kind* of genetic differences involved. Unfortunately, geneticists know very little about how genetic variation affects behavior in humans. They know that genes produce enzymes, but they have no way of comprehending the intricately complex relationship between enzyme concentrations and behavior. So we are left to speculate. Hereditarians might begin by speculating that the .50 heritability of IQ stems from differences in "mental efficiency" genes. Some people have genotypes which produce enzymes which facilitate alertness and concentration; others lack sufficient concentrations of these enzymes, and therefore have less efficient neural transmission in the cerebral cortex. Assuming this difference is relatively impervious to fluctuations in the environment, it is fair to attribute 50 percent of the variation to genetic factors.

But there are other possibilities. The .50 heritability might reflect genetically determined differences in the rate of maturation of neural structures. There is some evidence that genes may largely control rate of biological maturation.[19] It is plausible that at age six when children enter school there are important differences in how completely their cortical brain structures have matured. These may help to create an initial impression of brightness or dullness, and thereby serve as a basis for inducting children into upward or downward cycles of motivation and accomplishment. In this case it would be misleading to attribute the variation to differences in "mental maturation" genes. If schools systematically worked to make all children bright, then the behavioral differences due to rate of maturation conceivably would disappear by age ten or twelve. Instead they serve as a basis for permanent differences in IQ scores. But these differences are not really caused by the genes; they are caused by the social processes in schools. Genes are important as markers rather than as determiners.

A third possibility shows that their role could be even more indirect. Suppose there are genetic differences which affect the threshold at which a baby will start to cry in response to new stimuli. These differences in "baby crankiness" genes shape the baby's behavior in a way which differentially reinforces or punishes parents for trying to play with the infant. As a result, some young children may receive more parental stimulation than others, and be more likely to perform well in school. In this case genetic differences are important mainly insofar as they influence the home environment.

Finally, it is possible that genetic factors may influence a person's propensity to daydream. These "daydream proneness" genes may directly affect performance in school, since one of the causes and symptoms of dullness is excessive reverie. On the other hand, Chapter 13 presents evidence that a major attribute of genius is the tendency to engage in vivid daydreams. So, ironically, people with "poor" genotypes for developing high IQ scores might also have the genes most conducive to becoming a great artist or scientist.

The main point is that a heritability coefficient of .50 raises all these possibilities and confirms none of them. If all four kinds of differences are involved, then a .50 heritability might mean that about 10 or 15 percent of the variation is really attributable to genetic factors, and the remainder to either environment or some interaction of genes and environment. High heritability for a behavioral trait allows one to decide that genes determinine the trait *only* if one *assumes* that environment or experience does not. Using heritability estimates to prove that IQ scores are hereditary involves the same kind of tautological reasoning used by Galton.

Current evidence for the genetic determination of mental ability is superficially impressive but actually no more definitive than what existed in 1920, or for that matter, 1870. Debate over heritability has generated the mirage of a simple yardstick measuring the relative potency of genes and environment for determining IQ scores. In addition, it has provided fertile ground for the incubation of pseudoscience. A third view of the heritability debate is presented in Chapter 12— namely, that it has involved a clash between two scientifically naive but politically congenial hypotheses.

Theoretically, reliable heritability estimates could establish an upper limit to the amount of variation in IQ scores conceivably determined by heredity. This might constitute a worthwhile research goal, except for the fact that it is very unlikely that reliable estimates could be obtained. The technical difficulties involved in gathering unambiguous data are considerable. Even when the necessary data exist, there is no precise way of calculating heritability from them. Based upon an uncritical acceptance of existing data, various investigators have derived heritability coefficients ranging from .45 to .80.[20] Finally, it is well to remember that knowing the extent to which IQ scores were hereditary would not answer the basic question posed by Galton and Spencer: Are differing levels of *mental capacity* inherited? My own view is that this question is scientifically unanswerable now, just as it was a hundred years ago. If it could be solved, it would not be by estimating heritability, but by some sort of controlled breeding experiment. Readers interested in pursuing this question should examine Baron Von Zetnikoff's plan, found in the appendix.

8. Ethnic Minorities and IQ Tests: The Problem of Cultural Bias in Tests

At various times during the last forty years, instruments known as "culture-fair" IQ tests have served as vehicles for the transmission of pseudoscience. Although the tests show no real basis for using the culture-fair label, and are less valid as predictors of scholastic performance than conventional IQ tests, many people nevertheless persist in believing that such tests can provide trustworthy comparisons of the basic aptitudes of different races and ethnic groups. This is thought to be so because it is believed that the test items contain subject matter sufficiently universal that no ethnic or status group could have any special disadvantage attributable to the particularities of its culture. The reasoning which underlies this belief is clearly fallacious and easy to refute. The interesting question is why the belief has gained the degree of acceptance which it has.

The misunderstandings about culture-fair tests, like those about conventional IQ tests, have stemmed from a pretense of verification which is for the most part hidden from public view. People do not know exactly how these tests came to be called culture-fair. They merely read books and articles where the tests are called such, and assume on the basis of the label that the tests are indeed culture-fair.

For the tests to have acquired the label to begin with, the pretense had to be explicit and elaborate. Now, however, the common practice is merely to use the label, avoiding any discussion of its origin, and relying upon the label itself to convey the deception. So, for example, in discussions of racial differences in IQ scores, one will sometimes find statements like the following:

> So-called "culture-free" or "culture-fair" tests tend to give Negroes slightly lower scores, on the average, than more conventional IQ tests such as the Stanford-Binet and Wechsler scales. . . .The majority of studies show that Negroes perform relatively better on verbal than on nonverbal intelligence tests.[1]

The precise effect of such statements is difficult to measure, but undoubtedly they encourage at least some readers to dismiss the issue of cultural bias in tests and to assume that the racial comparisons are valid. To comprehend the deception involved, we must first understand the importance and complexity of the culture-bias issue. This can be done by looking at the matter historically and then examining current arguments.

The Problem in Historical Perspective

As several writers have shown, the use of IQ tests to compare intelligence levels of ethnic groups has a sordid history. "Scientific racism," the attempt to prove nonwhite races genetically inferior, first became prominent in the United States during the mid-nineteenth century. As slavery was becoming a burning controversy, its proponents turned increasingly to biological and religious doctrines which posited a *qualitative*[2] difference between blacks and whites. Thus, one popular idea of the time traced blacks' inferior social position to their imaginary descent from certain biblical ancestors.[3] Fifty years after emancipation, when blacks had acquired a token freedom but still resided at the bottom of the wage-labor system, they were acknowledged as equals in principle, but were seen as *quantitatively* inferior to whites, by a measure of fifteen IQ points. Since then, the economic position of most blacks has not improved much; nor have the psychometricians credited them with increased intelligence.

The stigma of a low IQ score has by no means been reserved exclusively for nonwhites. In the early twentieth century, when masses of white immigrants were living in poverty, facing an alien culture, and struggling to unionize, they too had test results which showed most of them to be mentally defective. Although test performance undoubtedly depended upon familiarity with American language and culture, the dominant interpretation of the First World War army data stressed that recent immigrants from southern and Eastern Europe had performed poorly because they were members of inferior races—Jews, Alpines, and Slavs, as opposed to Nordics who were superior. The correlation between test scores and number of years lived in America was explained by the fact that most of the earlier immigrants were from northern Europe and Great Britain while most of the recent ones were not. Carl Brigham, the primary author of this interpretation, received acclaim in psychology journals, influenced congressional debates over immigration restriction, and later came to head the College Entrance Examination Board.[4]

Of course, we now know better. During the 1930s opinion shifted. Even Brigham repudiated his interpretation.[5] What had made this outlook possible was an extremely shallow and ethnocentric conception of culture, together with a willingness to interpret ambiguous data carelessly. In the meantime, however, studies like Brigham's had fanned racist sentiments and promoted the passage of explicitly racist legislation.

While the early mental testers could be accused of promoting nativism and racial bigotry, on the charge of fostering sexism they must stand acquitted. Lewis Terman and others who followed deliberately designed their tests to show no sex differences in average levels of general intelligence. Galton and Spencer both had maintained that women were naturally less intelligent than men, and apparently women had performed worse on Galton's anthropometric tests. Even after Binet-type IQ tests were introduced, there was still considerable opportunity to label women inferior. On the army alpha test, given to soldiers in the First World War, women everywhere scored around ten points lower than men.[6] But Terman and other psychometricians were not satisfied with this result. They tried to maximize the number of test items which showed no difference in the performance of men and women, and to further balance the scores they chose equal numbers of items favoring each sex.[7] So, on the Stanford-Binet test, as on subsequent IQ tests modeled after it, objective measures of ability attested to a full equality of the sexes. Exactly why this happened is unclear. Perhaps the test designers had to reckon with the fact that girls usually performed better than boys in elementary schools. Perhaps they were responding to pressure generated by the strong women's movement of the period. Perhaps the fact that many of Terman's coworkers were women had some impact. Whatever the causes, women were accorded equal intelligence whereas blacks were not.

Most likely the early psychometricians did not have to connive or scheme in order to produce lower scores for blacks and Chicanos. The test designers themselves were white, middle-class academicians who had little if any familiarity with the cultures of ethnic minorities. There were hardly any nonwhites in the original standardization samples, so the testers could escape awareness of the special problems involved in communicating with children of disadvantaged minorities. They could churn out tests referenced toward white middle-class culture—the only culture they themselves understood—and assume that these were objective tests of ability. When it came time to interpret the low scores of blacks and Chicanos, they could fall back upon their own racial prejudice to eradicate any doubt about the results. Consider the tone of Terman's conclusion:

Do races differ in intelligence? A nation which draws its constituents from all corners of the earth and prides itself on being the melting pot of peoples cannot safely ignore this question. It is axiomatic that what comes out of the melting pot depends on what goes into it. A decade ago the majority of anthropologists and psychologists flouted the idea that there are any considerable differences in the native mental capacities of races or nationality groups. Today we have over-whelming evidence that they were mistaken. Army mental tests have shown that not more than 15 percent of American negroes equal or exceed in intelligence the average of our white population, and the intelligence of the average negro is vastly inferior to that of the average white man. The available data indicate that the average mulatto occupies about a mid-position between pure negro and pure white. The intelligence of the American Indian has also been over-rated, for mental tests indicate that it is not greatly superior to that of the average negro. Our Mexican population, which is largely of Indian extraction, makes little if any better showing.[8]

The charge of cultural bias could have been raised against IQ tests at any time since their inception. It did not become a major controversy, however, until after the Second World War. Several things had to happen first. One was an intellectual legitimization of the belief in racial equality. This was supplied by the growing influence of Franz Boas in anthropology. Another was the acknowledgement that experience and environment greatly affected performance on IQ tests. If the tests measured hereditary ability, then there could be no such thing as cultural bias. But if they measured learning in a particular cultural setting, then the charge could have credibility.

Most important was the national shift in attitudes toward racial segregation which occurred largely as a result of the war itself. War-induced labor shortages had enabled unprecedented numbers of blacks to get jobs in major industries. As Russell Marks points out, this helped business leaders "to realize the importance of fully utilizing Black labor," and therefore to see the advantages of integrating blacks into white society.

> The demands of industrial efficiency and social control were the driving forces that largely changed the liberals' and businessmen's attitude toward the Black. Once the Black was recognized as a capable productive unit, whose economic potential could only be realized through more fully integrating him into society, then prejudice and discrimination were wasteful.[9]

After the war it became fashionable to reinterpret test results in ways less conducive to theories of white racial superiority. At the University of Chicago, Allison Davis brought together researchers from several departments to investigate the matter of cultural bias in IQ tests.[10] The issue gained a respectability and an acknowledged importance which previously it had lacked. Even Lewis Terman came to doubt his earlier conclusions about the racial inferiority of blacks and Chicanos.[11]

Business support of racial integration created a favorable climate for the growth of the civil rights movement. The movement in turn challenged IQ tests for being discriminatory against minorities. A series of court battles helped to make the cultural bias of tests into a burning issue. The integration of universities meant growing numbers of black and Chicano psychologists would constitute a supply of competent professionals willing and able to challenge the tests. All these factors dictated that the issue of cultural bias could no longer be ignored.

Current Status of the Problem

As long as prevailing opinion was sufficiently racist, reports of the inferior intelligence of ethnic and racial minorities were likely to be accepted uncritically.[12] However, as overtly racist statements have become less fashionable, the meaning of blacks' fifteen-point deficit in IQ scores has become problematic. Several linguists have been influential in swaying opinion. William Labov, for example, has noted that until fairly recently many whites observing the language of black children have interpreted it as a symptom of mental inferiority. These observers have used test results glibly to promote concepts like "verbal deprivation," according to which,

> black children in the urban ghettos receive little verbal stimulation, hear very little well-formed language, and as a result are impoverished in their means of verbal expression: they cannot speak complete sentences, they do not know the names of common objects, cannot form concepts or convey logical thoughts.[13]

Some educational psychologists have used these ideas to argue that the vernacular of black children should be disregarded in the classroom, because it is a symptom of mental inferiority. However, competent linguists like Labov have shown this view to be largely a product of the ethnocentrism of observers who, because they are unfamiliar with the language of black children, assume it is illogical, ungrammatical, and conceptually deficient.[14] More careful examination of the language shows most of the charges to be clearly unwarranted. Stigmatizing children's normal language certainly cannot help them to learn in school and probably makes matters considerably more difficult. Hence, Labov points out, linguists "are unanimous in condeming this view as bad observation, bad theory, and bad practice."[15]

Others have stressed that differences in dialect may hinder a teacher's relationship with minority children even when the teacher intends to avoid all forms of bias. As Gumperz and Hernandez-Chavez conclude:

> culture plays a role in communication that is somewhat similar to the role of syntactic knowledge in the decoding of referential mean-

ings. Cultural differences, in other words, affect judgment both above and below the level of consciousness. A person may have every intention of avoiding cultural bias, yet, by subconsciously superimposing his own interpretation on the verbal performance of others, he may nevertheless bias his judgment of their general ability, efficiency, etc.[16]

The accusation of cultural bias in IQ tests is part of a larger critique which says that racism is institutionalized in the curricula, teaching methods, and evaluation procedure of public schools. According to the traditional view of psychometricians, schools and IQ tests both provide fair assessments of any minority group's mental abilities. Black and brown children perform worse in school than whites because they generally have lower aptitudes, and tests measure their lower aptitudes. According to the critique, black and brown children perform poorly because numerous subtle and not-so-subtle forms of discrimination in schools discourage them from doing their best. Their lower scores on IQ tests can be attributed to cultural bias in three different senses:

(1) Test items are selected which require information generally more accessible to white, middle-class children than to nonwhite minorities.

(2) Performance on tests depends greatly upon learning in school, hence lower test scores are a direct reflection of the various forms of discrimination in schools.

(3) Because black and brown children frequently have hostile or indifferent relationships with teachers and school authorities, they are not likely to be highly motivated to do well on tests. Hence, tests measure their negative attitudes towards tests rather than their capacities for learning.

The accusation of cultural bias in tests has confronted psychometricians with a tricky problem. On the one hand, the charge clearly has at least some validity. On the other hand, it is very difficult to know how much validity, since performance in school, the normal criterion against which tests are validated, is itself suspect. To know whether the black-white education gap is caused by the lower intelligence of blacks or the institutional racism of schools would require, at the very least, much painstaking observation of interactional processes in the classroom, a mammoth task for which most mental testers have neither the training nor the inclination. Even after this was done it is likely that evidence could be marshalled for either viewpoint, and the decision would come down to a moral and political choice of whether to blame the ethnic and racial minorities or the school system.

The problem is further compounded by the ability of black psychologists to design IQ tests referenced toward black culture. Because such tests have an obvious bias in favor of those familiar with ghetto language, whites tend to perform poorly on them. On the Black Intelligence Test of Cultural Homogeneity (BITCH), for example, a sample of blacks produces an average score 36 points above that of the sample of whites.[17] Clearly, valid comparisons of ethnic groups would require some objective standard of culture-fairness. But thus far no one has been able to devise such a standard.

Most contemporary psychometricians have disdained interest in the theoretical question of comparing minority groups' intelligence levels. They have chosen to ignore the larger issue of cultural bias in tests and schools, and instead have focused on the more limited question of *selection bias in the tests as they are used for job selection and admission to schools.* A number of statistical approaches to this problem have been designed, all of which presuppose that the criterion performance measure (for example, college grade point average) is fair by definition. Selection procedures using tests are seen as fair or biased depending upon how well the tests predict subsequent performance. One popular approach, for example, claims that a test is fair for selection purposes if it predicts grade point average as well for blacks as it does for whites.[18] Another approach contends that selection is fair when the percentage of minority applicants admitted is the same as the percentage reaching some specified level of criterion performance.[19]

While all the approaches address themselves to important issues of selection, none are of much use in answering the basic question: Are the lower scores of ethnic minorities attributable to culture-bias or do they reflect genuinely lower capacities? The eugenics paradigm has specified this as an important question, and for the investigators who continue to work within the paradigm, culture-fair IQ tests have seemed to furnish the best strategy for answering the question.

Deficiencies of Culture-Fair IQ Tests

Culture-fair tests have maintained a considerable mystique. It is not uncommon to hear that they measure basic capacities which are largely unaffected by culture and learning. On the other hand, examination of the pertinent evidence shows the tests to be seriously deficient in two respects: their predictive validity appears to be considerably lower than that of conventional IQ tests, and their pretense of being impervious to cultural variations is unsupported and most likely false. Briefly reviewing the two most popular of these tests will make the point.

The two most widely acclaimed culture-fair tests have been Raven's *Progressive Matrices* and Cattell's *Culture-Fair Tests of g,* originally designed in 1938 and 1940, respectively. These two have followed the dominant approach of "employing simple figural materials [and] requiring subjects to engage in reasoning, inference, generalization, and other basic mental processes in terms of relationships between geometric forms, patterns, etc."[20] For example, the four subtests for young children considered fully culture-fair by Cattell involve copying symbols, classifying pictures, tracing paths through mazes, and identifying similar drawings. Older children and adults are required to complete sequences of drawings by selecting from among five options, to pick out the drawing which differs from the others in a series, and so forth.[21] Raven's matrices consist of geometrical designs from which the subject chooses the alternative which properly completes the sequence.

While no IQ test has a predictive validity sufficiently broad to justify use of the general intelligence concept, some of the standard tests, like the Stanford-Binet and Wechsler scales, are at least moderately able to predict performance in school. This establishes a baseline for what constitutes a valid IQ test. Although Raven's and Cattell's tests have been in existence for over thirty years, there appears to be virtually no evidence that they attain even this baseline of predictive validity. Reviewers generally sympathetic to the tests have noted this deficiency. About Cattell's test, one states that, "the evidence on the validity of the tests in predicting scholastic achievement is not impressive," and then he mentions one study showing a low correlation with performance on the Stanford Achievement Test for a small sample of only twenty-eight children. He also notes that the most recent handbook of the test lacks evidence relating to the test's validity. The other reviewer states that he "would need to see some real longitudinal validity data," before he could endorse the test.[22] The situation is basically similar for the *Progressive Matrices* test. One reviewer says that the literature dealing with test validity and reliability is "equivocal," and that the test's "relevance to intellectual functioning in general remains to be documented." Another proclaims that "no really satisfactory conclusions as to validity are possible," on the basis of data reported.

> The author warns us against taking the test as one of "general intelligence," but has nevertheless himself proceeded on some such basis to draw what appear to be inappropriate conclusions about "The Development and Decline of *Mental Ability*" [reviewer's italics] and specifically describes his five rough screening grades as "intellectually superior," . . . "definitely above average in intellectual capacity," . . . "intellectually average" and "definitely below average in intellectual ability," . . . and "intellectually defective."[23]

Some effort is made to circumvent the question of predictive validity by proposing as a substitute criterion the g-factor loading of the tests (that is, the extent to which test items are similar to one another in what they measure). Since the tests were designed deliberately to maximize this loading by eliminating items and subtests not highly saturated with g, it is to be expected that the g-factor loadings will be high for both tests.[24] But all this means is that the items on each test are similar to one another. It says nothing about the tests as measures of mental capacity outside of an IQ-type test situation. In short, there can be no substitute for evidence of predictive validity, and on this criterion the leading culture-fair tests appear to be quite weak.

Of course, it could be argued that the predictive validity of conventional IQ tests stems precisely from their cultural biases; that is, the fact that they contain subject matter familiar in school curricula is what makes them effective predictors of classroom performance. This line of reasoning suggests that it would be very difficult to construct a valid IQ test which was not obviously culture-bound. As Anne Anastasi has argued, "a test constructed entirely from elements that are equally familiar in many cultures might measure trivial functions and possess little theoretical or practical validity in any culture."[25]

The fact that Raven's and Cattell's tests use geometrical forms rather than words makes them less obviously culture-bound than conventional tests, since geometry is presumably universal to all cultures. Also, average scores appear to be the same for a variety of cultures—French,

Taiwanese, British, and American whites, for example. But scores tend to be lower for many nonwhite groups—people of India, Puerto Ricans, and American blacks.[26] Some investigators are tempted to conclude that these nonwhite groups have less capacity to reason abstractly, but there is an obvious alternative explanation which casts serious doubt upon any such conclusion. The lower scoring populations may simply be less oriented to solving geometrical design problems. They may have grown up using different shaped blocks as toys less often than the higher-scoring populations. Or they may have less experience with the systematic exploration of two-dimensional surfaces, like the pages of a test booklet. Games with dominoes are sometimes used as culture-fair IQ tests. But little effort is made to see how much time children from different races and strata actually spend playing with dominoes. It could be that children from relatively affluent families spend more time playing solitary, indoor games which resemble IQ test items because they have their own rooms, whereas lower class children usually do not have their own rooms. So the latter are more oriented to communal, outdoor games and do not do as well on geometrical tests.

These differences may be especially important because familiarity with test items can greatly affect scores. As one reviewer says about Raven's *Progressive Matrices* test:

> The graceful will o' the wisp of "innate capacity" is perhaps even more enticing in the geometrical jungle, but recently published results of the Heim's experiments in Cambridge and other evidence seems to suggest that considerable gain in scores may be expected in well motivated repeated testing in [the test's 1938 version] without any knowledge of results.[27]

Nonverbal tests may contain tremendous cultural biases, but these are camouflaged by the fact that only a cumulative record of children's play habits could reveal their true extent. Needless to say, such records are not sought by the tests' proponents. In short, the fact that a given test is *less obviously* biased does not mean that it is *less* biased.

Quite apart from any questions of test content, the testing situation itself may discriminate against minority children. Frank Riessman points out that the low scores of many black children may be due to poor rapport with examiners, low motivation to perform on tests, and a lack of meaningful, directed practice in taking tests.[28] When

Ernest Haggard trained examiners to establish better rapport, offered special incentives for doing well, and gave disadvantaged children three hours of practice with tests, the result was a dramatic improvement in their average IQ.[29]

Critically examining the arguments made in favor of culture-fair tests raises the question of why test proponents have relied upon this defective reasoning. Why, for example, have some been willing to conclude that a high g-factor loading is sufficient evidence of the test's validity? Why has the comparability of some ethnic or racial groups' scores been seen as showing that the tests provide fair comparisons for all minority groups? What justification has there been for deciding that performance on geometrical design problems is largely unaffected by learning; or alternatively, that the relevant sorts of learning are equally present in all cultures? To answer these questions we must recall the illusions under which proponents labored when the tests were created.

The Recurring Mirages of Spearman's g and Measurable Fluid Intelligence

The first culture-fair IQ tests originated during the 1920s an 1930s in the laboratory of Charles Spearman, the British psychometrician responsible for the use of factor analysis and the concept of *g*. To Spearman this concept meant two things—it was the general factor in scores on parts of IQ tests, and it was a measure of a person's innately determined level of mental energy, a sort of horsepower of the mind. As such it was the central core of Galtonian natural ability. Spearman's definition gained wide acceptance, but after 1925 a steady steam of evidence cast doubt upon it. As long as the leading psychometricians had maintained that IQ tests measured innately determined mental capacity, then the theoretical meaning of g could be seen as congruent with its practical representation in the test scores. However, when it became generally conceded that IQ scores were greatly affected by learning and environment, then the congruence disappeared. For Spearman and his disciples who continued to believe in Galton's theory, this created a need for new kinds of IQ tests, the scores on which would not be greatly affected by learning. Tests employing simple figural materials and geometrical designs not in the ordinary school curriculum seemed to provide a promising approach.

As these new "culture-free" tests were being created, the problem arose of how to reconcile the two divergent conceptions of general intelligence: one the one hand, it meant genetically determined mental capacity, or energy level; on the other, it denoted the common factor in performance on parts of conventional Binet-type IQ tests. Raymond Cattell solved this problem by concluding that there were two types of general intelligence rather than one. In 1941 he formally announced his theory of *fluid* and *crystallized* intelligence.

Crystallized ability, according to Cattell, is measured by conventional IQ tests and involves using memory to recall judgments and concepts which have been taught previously. Fluid intelligence, on the other hand, is measured by Cattell's test and others like it. Fluid intelligence supposedly is "unconnected with cultural skills," "rises at its own rate and falls despite cultural stimulus," and "has the 'fluid' quality of being directable to almost any problem." It is "an expression of the level of complexity of relationships which an individual can perceive and act upon when he does not have recourse to answers to such complex issues already stored in memory."[30]

As a conceptualization of mental processes, the distinction between fluid and crystallized ability is rather simple, but probably not completely wrong. The unique and striking feature of Cattell's theory is his claim that culture-fair tests measure fluid intelligence. If this were true, then the tests would have to be culture-fair because fluid intelligence is "unconnected with cultural skills." Moreover, once one had a test which measured this precious quality, then factor analysis could be used to determine the extent to which other tests also measured it. Because Cattell's pretense of verification has been so influential in the development of culture-fair tests, it is worth looking at the evidence he has been able to put forward. This evidence is conscientiously listed in his book, *Abilities: Their Structure, Growth and Action* (1971).

At the same convention where Cattell announced his theory, Donald Hebb, the noted physiological psychologist, reported the following:

> In any test performance there are two factors involved, the relative importance of which varies with the test: one factor being present intellectual power, of the kind essential to normal intellectual development; the other being the lasting changes of perceptual organization and behavior induced by the first factor during the period of development. . . . The contrast is not between intelligence and

knowledge, but between capacity to develop new patterns of response and the functioning of those already developed.[31]

Hebb demonstrated that adults with brain injuries showed more deterioration on tests stressing the former type of ability than on tests stressing the latter. Thus far the distinction between fluid and crystallized ability is valid, but Cattell's claims go much further. He contends that the fluid ability measured by his test is ability in general rather than ability on geometrical tests, and that it is largely unaffected by previous learning and experience. Neither of these claims is supported by evidence, and both are implausible. What is more likely is that two kinds of ability are involved, both of which are learned. In the one case actual answers are learned previously and recalled from memory; in the other a predisposition to concentrate or not concentrate on test items is learned. While correct answers have to be figured out for the first time during the test, the likelihood that they will be figured out is determined by previous experience with similar figural materials. So performance indicates only ability in that type of situation, not ability in general.

Cattell lists further evidence that led him to his "discovery." But none of it is very compelling. In addition to Hebb's data about brain injuries and test scores, there were high correlations among scores on tests developed in Spearman's laboratory. Indeed, such tests were probably quite similar to one another. There was some disagreement about how many general intelligence factors to have. Spearman had insisted upon one; Burt had suggested three. Two must have seemed like a reasonable compromise.[32] Early use of culture-fair IQ tests showed standard deviations of around 24 points instead of the usual 16. But this means nothing by itself. A test designer can establish whatever standard deviation is desired, merely by how he or she chooses to standardize the test. Curves of change in ability with age differed for culture-fair and conventional IQ tests. On the former, performance improved until around age thirteen and then declined steadily after age twenty or twenty-five. On the latter, it improved until around age sixteen or seventeen and then either remained constant or continued to rise.[33] But again, this is to be expected. Many people play with blocks and dominoes when they are young, and practice concentrating on geometrical figures little during adulthood. But they continue to exercise the verbal and numerical abilities measured by conventional IQ tests.

The above evidence does not contradict Cattell's implausible theory, but neither does it justify acceptance of the theory. To Cattell "the ultimate foundation of the fluid and crystallized intelligence concepts rested on the way in which *all* of the above six diverse sources 'clicked into place' when put together, and without all of them the full properties of the concepts could not be realized."[34] Most likely this is an honest account of what went through his mind, but we may suggest that the real causes of Cattell's discovery lie not in the evidence he cites, but in the predicament faced by eugenics paradigm advocates at the time.

The early mental testers' pretense that Binet-type IQ tests could measure Galtonian natural ability lay at the heart of their efforts to construct a science of eugenics. They had hoped that such tests could be used to solve all major problems of the paradigm, including the matter of racial comparisons. As Terman's and Spearman's mirage faded in the face of contradictory evidence, the strong need which originally had inspired it remained. Cattell and others loyal to the paradigm created a new mirage by projecting the same illusion onto a new type of test. Thus, Cattell informs us that fluid intelligence is something very much like Spearman's original conception of g.[35] To have said that the new culture-fair tests measured true intelligence and the conventional Binet-type did not would have been unwise because the latter predicted school performance more effectively, and its proponents were more numerous and powerful than the Galtonians, especially in the United States. So everything "clicked together" and Cattell concluded that there were two types of intelligence—one sustained the mirage, and the other allowed the majority of psychometricians to continue using the term. The supporting evidence Cattell reports was sufficient to elicit the illusion of a true discovery, although it certainly does not support the claim of such a discovery in any scientific sense. Once the false discovery was made, and the test labeled culture-fair, subsequent proponents of white racial superiority could then use the label without explanation as a convenient way of dismissing the otherwise thorny issue of culture-bias in tests.

9. The Restorationists

The eugenics movement has never regained the strength it had prior to 1930. During the last decade, however, there has occurred a remarkable resurgence of interest in the eugenics paradigm. This revival of interest is usually traced to the publication of Arthur Jensen's article, "How Much Can We Boost IQ and Scholastic Achievement?" in 1969.[1] Actually, the paradigm has had advocates continuously since its inception; research in eugenics was merely deemphasized prior to Jensen's article. After the Second World War it received little publicity and was not considered urgent or important by government planners. Within the fields of psychology and education, eugenics was forced to assume a low profile. The nature-nurture question was rejected as unresolvable by most psychometricians, although some importance of heredity continued to be professed. The question of innate racial differences in intelligence was dismissed for the same reason. The hereditarian position was never disproved, but the defectiveness of the eugenics paradigm was tacitly acknowledged.

Before 1968 the leading spokesman for eugenics was Sir Cyril Burt, the English psychometrician whose career had spanned half a century.

Toward the end of his career Burt lamented the decline of interest in his field:

> With the advent of behaviourism, investigations [in eugenics] virtually ceased. Even to ask such questions is to incur the old jibe that we are "raising the discredited problem of nature versus nurture." Nevertheless, let us hope a small band of enthusiasts will still come forward to explore this urgent and fascinating field of research.[2]

But unbeknownst to himself, Burt already had played an important role in stimulating renewed interest. Some ten years earlier he had delivered a lecture in London at which one of the persons in attendance was the American educational psychologist, Arthur Jensen. Jensen reported that the lecture was "impressive indeed," and "probably the best lecture [he] ever heard."[3] Jensen did not immediately begin work in eugenics, but the talk had planted a seed in his mind which would come to fruition twelve years later in the 1969 article. Why 1969?

During the 1960s the liberal response to the civil rights movement had been to view the educational system as the major vehicle for achieving racial equality. Educational psychologists were called upon to examine the particular problems of disadvantaged minorities. By 1967 Jensen was writing a book on this topic. Part of what had to be explained was the failure of preschool compensatory education programs to dramatically affect the scholastic achievement of black youths. Different types of explanations were possible. One approach was to acknowledge the superficiality of the programs and to move toward a deeper critique of institutionalized racism in the schools. This, however, was not an easy path for the majority of educational psychologists, who preferred not to drift too far outside of the national political mainstream. The obvious alternative approach was to resurrect a modernized version of Galton's theory by contending that the programs had failed because many black youths were innately uneducable. Indeed, Galton's theory had been used periodically throughout the late nineteenth century to account for the failure of school reform movements, so it is not surprising that it could be used this way again.[4] Jensen's article began by proclaiming the failure of compensatory education and moved gradually to the conclusion that this was likely due to a possible genetic inferiority of the children involved. Once published, the article was destined to attract considerable attention. It clearly offended the liberal biases of many academics and thereby aroused a storm of criticism. On the other hand, it justified inequality and seemed to provide a justification for conservative policymakers wishing to eliminate programs like compensatory education. The fact that its publication in winter 1969 coincided with the inauguration of a conservative president intent on dismantling such programs guaranteed that the article would receive widespread publicity, both favorable and unfavorable.

The Jensen article provided a rallying point for hereditarians generally, and encouraged them to become more bold in professing previously discredited hypotheses. Popularized versions of Jensen's work were published in England by Hans Eysenck and in America by Richard Herrnstein.[5] William Shockley, the Nobel laureate campaigning for eugenical sterilization, became another public supporter. Raymond Cattell joined the cause, as did a number of others. Most recently, John Loehlin, Gardner Lindzey, and J. N. Spuhler together have published *Race Differences in Intelligence* which is reputed to be the most comprehensive and objective treatment of the controversy raised by Jensen.

These people are referred to collectively as *restorationists,* because they seek to restore interest in the eugenics paradigm. They have revived the nature-nurture controversy along with the issue of innate racial differences in IQ scores. They have also brought about a renewed interest in IQ tests as measures of intellectual capacity, and have proposed to study how breeding patterns are affecting the national intelligence. Their interest in eugenics per se ranges from mere passing reference to "possible dysgenic trends" to actual proposals for making welfare payments contingent upon voluntary sterilization.[6]

The restorationists have produced some new evidence, but have relied mainly upon findings which other investigators accumulated during the last fifty years. So, many of the problems with their work are problems with the work of those they cite (e.g., Terman, Burt, Cattell, etc.). But, also, the restorationists have added some original distortions and misinterpretations which have helped to make their arguments appear convincing. Many specific errors can be cited,[7] but to view the restorationists simply as careless or incompetent scientists is to obscure their historical significance. They are the inheritors of a tradition of pseudoscience. Their task is to renew the credibility of a discipline and to dissolve the prejudices which have led to its being deemphasized within the field of psychology. Thus far they have had a fair amount of success, and it is important to understand why and how they have done so.

The roots of their success lie in the way in which psychologists have dealt with previous instances of pseudoscience. Most people with expertise in the testing field have been reluctant to issue any clear denunciation of past work. Where major defects have been comprehended, the conventional response has been to dismiss the results quietly and not to dwell upon how false conclusions ever could have been established so authoritatively. This policy of benign neglect promotes the appearance of uninterrupted scientific progress, but it increases the risk of previously outmoded pseudoscience recurring in a slightly altered form.

Specifically, the restorationists have been providing answers to questions previously acknowledged as unanswerable. They argue, quite correctly, that no one has ever proven the opposite of their hypotheses. Critics merely have demonstrated the futility of the questions. But to say a problem is insoluble seems like a weak response when someone else appears to be providing a solution. This is so *unless* one can prove the proponent untrustworthy by either showing him to be a deliberate fraud or explaining how he relies upon a history of systematic distortion for the credibility of his apparent solution. In the case of Jensen et al., the former is not true, and the latter, while true, is difficult for critics to express coherently because of the general reluctance to acknowledge the impact of pseudoscience.

Because the reader's assumptions typically bear the imprint of past pseudoscience, he is frequently slow to comprehend the major fallacies in the restorationists' argument. Even when the critic is able to expose the fallacies clearly, and the reader understands them intellectually, they may strike the reader as minor quibbles rather than vital, central issues, because his or her deeper emotional response is governed by a faith in the familiar conclusions of pseudoscience. Under these conditions, the restorationist's best strategy is to portray hostile critics as obscurantists who stand in the way of inquiry merely because the results are not congenial to their particular ideology. For example, Jensen writes:

What struck me as most peculiar as I worked my way through the vast bulk of literature on the disadvantaged was the almost complete lack of any mention of the possible role of genetic factors in individual differences in intelligence and scholastic performance. In the few instances where genetics was mentioned, it was usually to dismiss the issue as outmoded, irrelevant, or unimportant, or to denigrate the genetic study of human differences and proclaim the all-importance of the social and cultural environment as the only source of individual and group differences in the mental abilities relevant to scholastic performance. So strongly expressed was this bias in some cases, and so inadequately buttressed by any evidence, that I began to surmise that the topic of genetics was ignored more because of the particular author's social philosophy than because the importance of genetic factors in human differences had been scientifically disproved.[8]

Of course, there have been good reasons for this refusal to consider genetic explanations. Defects in the available methodologies preclude the possibility of any sound answer to such questions. These defects enable critics to raise objections which cannot be met head on, and have to be dismissed in a roundabout manner. So part of the restorationists' strategy is to use a variety of rhetorical tricks to help conceal the defectiveness of their paradigm. When valid objections are dismissed in this way, critics face a dilemma. They can remain scholarly and speak only to the issues, in which case they will win the scientific debate but appear to lose it. Or they can escalate the contest by challenging the proponent's competence or integrity, in which case they risk appearing dogmatic and intolerant of others' views.

This predicament becomes clear when we examine the major defects in the restorationists' argument, along with the efforts to circumvent them. The preceding three chapters have discussed four cardinal defects of contemporary work in eugenics. Two concern the use of IQ tests as measures of intellectual capacity, and two deal with heritability estimates. Briefly, these four defects are as follows.

1. *The Limited Validity of IQ Tests*

IQ tests do not predict performance in nonscholastic activities, so it is unreasonable to call them measures of general intelligence or mental capacity. They measure specific kinds of ability which are closely related to doing well on tests.

2. The Cultural Bias of IQ Tests

Test items consist of activities which are probably more familiar to certain ethnic and cultural groups than to others. Since differences in test performance may be largely a function of different attitudes toward test material and the testing situation, the average IQ socres of different groups may tell very little about how the groups would perform on the average in situations not closely resembling an IQ test. Comparisons which suggest that tests measure the relative general intelligence of various groups probably are unfair to one group or another.

3. The Inflation of Current Heritability Estimates

Reliance on faulty data combined with systematic exaggeration of results has greatly inflated estimates of the heritability of IQ scores. The magnitude of this effect appears to be very large, but is impossible to calculate precisely.

4. The Meaning of Heritability

When heritability coefficients are calculated for characteristics considered modifiable by the environment they do *not* represent the proportion of variance attributable to genetic factors because they do not distinguish between genes-as-determiners and genes-as-markers, a problem which can be referred to as the markers vs. determiners confound.

To ascertain how the restorationists respond to these objections we may turn to the current writings of Arthur Jensen, and also to Loehlin, Lindzey, and Spuhler's *Race Differences in Intelligence*. Jensen is the most forceful and imaginative proponent of the eugenics paradigm. *Race Differences in Intelligence* was prepared under the auspices of the Social Science Research Council and has an impeccable reputation among psychologists.

1. The Limited Validity of IQ Tests

Terman and other early psychometricians popularized a broad definition of intelligence as being virtually synonymous with mental capacity, and persuaded many to believe that IQ tests measured intelligence conceived in this way. Since then, new evidence has contradicted this assertion. The restorationist's task is to preserve the broad connotation of intelligence in the reader's mind, and at the same time establish clearly that IQ tests measure intelligence. Jensen accomplishes this task by splitting in two the definition of intelligence:

> The term "intelligence" should be reserved for the rather specific meaning I have assigned it, namely, the general factor common to standard tests of intelligence. Any one verbal definition of this factor is really inadequate, but if we must define it in so many words, it is probably best thought of as a capacity for abstract reasoning and problem solving.[9]

The first part of the definition establishes a priori that IQ tests measure intelligence. The second part reminds the reader that intelligence is not just test performance, but the ability to think and solve problems. To buffer the second part of his definition from any sharp refutation Jensen stresses that it is "really inadequate." It is there to be believed by the reader, but not examined too closely.

Jensen recapitulates Terman's arguments and evidence for the validity of IQ tests. Like Terman, he assumes the meritocracy interpretation is correct and he proudly presents the Barr Scale of occupational intelligence demands. He ignores all subsequent evidence which casts doubt on the validity of the tests.[10] Probably he is aware of such evidence, because he states that intelligence "should not be regarded as completely synonymous with . . . the totality of a person's mental capabilities."[11] However, having made this qualification he is free to make several other statements, unsupported by evidence, which suggest that IQ scores are indeed a measure of mental capacity:

> There can be little doubt that certain educational and occupational attainments depend more upon g than upon any other single ability.[12]

> Since intelligence tests get at learning that occurs in the total life experience of the individual, it is a more general and more valid measure of his learning potential than are scholastic achievement tests.[13]

> Intelligence thus can be thought of psychologically as that aspect of mental ability which *consolidates* learning and experience in an integrated, organized way, relating it to past learning and encoding it in ways that permit its retrieval in relevant new situations.[14]

The above are best viewed as statements of Jensen's faith in IQ tests rather than deliberate deceptions on his part.

Loehlin, Lindzey, and Spuhler do not review evidence relating to the validity of IQ tests. They merely state that the validity of a test depends upon the population in which it is used. They define intelligence as the ability to appraise situations in which others are floundering, to select effective courses of action, and to do so repeatedly in a wide variety of situations. Each IQ test item is viewed as a situation, so the tests by definition include a wide variety of situations.[15] The authors do not question the extent to which test items are representative of real-life situations other than test-taking, but they must presume it is great since they use the terms, *intelligence, IQ,* and *test scores* interchangeably. In a section entitled, "How Important is IQ?," they cite Jensen's discussion of the Barr Scale along with contradictory opinions of several other researchers, and then take a position solidly in the middle: "On the whole then, we conclude that while IQ is of some genuine importance it is very far from all-important in determining what life will be like for most persons in the United States at the present time."[16]

2. *The Cultural Bias of IQ Tests*

Jensen quickly dismisses this issue by comparing the performance of blacks on so-called culture-fair tests with their performance on conventional IQ tests. Noting that they do as well or better on the conventional tests, he concludes that cultural bias is not an important component of black-white IQ score differences.[17] He deals with none of the complexities mentioned in the previous chapter and appears content to assume that biases which are not immediately obvious do not exist. Building upon a foundation of past pseudoscience, he accepts claims about culture-fair tests uncritically. In particular he makes no mention of the validity of such tests.

Loehlin, Lindzey, and Spuhler acknowledge that cultural bias in tests is a weighty issue. They discuss the importance of maintaining good rapport in the testing situation, and write:

> Matters of this kind have been of concern to intelligence testers since the beginning of intelligence testing. In the training of psychologists to administer individual intelligence tests, great emphasis is placed on developing and maintaining good rapport with the

testee, and on taking the testee's background into account in the choice of tests—and by using appropriate nonverbal tests with persons whose language backgrounds might handicap them on standard tests, and so on.[18]

The authors stress the psychologists' *concern* but do not hazard a guess as to how successful efforts to transcend cultural bias have been. Rather, they cite a few studies and conclude:

All in all, while the existence of some amount of cultural bias in some IQ tests for some intergroup comparisons can hardly be doubted, we are a long way from being able to assess with confidence the precise importance of such biases for particular group comparisons.[19]

3. *The Inflation of Current Heritability Estimates*

Prior to Leon Kamin's critical review of the literature, studies of separated twins and adopted children had been interpreted as providing strong evidence for a heritability of IQ scores in the .60 to .80 range. Kamin has undermined these estimates by uncovering major ambiguities in the data and gross exaggerations in the reporting of it. Since heritability estimates are the most popular way of implying large-scale genetic determination of IQ ability, the restorationist's task is to discredit Kamin's work so the old estimates will again be taken seriously. Jensen's current works were all written prior to Kamin's critique, so they cannot be expected to contain a response. *Race Differences in Intelligence*, on the other hand, includes an eight-page appendix sharply attacking Kamin.[20]

The main text of the book presents a heritability coefficient of .75 for IQ scores among whites in the United States. The .75 is neatly divided into separate components: .52 additive variance, .12 assortative mating, and .11 dominance. However, on the page following these findings, the authors write that, "the reader is cautioned not to take these numerical estimates too literally. The genetic model employed is oversimplified." They proceed to mention a number of ambiguities and to cite several widely discrepant heritability estimates. While doing so they take refuge in a statement that precise heritability does not matter anyway:

Fortunately, none of the conclusions to be drawn in the present book depend very heavily on exact figures for the heritability of

IQ, provided only that its heritability is appreciable. Whether the true figure for [broad heritability] is closer to .40, .60, .75, or .90 might sometimes affect matters of emphasis, but rarely matters of substance.[21]

This disclaimer proves convenient when it comes to evaluating Kamin's work, since the authors concede that several of his points are valid. For example, they agree that "to use Burt's data one must take a lot on faith," and say that Kamin "correctly notes that the degree of separation in [twin] studies is often exaggerated in secondary accounts."[22] On the other hand, they accuse Kamin of having an environmentalist bias which leads him to exaggerate the extent of uncertainties in the data:

> In short, while an explanation of the data from adoption studies in purely environmental terms may be logically possible, on the whole Kamin's interpretation seems much less plausible than a view that allows a place for substantial genetic factors—unless, perhaps, one begins with a strong a priori commitment to a purely environmentalistic position.[23]

In particular they reject Kamin's conclusion that there is no good evidence to disprove the hypothesis of zero heritability:

> On the whole, then, although Kamin's critique emphasizes some methodological points worthy of attention in conducting and evaluating studies in this area, it does not, in our view, constitute an unbiased survey of the literature, and it suffers from enough logical and statistical difficulties that Kamin's "reasonably prudent man" will want to think twice before accepting its conclusions.

> We suspect that for some time to come the individual social scientist's preference will have some bearing on the exact heritability figure he most favors for IQ in the U.S. population. But we believe that the data do place some real constraints on the plausible values of this index, and that for at least the last 30 years these values have not included either zero or one.[24]

This sounds very reasonable, but it involves a substantial retreat from the authors' earlier claim that IQ scores have a heritability of around .75. Now they merely say that zero is not a plausible value. How far above zero can estimates rise with the authors still being confident that they are not too high? We are left to speculate. Loehlin, Lindzey, and Spuhler do not suggest that Kamin's critique should be ignored, but neither do they attempt to specify the range of plausible estimates in light of the critique.

The issue of precise heritability is, unfortunately, more important than the authors contend. If estimates can be kept close to 1.00, as those of the late Cyril Burt always were,[25] then it logically is possible but very implausible that the figures would signify no genetic determination of IQ scoring. But the more heritability estimates drop below .50, the more likely it becomes that they signify genes acting only as markers and not at all as determiners. So, abandoning exact estimates makes it especially important to understand the actual meaning of heritability.

4. *The Meaning of Heritability Coefficients*

The confounding of genes-as-determiners with genes-as-markers constitutes a fatal and irremediable flaw in the hereditarian argument. This problem exists because genes do not shape behavioral traits directly, but through a series of complex interactions with the environment. Critics of the eugenics paradigm have argued that because these interactions are complex and unknown, there can be no way of disentangling the separate influences of genetic and environmental factors. Jensen summarizes their argument:

> although there may be significant genetic differences at the time of conception, the organism's development involves such complex interactions with the environment that the genetic blueprint, so to speak, becomes completely hidden or obscured beneath an impenetrable overlay of environmental influences. . . . The whole notion of heritability is, in effect, dismissed. The question of the relative importance of heredity and environment in determining individual differences in the development of a characteristic is viewed as fundamentally unanswerable.[26]

This position, sometimes known as "interactionism," is substantially correct, but fails to express the problem adequately because it does not show clearly how heritability coefficients over-estimate the actual extent of genetic determination of IQ scores. It has the additional drawback that the term *interaction* has another, more specific meaning in population genetics. Jensen capitalizes upon the ensuing confusion by arguing that the interactionist position "has arisen from a failure to understand the real meaning of the term 'interaction' as it is used in population genetics."[27] In other words, he implies that because critics use the term *interaction* in a different manner, their argument is incorrect. But that, of course, does not follow logically.

Jensen adopts the narrow, technical definition of genotype-environment interaction and estimates its effect to be quite small.[28] The estimate cannot be trusted, given the problems with the data base. But that is all beside the point because the broad "interaction effects" discussed by critics are now considered under the separate category of "genotype-environment correlation," or "genotype-environment covariance."[29] Such correlation may be of two types. In one case inherently superior genes are matched with superior environments. In the other case genes not inherently superior serve as a basis for phenotypic superiority by virtue of some social process which discriminates in favor of that genotype. To the extent that the latter type of correlation exists, heritability estimates exaggerate the degree of genetic determination. Jensen does not deny the existence of this latter type; he merely overlooks it. His examples of genotype-environment correlation stress only the former type:

> Children with better than average genetic endowment for intelligence have a greater than chance likelihood of having parents of better than average intelligence who are capable of providing environmental advantages that foster intellectual development. Even among children within the same family, parents and teachers will often give special attention and opportunities to the child who displays exceptional abilities. . . .A bright child may also create a more intellectually stimulating environment for himself in terms of the kinds of activities that engage his interest and energy. And the social rewards that come to the individual who excels in some activity reinforce its further development.[30]

Jensen's overall strategy is to forestall awareness of the markers vs. determiners confound by taking each of the terms by which the confound would be expressed (e.g., gene-environment interaction, gene-environment correlation) and discussing it in a way which excludes any mention of the confound. Critics who try to argue that Jensen has not considered the interaction or correlation of genes and environment are easily foiled. He has considered them; he merely has not considered the relevant meanings of the terms *interaction* and *correlation*.

He concludes the issue by stating that, "Since most estimates of the heritability of intelligence are intended to reflect the existing state of affairs, they usually include the covariance in the proportion of variance due to heredity."[31] In other words, since the estimates are intended to reflect the existing state of affairs, whenever environmental effects are distributed on the basis of genetic differences, they may be counted as purely genetic influences.

The absurdity of this position becomes clear if we apply it to a hypothetical example of covariance: in a given racially mixed population, variance in income is determined mainly by racial discrimination. Because skin color is primarily a genetic characteristic, the trait "personal income" has a very high heritability. Because persons with "poor" genotypes (i.e., dark skin) also have poor environments (i.e., racial discrimination against them), there is substantial gene-environment covariance. Applying Jensen's logic, we learn that, the variation in income caused by racial discrimination is really caused by genetic differences exclusively. We may conclude this because our heritability estimate is "intended to reflect the existing state of affairs" in which discrimination is based upon genetic differences.

Unlike Jensen, Loehlin, Lindzey, and Spuhler acknowledge the marker vs. determiners confound. Referring to the problem as "feedback-based gene-environment correlation," they admit that heritability estimates may be inflated by "genetic involvement [which] could conceivably be irrelevant to the trait in any direct biological sense." They point out that traditional methods of estimating gene-environment correlation do not apply to this type, since it is:

a potential correlation between genes and environmental input that is tied to the individual himself, and escapes our experimental control by moving with him into an adoptive family.[32]

Having agreed that such an effect is possible, the authors must find some way of estimating its magnitude, lest the entire procedure of calculating heritability be rendered meaningless. They suggest that,

One possibiltiy is to find subgroups within the population in which such feedbacks can reasonably be postulated to be more or less strongly operative, and compare heritability estimates in these groups.[33]

Specifically, they state that blacks *may* have less feedback-based correlation than whites because their environments are more restricted or suppressive for developing high IQ scores. If such feedback were a substantial part of the calculated heritability, then one would expect heritability of IQ scores to be much higher among whites than blacks. After noting the additional complication that restricted environments could raise heritability by lowering the amount of environmental variance, the authors compare heritabilities of IQ scores for the two groups. They sift through some painfully ambiguous data and conclude that certain methods "tend not to show consistent differences," while others "sometimes suggest lower IQ heritabilities for blacks, although more often they do not." This leads the authors to declare that,

> the data do not provide much evidence for black-white differences in gene-environment correlations that derive from the response of the environment to the individual, since the effects of this should be observable in heritability estimates derived from within-family variation. This offers little support for views that place heavy emphasis on a gene-environment covariance component in IQ variation, although it remains possible that such a component exists but does not differ between blacks and whites in these studies.[34]

This passage appears at first glance to be saying that the data show there is little likelihood of feedback-based correlations greatly inflating heritability estimates. Literally, the passage does not say that. It says that the black-white heritability comparison "offers little support" for such a view. This is true. It is also true that the comparison offers little refutation. To show how far the comparison is from being any kind of test of feedback-based correlation we need only diagram the authors' argument.

Proposition	*Truth value of proposition*
(P) Substantial feedback-based gene-environment correlation exists among whites.	To be discerned.
(1) Compared to whites, blacks have more restricted or suppressive environments for developing high IQ scores.	Probably true.

(2) IQ ability among blacks has much less feedback-based gene-environment correlation than it does among whites.

Completely unknown.

(3) Among blacks the heritability of IQ scores is raised by the fact that there is less variation in relevant environmental factors than there is among whites.

Completely unknown.

(4) Heritability of IQ ability is much lower among blacks than it is among whites.

Probably false but still uncertain.

The Authors' Argument

(3) is false.

Completely unknown.

If (P) is true and (3) is false, then (2) implies (4)

Correct deduction based upon a proposition whose truth value is completely unknown.

If (P) is true, then (2) implies (4)

Correct deduction based upon a proposition whose truth value is completely unknown.

(1) is true.

Probably true.

(1) implies (2).

Completely unknown.

If (P) is true, then (1) implies (4).

Correct deduction based upon two propositions whose truth value is completely unknown.

If (P) is true, then (4) is true.

Correct deduction based upon two propositions whose truth value is completely unknown.

(4) is false.

Probably true but uncertain.

Therefore (P) is false.

Correct deduction based upon two propositions whose truth value is completely unknown, and two which are probably true but uncertain.

This argument has the form of hypothesis testing, but lacks the substance because most of the premises used to test the proposition could themselves be either true or false. Since there is no real way of knowing whether they are true or false, comparing heritabilities of IQ scores among different groups is not a very promising approach to the problem of distinguishing genes-as-determiners from genes-as-markers. In fact, no one has thought of a promising approach. The problem appears to be insoluble.

The Race Question: Is Further Research Really Needed?

The major difference between Arthur Jensen and the more "moderate" restorationists like Loehlin, Lindzey, and Spuhler is typified by their divergent conclusions about the possibility of black genetic inferiority. Jensen ignores the cardinal defects in eugenics research, stacks all the evidence on one side, and concludes:

> All the major facts would seem to be comprehended quite well by the hypothesis that something between one-half and three-fourths of the average IQ difference between American Negroes and whites is attributable to genetic factors, and the remainder to environmental factors and their interaction with genetic differences.[35]

The authors of *Race Differences in Intelligence* acknowledge some of the defects, present evidence on both sides, and finally state that they cannot discern the relative importance of cultural bias in tests, environmental conditions, and genetic factors for creating the black-white IQ score differences. They speculate that all three probably are involved to some extent, and they stress that the range of differences between individuals is much greater than that between ethnic groups. They declare that, "On the whole, these are rather limited conclusions. It does not appear to us, however, that the state of scientific evidence at the present time justifies stronger ones."[36]

Loehlin, Lindzey, and Spuhler are concerned primarily with encouraging further research in the field, rather than with reaching firm conclusions themselves. They suggest further investigation in ten specific areas relevant to the race question, and insist that, "The factual questions involved, if phrased in limited and specific form, should indeed be answerable, and it is probably worth society's time and money to answer a good number of them."[37] Here we arrive at the crux of the matter: To what extent are the questions of inherited mental ability and innate, racial ability differences answerable scientifically? And if they are essentially unresolvable, then why is it "worth society's time and money" to try to answer them?

Although the authors of *Race Differences in Intelligence* appear confident that the central questions can be answered, their book may be interpreted as providing some indications to the contrary. It contains some seemingly strong evidence against the hypothesis of black genetic inferiority. There is the well-documented estimate that only 6 percent of the total human genetic variation is variation between races. So a white person picked at random is likely to have almost as many genes in common with any given black person as he does with another white.[38] Studies of racial mixture consistently have shown: (1) that there is a positive correlation between lightness of skin color and IQ score; but (2) having a greater percentage of characteristically European genes does not raise the IQ score of blacks, except insofar as it lightens skin color.[39] This would seem to indicate that black-white IQ score differences are caused by discrimination based on skin color rather than by racial differences in "ability" genes. But the alternative hypothesis that variation in "ability" genes is directly linked to variation in skin color genes cannot be ruled out completely. Also, the authors stress that whites mating with blacks may not be a representative sample of the entire white population, and that sample bias may account for the negative results. The inference is that these miscegenating whites may themselves be inferior.

The authors conclude that, "On balance, such studies can probably be assessed as offering fewer explanatory difficulties to environmentalists than to hereditarians, although they admit interpretation from a range of viewpoints."[40] Undoubtedly this is correct. The hypothesis of black genetic inferiority is such that it cannot be disproved absolutely as long as black-white IQ score differences exist. Even when the evidence makes it appear implausible, there can always be new doubts and an apparent need for further research. Until the day comes when blacks have sufficient influence among mental testers to force a restructuring of tests which eradicates the black-white IQ score difference, it is very unlikely that there will be any clear vindication of racial equality from psychometricians.

Confirming the hypothesis of black genetic inferiority would be even more difficult than disproving it. Each of the four cardinal defects presents a formidable obstacle, and none of the restorationists has shown how any of these could be surmounted. Loehlin, Lindzey, and Spuhler have attempted to resolve the markers vs. determiners confound, but their approach does not seem promising. Their ten suggested areas of further research conceivably could produce more trustworthy heritability estimates, but at present show no prospect of dispelling doubts based upon limited test validity, cultural bias in tests, or the meaning of heritability.

The race question produces a reenactment of the eugenicist's classic dilemma. Any affirmative answer necessarily is predicated upon acceptance of major flaws and vital ambiguities in the argument. The individual scientist must either restrict his or her vision and rely heavily upon pseudoscience to make a case, or admit that an affirmative answer cannot be reached scientifically. Jensen takes the first alternative and systematically ignores the four defects. Loehlin, Lindsey, and Spuhler acknowledge the defects for the present, but forget about them for the future. They assume that key defects will somehow be remedied, even though no one has presented a viable strategy for remedying them.

Why, then, do scientists even bother with the race question? Part of the reason probably stems from government policymakers' response to the black power movement of the 1960s. When that movement demanded community control of schools, it made a political issue out of the educational failure of black children. Its demands for control were based upon charges of institutional racism. Rejecting those demands put policymakers in the position of arguing that such failure was due to something other than racism, and the backlog of IQ data made "inferior intelligence of blacks" seem like a plausible alternative. Having a vested interest in rejecting charges of racism made administrators prone to believing that blacks were less intelligent than whites. Facing a political controversy made them feel it was important to discover why blacks did so poorly on IQ tests. Hence a social climate conducive to revival of the nature-nurture race issue was established.

Debating the importance of genetic and environmental causes of racial IQ score differences has the side effect of propagating the belief that blacks are indeed less intelligent than whites. Regardless of the debate's outcome or lack of outcome, the importance of blacks' lower IQ scores is highlighted and exaggerated in the public's mind. People assume that scientists would not spend much time arguing over the causes of something which did not exist. So the mere fact of the debate itself reinforces the notion of black intellectual inferiority.

Several writers have posited three basic positions in the race controversy: the *dogmatic racist* who believes his or her race is superior regardless of evidence; the *ignoracist* who refuses to consider the possibility of innate race differences in intelligence; and the *scientist* who examines pertinent data objectively.[41] Perusal of the restorationists' writings suggests that there are four positions rather than three. In between the dogmatic racist and the ignoracist are found two varieties of *scientific pretenders*. They are pretenders because they claim unjustifiably that science has resolved or will resolve the race question. One variety is the *quasiempirical racist,* who examines evidence but projects his own biased conclusions onto it. The other is the *perpetually noncommittal empiricist,* who insists on studying the question but always declines to answer it. Given this range of alternatives, and the obnoxious social consequences of debating the issue, it is perhaps not entirely unreasonable or antiscientific to adopt the ignoracist position and suggest that the question of race differences in intelligence simply be abandoned.

10. "Creativity" Tests

Recent attempts to measure creativity have spawned the belief that creativity and intelligence are separate traits, and that each can be measured by the appropriate test. The factual underpinnings of this view are that doing well in school and scoring high on IQ tests differ enormously from having the ability to generate some valued artistic or intellectual product. On the other hand, it is not true that existing tests measure creative potential, and it is unlikely that any tests ever will. The excessive faith shown by educators and the public in creativity tests has no scientific justification. Yet it *seems* to stem from scientific inquiry. People commonly point to the work of creativity testers as showing that creative potential can be measured. Somewhere along the line deception and misunderstanding have occurred, but it is difficult to pinpoint the exact locus. Fifty years' experience with mental tests has imbued modern test designers with a greater sophistication so that they exhibit none of the gross self-deception or testimonials of faith which characterized the early IQ test proponents.

Nevertheless, pseudoscience continues to function obliquely. Creativity testers have conducted studies resulting in ambiguously worded conclusions which have encouraged the public to believe that certain tests measure a person's creative capacity. For example, the authors of the well-known *Remote Associates Test* (RAT) have said that their instrument measures "an ability fundamental to the creative thinking process."[1] In one sense this is true. To associate concepts and ideas in unusual ways is part of creative thinking, and many kinds of tasks require this ability. Two activities which require it extensively are the RAT and crossword puzzles. One would not think to use crossword puzzle-solving performance as a measure of creative potential, but the RAT manual states that the test is "a measure of the ability to think creatively," thereby encouraging undiscerning users to believe that the test measures capacity for creative accomplishment.[2] The *Torrance Tests of Creative Thinking* (TTCT) have accumulated much evidence which suggests that they do not measure creative ability. Proponents respond that this is all-right because the tests' major purpose is to encourage further research. However, by publishing the tests commercially with the recommendation that they be used to assess individual students' potentials, the author guaranteed that educators and the public would develop highly exaggerated notions of the tests' validity. As one rival test designer says about TTCT,

> Although called a "research edition," advertising matter presents the tests, together with a series of workbooks and phonograph records, as "a complete program in creative development." The intent, then, is to make available for general use instruments that are presumed to be not just tests of intelligence but tests of creative thinking.[3]

Far more than the early IQ testers, modern proponents of creativity tests are aware of their instruments' limitations. The problem is less what Lippmann called "self-deception as the preliminary to public deception," than it is a willingness to make disingenuous statements and market products of dubious validity. The public and the psychometricians jointly concoct the deception. On one side there is a strong will to believe, on the other a readiness to be misinterpreted. This makes it difficult to specify who is fooling whom, but does not necessarily reduce the overall volume of false persuasion. Although contemporary pseudoscience in the creativity field has a different format than its predecessor of fifty years ago, the sources of the two have a remarkable similarity. In each case there is the familiar triad of an essentially unsolvable problem, a pressing social need to solve it, and an inclination to overlook crucial defects in the basic approach which precludes any possibility of an acceptable scientific solution.

First of all, why is the problem essentially unsolvable? Designing tests of creative potential is likely to be an ill-fated enterprise because the situation of taking a test is inherently different from the situation of doing genuinely creative work. To a large extent this is true regardless of the test's specific content. The fact that no close simulation of the creative process is possible means it is very improbable that any test will be able to identify people with creative talent. There are several important differences between the process of doing creative work in the arts and sciences and the activity of taking an IQ test:

(1) To do well on IQ tests one must repeatedly choose a single correct answer from among alternatives rather than generating novel but appropriate responses as is required in creative thinking.

(2) Only in the test situation does one work within an externally imposed time limit of an hour or two.

(3) When taking an IQ test one solves many small problems which are largely unrelated to each other. Real creative work involves solving a few large problems, the parts of which are interconnected.

(4) One has no specific preparation for an IQ test, and one ceases to work on test questions after leaving the room in which the test was given. Real creative work is an ongoing process in which present activity is related to past accomplishments and directed toward future goals.

(5) In the test situation one performs tasks which are uniformly assigned to everyone in the group. This differs from creative work where particular interests are followed by engaging in self-directed, self-regulated activity.

Psychometricians wanted to construct tests which simulated the creative process more closely than the old format did. But what could they change? Only the first difference could be eliminated conveniently. The other four are necessary limits to any standardized test. To make scores comparable, uniform tasks must be assigned. To make administration of the test feasible it must be restricted to a fairly short time duration. To guarantee that a wide range of specific problems is sampled in the test, each problem must be restricted. To insure comparable results, people must be allowed to work on questions only in the immediate testing situation. In short, psychometricians were forced to hope that the first difference was the critical one, and that eliminating it could give them tests of creative ability.

In the 1950s J. P. Guilford and then E. P. Torrance designed tests to measure what they called *divergent thinking ability*. These required people to give numerous responses to a variety of openended questions. For example, test subjects were asked to list as many unusual uses of bricks or cardboard boxes as they could. They were asked to list ways of improving various products, to give detailed interpretations of pictures shown to them, and to draw pictures of their own. Responses were graded on their number, elaborateness, and originality. These tests were seen as measures of creativity, and were contrasted with intelligence tests which were thought to measure *convergent thinking ability* because they required people to select particular correct answers.

The proponents' first task was to demonstrate that convergent and divergent thinking abilities were separate traits. If the correlation between creativity test scores and IQ scores were too high, then it could be argued that the "creativity" tests were really another variety of intelligence test. Both Guilford and Torrance deliberately sought to minimize this correlation, and in this way succeeded in holding it to moderate levels. However, the correlations among their various subtests (for example, unusual uses, product improvement, interpreting figures, drawing pictures) tended to be quite low, and in many cases were lower than the correlations between scores on subtests and IQ tests.[4] In other words, the evidence suggested that there was no consistent trait of divergent thinking ability, but that some people liked to think about cardboard boxes while others liked to draw andothers liked to interpret figures. This did not augur well for the tests as measures of creative potential. Subsequent test batteries (for example, Wallach and Kogan's tests) raised the correlation between subtests by selecting tasks more similar to each other, and by counting only the number of responses and not assessing their quality. But this did not establish a consistent trait; it merely made the absence of such a trait less visible.

The next task was to demonstrate the tests' predictive validity by showing high correlations between test scores and real-life creative achievement. Here the remaining four differences between test situation and creative process proved decisive, guaranteeing that the evidence of predictive validity would be on the whole very disappointing. Guilford's tests were intended for use with adults; hence scores could be contrasted with measures and ratings of actual achievement. As a result the tests confronted much disconfirming evidence and were subjected to a number of harsh appraisals, like the following by Mac-Kinnon:

> In an intensive study of research scientists in the Air Force Guilford's tests of creativity failed to predict the criterion and in our own studies these same tests have likewise shown essentially zero correlation with the criterion. In view of such negative findings the use of Guilford's battery of creativity tests for the identification of creative persons would be, to say the least, questionable.[5]

Torrance's tests were used mainly with children, so there could be no clear criterion of creative accomplishment, and the disconfirming evidence could never be as decisive. Nevertheless, scores were contrasted with a variety of peer and teachers' ratings of creativity, and the correlations generally were negligible or unimpressive. As one reviewer states, "The predictive ability of the tests is quite in line with other, unpublished, measures of creative potential—low."[6]

The RAT at first produced some seemingly impressive evidence of predictive validity. Fairly high correlations were obtained between scores and instructors' ratings of creativity among architecture and psychology students.[7] But two additional considerations diminish the significance of these results. Scores on the RAT correlate quite highly with IQ test results, and there is strong evidence that when teachers rate students, they fail to distinguish creativity from academic aptitude or general verbal facility.[8] Subsequent studies with larger samples and better measures of creativity have shown little or no relation between RAT scores and creative achievement.[9] While validating evidence for the RAT is less unequivocally negative than it is for Guilford's and Torrance's tests, it is certainly not sufficiently impressive to justify calling the test a measure of creative potential.

Overall, it appears that the more an investigator is willing to depart from using a standardized test format, the more likely he is to be successful in identifying creative people. Creativity tests have yielded poor results. Measures of aesthetic preferences, such as the tendency to like complex figures or generate unusual words, have been somewhat more successful.[10] Personality ratings show some meaningful differences between creative and uncreative people, and the most striking contrast is found in their own self-descriptions.[11]

The tests' failure is easily understood in light of the basic differences between taking a test and doing creative work. Simply having or not having a time limit can greatly affect performance. For example, Torrance administered his tests to seventy-five sixth grade children in a group setting with the standard five-minute limit for each subtest. Then the children were asked to work on the tests for the next twenty-four hours, adding ideas as they occurred. The correlation between the two sets of scores was only .23, thus showing that how a person performs in a normal testing situation may have little to do with how he or she performs the same tasks at leisure.[12]

The strongest evidence that creativity tests measure anything related to occupational performance has been the relationship between scores on the Torrance tests and ability as a salesperson.[13] Department store employees classified as having a high sales volume produced scores averaging around 135, while the average of employees with low sales volume was only 111. Torrance interpreted this significant finding to mean that creativity was an important aspect of a good salesperson. However, given the lack of evidence that the tests correlate with other kinds of creative accomplishment, one could just as well conclude that the tests measure sales ability. Certainly the situation of a salesperson more closely resembles that of a creativity test-taker than the situation of either salesperson or test-taker resembles that of a creative artist or scientist. To do well on the Torrance tests one must be spontaneously fluent and generate a large number of novel but appropriate responses related to matters not of one's own choosing, precisely what one must do to excel as a salesperson.

The problem of designing a valid creativity test is certainly unsolved, and by all appearances unsolvable. But this has not prevented large segments of the public from believing in the tests because, as Cronbach points out, "most of the tests have been announced to the world prior to any solid validity studies."[14] The primary reason for this lack of caution has been the pressing demand for usable creativity tests. The demand may be seen as accruing partly from developments within psychometrics and partly from imperatives thrust upon the school system by the Cold War.

Creativity testing is an American fad which began around 1950. In 1949 the *Psychological Abstracts* listed only 7 studies done in that year under the heading of creativity. A steady growth of interest over the next two decades brought the corresponding number to 218 in 1969.[15] The fad has grown in response to the proliferation of evidence that IQ tests cannot predict creative achievement. The early psychometricians had led the public to believe that IQ tests could predict intellectual achievement. The term *intelligence* was virtually synonymous with mental capacity, and outstanding creative accomplishments were seen as beyond the reach of all but the very highly intelligent—that is, those with the highest IQ scores. As actual data began to contradict the conclusions previously established by pseudoscience, the mental testers faced a dilemma. They could either admit that IQ tests did not adequately measure intelligence, or they could reduce the scope of the meaning of the concept intelligence. They opted for the latter because abandoning the equation of IQ score and intelligence would have left the concept without any clear definition or agreed-upon measure, and this would have rendered it so amorphous as to be useless. Proponents became increasingly vague and equivocal about what intelligence meant, no longer viewing it as capacity for achievement, but merely as one important aspect of such capacity.

This contraction in the meaning of intelligence left a void because psychometricians had grown accustomed to believing that they could measure mental capacity. They needed some new quantifiable trait which, together with IQ scores, could do what they once believed the IQ score alone had done. Creativity was the logical candidate because it denoted having significant, recognizable achievements, and these were precisely what IQ tests failed to predict. So test designers departed from the traditional format, produced tests which had fairly low correlations with IQ score, and used these correlations to reinforce their original supposition that creativity and intelligence were separate traits.

The early psychometricians had succeeded in getting schools to teach students differently depending upon their mental capacities, and to use tests as measures of that capacity. This guaranteed that as the conceptualization of mental capacity became more differentiated, there would be an automatic demand for tests to measure each new component trait. The demand for creativity tests also was exacerbated by a growing national obsession with science and technology in the period following the Second World War. Previously, schools had been called upon to transmit culture, inculcate work discipline, and prepare students for a variety of occupations. In the wake of the great science boom, however, schools were pressed to make a special effort to train scientists and encourage the development of scientific creativity. In part the science boom represented an awareness of a long-term economic trend. Since the Civil War, economic growth had depended increasingly upon technological advance. The boom also was fueled by plans for global hegemony, and by the concern with military technology which this brought. The feeling that victory in the Cold War depended upon science did much to foster the government's enthusiasm for scientific creativity.

Largely because of the science boom, creativity became a prominently cherished American value. The growing concern with creativity activated a number of educational critics like Paul Goodman who accused the schools of being repressive agents of social control, whose very operation was inimical to creativity.[16] The critics' point was well taken. There was a glaring contradiction between adapting students for work in offices and factories by training them to obey a chain of command, and training them to be creative. Schools traditionally had concentrated on the former objective, and therefore had failed to achieve the latter. The science boom intensified pressures for educational reform designed to encourage creativity in the schools. It lent a new credibility to the claims of progressive educators that schools should be child centered and encourage free self-expression. However, if the reforms were applied universally throughout the school system, they would interfere with the schools' traditional functions of social control and reproducing class divisions. Progressive reforms would be feasible politically only if their application were restricted to an elite group of creative children destined for professional careers. The problem then became how to select these children. The fact that only a small percentage could be selected discouraged educators from believing that all children had creative potential. From a faith in the benevolence of the educational system, it followed that if only a few could have their creativity nurtured, then only a few had creativity worth nurturing. How, then, could educators select the children on whom special attention would not be wasted? Traditional measures of scholastic ability like IQ score and grade point average had failed to predict scientific creativity, so schools needed new tests for this purpose. Utopian critics like Paul Goodman wrote longingly about transforming the entire educational system, but pragmatic reformers looked to psychometricians for tests of creativity.

Reformers presented two kinds of arguments. One was that the right type of education would actually cultivate creativity. But nobody could be sure what the right type was. For an educational program to claim that it fostered creativity, it needed a way of showing that children completed the program more creative than when they entered it. Thus it needed a convenient, precise measure of creativity which could be administered twice. Creativity tests were intended to be such a measure. The other argument was that certain children were naturally creative, and that conventional schooling stifled their creativity. Society needed to place these children in special environments to preserve their natural creative impulses. Reform was needed to produce a sanctuary for this type of gifted child.[17] But the sanctuaries would be useless unless one had some way of identifying the naturally creative. It would do no good to place uncreative children in these special environments. Again, the argument for reform depended upon having convenient and precise measures of creativity. As a result, attempts to initiate progressive reform wound up adding to the demand for creativity tests, and influenced the research priorities of government funding agencies accordingly.

The pressing demand for a valid creativity test of course did not mean that such a thing was possible. To project the illusion of a valid test psychometricians had to overlook or downplay the importance of major defects, the most important of which was the tests' inability to predict creative achievement. The mental testers' experience with IQ tests had in several ways imbued them with the myopia necessary for the continuation of pseudoscience. By developing IQ tests, the field of psychometrics had established uneven standards of scientific rigor. On the one hand, the tests made it possible to speak of intelligence as a trait which could be measured quantitatively. This set the precedent that other traits, including creativity, could not be discussed authoritatively without quantitative measurement. On the other hand, psychometricians' acceptance of IQ tests accustomed them to making lenient judgments about predictive validity. It established that a test could be called a measure of something if scores showed a moderate correlation with it. This lenience was extended to measures of other traits, including creativity. The lenient judgments about test validity made possible the promotion of creativity tests, and the demand for quantitative precision made it necessary.

Believing that IQ tests measured all-around intelligence led psychologists to the more general proposition that a test need not closely resemble any activity in order to measure ability in it. This enabled them to escape the conclusion that their problem was unsolvable, and allowed them to see negative results as always indicating some inadequacy with the particular test, never with the basic approach of designing creativity tests. Finally, having to incorporate past pseudoscience in the IQ-test field habituated testers to the practice of making provocative ambiguous statements which project extravagant claims without professing them literally. Such statements have become an important vehicle of false persuasion in the creativity assessment field as well.

The creativity tests' lack of validity is a serious problem only if they are viewed as attempts to measure an existing trait. If, instead, they are seen as instruments of social reform, then their lack of validity becomes less problematic. Suppose schools accepted a particular test as a measure of creativity and proceeded to label children "creative" who scored high on that test. If teachers taught these children to view themselves as creative, and encouraged free expression of their ideas, it is likely that the children would in fact become more creative than average. The test would then acquire evidence for its predictive validity because it had been used as the basis for a self-fulfilling prophecy. Pseudoscience, having helped to secure acceptance of the test, would then become less necessary.

Overview and Appraisal

The preceding two sections have focused on past and present forms of pseudoscience in the field of mental measurement. It is difficult to estimate the influence of this distortion and pretense, but undoubtedly it has been substantial and widespread, since many common beliefs about mental ability appear to have no other scientific source.

This section offers several types of overview, the first of which focuses on the concept of pseudoscience. It asks how the distortion and pretense are possible, given that science is supposed to be self-correcting. Certainly errors are normal and to be expected, but the magnitude, tenaciousness, and persuasive effect of these errors are clearly anomalous. The only other known example of pseudoscience on this large a scale is the Russian variant of Lamarckian biology called Lysenkoism. Chapter 11 compares the two cases, seeking to determine what is common in their origin and development.

Chapter 12 considers the political significance of IQ tests, noting how beliefs about them have been shaped by a desire to attribute social class differences to variation in ability. Since this commitment to merito-cratic ideology has inspired many of the testers' exaggerated claims, it is reasonable to see the pseudoscience as a type of ideological distortion that can best be understood by examining the ideology it supports. Accordingly, the chapter focuses on the concept of meritocracy, tracing its evolution over the last hundred years, and showing how it provides a limited, misleading view of the stratification process.

Psychometric pseudoscience has left the public with an image of mental ability that is fundamentally mistaken. The concluding chapter is an attempt to alter this image. By sorting out beliefs based primarily on pseudoscience, it seeks to clarify what is really known. By reporting on observations of people with exceptional creative talent, it provides grounds for an alternative conception. In short, it seeks to correct the popular misconceptions which have arisen from the ill-fated effort to construct a science of eugenics.

11. The Pseudoscience Phenomenon

Since scientific verification has become accepted as the most authoritative proof by most people in advanced industrial societies, there inevitably have developed numerous instances of sham science being used to support ideas which could not be supported by real science. This process is sufficiently widespread and has enough impact on popular views that some concept of pseudoscience is needed to describe it. A precise definition is difficult because there is no sharp dividing line between actual pseudoscience and normal cases of fallibility by scientists. There are cases sufficiently flagrant, nonetheless, that are qualitatively different from mere scientific error, and these need to be explained.

Pseudoscience may be defined, somewhat more formally than initially stated in the Introduction, as *a sustained process of false persuasion transacted by simulation or distortion of scientific inquiry and hypothesis-testing.* There are four parts to the definition: (1) essentially incorrect results are generated; (2) these are successfully and persuasively disseminated to a substantial audience; (3) dissemination occurs by a process of convincing the audience that results are bona fide scientific conclusions; (4) the normal processes of error correction in science are retarded or prevented from functioning, so that the incorrect beliefs generated are sustained over time.

This definition excludes astrology, for example, which usually is accepted in spite of the knowledge that it is not scientific, rather than because of a belief that it is. The definition does not include most cases of scientists simply giving false opinions, because usually these will be recognized as only opinions unless some effort is made to create the appearance of empirical verification. For this process of false persuasion to occur, the originators must be viewed as reputable scientists by the receptive audience, but not necessarily by specialists in related fields. Results cannot be considered "essentially incorrect" simply because they contain errors or misleading statements; the major conclusions must be erroneous in some fundamental way. The ideas professed, however, need not be completely false. It is sufficient that the claim of scientific verification remain in question or that the conclusions drawn are a major exaggeration of something which is true to a much smaller degree or under very limited circumstances.

Pseudoscience is most likely to develop in areas of pressing human concern—health, sexuality, drug addiction, and other major social issues. Typically, it serves as a kind of wish-fulfillment, enabling people to discover what they would like to believe. Often this involves discovering some miracle cure or some horror which legitimizes existing policies, prohibitions, and moral codes.

Most recognized instances fall under the category of *petit pseudoscience.* This is when small, independent originators profess eccentric theories without the benefit of significant institutional support. They usually work in almost total isolation from their colleagues, and are excluded from the scientific journals and societies which define them as quacks or cranks. A number of instances of this type are described in Martin Gardner's *Fads and Fallacies in the Name of Science.* Some have built up substantial cults, but aside from their followers they are held in disrepute. Their pseudoscience has a clearly limited domain, outside of which it simply fails to persuade.

Far more unusual, and perhaps more significant, are the few known instances of *grand pseudoscience,* where the domain is an entire nation or group of nations, and the false beliefs are openly professed as valid science by respected authorities in major educational institutions. Opposition exists, but the proponents have gained a sufficiently strong foothold within strategic institutions that the preponderance of educated opinion comes to favor the conclusions established by pseudoscience. For this to occur, proponents must have the support of powerful agencies, but such support does not automatically result in grand pseudoscience. Recourse to pseudoscience is probably frequent in large organizations. Corporations needing to justify profitmaking policies as in the public interest, and government bureaus needing to cover up past mistakes[1] can be expected to take refuge in false scientific persuasion. But such instances seldom produce grand pseudoscience because the major goal of those employing pseudoscience is usually only to obfuscate or falsify a specific issue. Little effort is made to construct enduring theoretical truths, so the false conclusions do not appear in textbooks and journals, and do not greatly influence which ideas the public regards as factual scientific knowledge.

The twentieth century's two clearest instances of grand pseudoscience have been Lysenkoism in the Soviet Union, also known as Michurinist biology and neo-Lamarckian genetics; and the various offshoots of Galton's theory developed in the United States and Great Britain, first under the titles of eugenics and biometrics, and later referred to as psychometrics and behavior genetics.[2] Lysenkoism achieved a dominant position in Russian genetics and agricultural science during the late 1930s, and maintained its position until 1964. Since then it has been in retreat, so that by now only faint traces of the earlier pseudoscience remain.[3] The Anglo-American pseudoscience, which we shall call eugenics-psychometrics, developed most aggressively during the first three decades of the twentieth century, was forced to retreat in the face of strong opposition during the next forty years, but has experienced a moderate resurgence during the last decade.

Both Lysenkoism and eugenics-psychometrics have profoundly influenced the thought of many people, including scientists, in their respective countries. In each case the most significant influence has occurred through a process of pseudoscience. The chief results of Lysenkoism have been: an acceptance of neo-Lamarckian theory, which posits the inheritance of acquired adaptive characteristics; persistent faith in a variety of bogus agricultural remedies; and a belief in the transformation of species (that is, that the seeds of one plant can under certain conditions develop into a plant of another species). The major results of eugenics-psychometrics have been: highly exaggerated notions of what

IQ and creativity tests are able to measure; a belief that variations in mental ability are determined largely by genetic differences; the belief that certain races are demonstrably more intelligent than others; and a maintenance of the doctrine that social inequality is caused by variation in the biological fitness of individuals.

The preceding ten chapters implicitly have sought to develop a theory of pseudoscience. By attempting to explain the rise and development of eugenics-psychometrics we have been led to put forward hypotheses about the conditions under which grand pseudoscience will occur and the manner in which it will be sustained. If we now formalize this theory and question its applicability to the case of Lysenkoism, we may begin to separate those elements of the history of eugenics-psychometrics which are unique and specific from those which are best seen as manifestations of a general pseudoscience phenomenon. The goal in this process is to develop a more precise theory which adequately describes a recurring cultural pattern. Such a theory might then be useful for identifying future instances of grand pseudoscience as well as those which could already exist, but not yet be recognized.

The Comparison of Lysenkoism and Eugenics-Psychometrics

1. The Mimicry of Scientific Procedures

Lysenkoists in the Soviet Union conducted experiments, gathered empirical evidence, published results in journals they controlled, and developed their own elaborate quasiscientific terminology.[4] Galtonians in the United States and England did these things, so in each case there developed a sizable community of scientific pretenders. Both communities have relied upon crucial ambiguities to maintain their credibility. The meaning of key concepts has been kept deliberately vague so theories employing them could not be refuted. Such has been the case with Lysenko's vaunted "stage theory" of plant development, as well as with the Western concept of intelligence. Both Lysenkoists and eugenicists have engaged in a variety of departures from normal scientific methods, but have differed in their defenses. Proponents of eugenics-psychometrics have strongly supported the idea of rigorous science, and when confronted with their own departures from it have chosen either to deny that these exist, or to admit them, claiming that imperfection and uncertainty are necessary parts of science. Lysenkoists, by contrast, have heartily endorsed their own methodological deficiencies. They have favored science per se, but have denounced the use of experimental control groups as unnecessary, and the use of statistics as "mathematical fetishism."[5] Ironically, psychometrics has spawned some of the major advances in statistical theory while being a locus of grand pseudoscience.

The source of their differences is easily understood. Lysenkoism developed in opposition to an established science of genetics. Its proponents have tended to be "young, poorly educated, subordinate, anti-intellectual nativists."[6] Lysenko himself was originally an untrained agricultural extension worker. Needing to reject a methodologically sophisticated science, Lysenkoists saw methodological sophistication as evidence of false, reactionary, bourgeois science. Their own "true, proletarian science" followed the dictum of the plant breeder, Michurin, that the best results could be obtained only by experience and not by reading books. The conclusions of eugenics-psychometrics, on the other hand, did not contradict those of any established science. Its proponents could thus afford to be enthusiastic about scientific rigor in the abstract.

2. The Defective Paradigm

A defective paradigm differs from a superseded one in that it never gives rise to important scientific discoveries in its central areas of concern. The superseded paradigm, while no longer seen as correct, at least at one time directed scientists to the solution of problems then viewed as important. It breaks down, however, when interest shifts to new problems which cannot be solved within it.[7] A superseded paradigm logically may or may not give rise to pseudoscience, depending upon whether its proponents feel compelled to establish and maintain their own solutions to the new problems. A defective paradigm, on the other hand, is almost certain to generate pseudoscience because the central problems initially specified are themselves unsolvable given the available methods for seeking a solution. This creates a situation in which proponents must either distort or fail, a dilemma likely to inspire recurring mirages where imaginary solutions are projected onto ambiguous data. The more cautious scientists do not become eminent because they fail to provide solutions to the problems regarded as central. Other scientists then seek to emulate the field's "successful" leaders, so both the defective arguments and false conclusions become institutionalized.

Pseudoscience can develop among investigators who do not share a paradigm, but it is not likely to develop on a grand scale. Individuals strongly dedicated to proving false theories can be expected to engage in false persuasion, but they will continue to do so as individuals unless their dedication is shared by many others. Adoption of a defective paradigm means that an entire community of scientists is committed to establishing the same unverifiable theory. So the mirages discovered by individuals are likely to be shared by the community, and this collective agreement will tend to make the proponents more bold in professing their false solutions, since it protects them from the charge that they are simply isolated cranks.

Lysenkoist pseudoscience began without any unifying paradigm. There was only a commitment to solving practical problems of Soviet agriculture, and a number of false panaceas for which a pretense of scientific verification had to be developed. Lysenko called for the adoption of the neo-Lamarckian paradigm in the late 1930s because he felt that it offered possibilities for breeding new varieties of plants more rapidly than could be done using traditional Mendelian genetics. According to this paradigm, one can alter the hereditary characteristics of plants by changing their environmental conditions (e.g., soaking the seeds, raising or lowering temperatures, changing the soil). Adoption of the paradigm produced a considerable expansion of Lysenkoist pseudoscience, since it put forward a general theory of heredity which could be tested experimentally in almost any location. The number of Lysenkoists multiplied as many young followers sought to "shatter the heredity" of plants, making the seeds of one species grow into adults of another.

> In nearly every issue of the journal [*Agrobiologiya*] from 1950 to 1955 articles appeared in which were seriously reported transformations of wheat into rye and vice versa, barley into oats, peas into vetch, vetch into lentils, cabbage into swedes, firs into pines, hazelnuts into hornbeans, alders into birches, sunflowers into strangelweed.[8]

Because such results invariably stemmed from the use of contaminated seed samples (for example, some rye seeds would be mixed in with the wheat), Lysenkoists made a point not to use experimental controls which would detect contamination.

For the community of eugenicists and psychometricians, the defective paradigm was influential from the outset. Having already been formed by the theories of Galton and Spencer, and the research strategies of Galton and Pearson, the eugenics paradigm needed only Binet's concept of an intelligence test to complete it. Henceforth it motivated recurring instances of pseudoscience. Even after interest in the nature-nurture question declined, pseudoscience continued because intelligence testers' early commitment to the eugenics paradigm had led them to devise false solutions to the unsolvable problem of designing culture-fair tests that measured mental capacity in general. And of course the current group of restorationists has sought to revive the eugenics paradigm in full.

Because the United States and England have fallen within the domain of eugenics-psychometrics, but outside the domain of Lysenkoism, we are accustomed to believing that the inheritance of mental ability is a proven fact, while the inheritance of acquired characteristics is an erroneous notion which has been disproved conclusively. Ironically, recent biochemical discoveries and a historical reexamination of Galtonian pseudoscience now suggest that the two ideas ought to be recognized as having comparable truth value.[9] Both are possibly true to some extent, but unconfirmed by scientific investigation. The manner and extent to which each is true is unknown and likely to remain that way for some time to come. In each case the crude, extreme versions of the theory, put forward by Lysenko on the one hand and Jensen on the other, are clearly false. But we cannot rule out the possibility that more limited versions of both will someday be proven valid. To do this would require the development of methodologies not currently imaginable, and even if it were done, it would not alter our evaluation of past pseudoscience.[10] In each case the claims of scientific verification and the specific formulations of the theories were false and would remain that way even if the general theories turned out to have some validity. A defective paradigm can be defective simply because it fails to specify methods which could confirm the theory; this is the case regardless of whether or not the theory is entirely false.

3. The Interdependence of Self-Deception and Deliberate Distortion

The question arises as to whether grand pseudoscience occurs primarily through the self-deception of its proponents or through their willful, deliberate deception of others. The answer is that both are involved, and that each depends upon the other. It is possible to cite specific instances which clearly involve deliberate charlatanism[11] as well as some which seem to involve merely honest error, but the general pattern appears to show a mixture of the two.

Those who examine the major proponents of grand pseudoscience encounter a convincing display of sincerity which would be difficult to effect and maintain entirely by willful pretense.[12] Grand pseudoscience also maintains itself over time by inaugurating new members into the community of proponents. If the major conclusions were disseminated primarily by deliberate fraud, then the new members would have to be informed of this so they too could become conscious charlatans. We would thus expect to find recurring instances of unsuccessful recruitment in which disillusioned scientists would reveal the deliberately fraudulent nature of the enterprise. Since these have not been found for either Lysenkoism or eugenics-psychometrics, we must conclude that something other than simple fraud is involved.

However, the proponents in each case have not behaved as if they were fully committed to the discovery of truth. When valid objections have been raised against their work, they have sought repeatedly to circumvent and dismiss those objections which could not be refuted. This pattern of apparently deliberate distortion has appeared in Terman's responses to Lippmann, as well as more recently in Jensen's evasive use of the terms *covariance* and *interaction,* in the attempts to dismiss Kamin's critique, and in the refusal to cite studies with evidence contradicting the meritocracy interpretation.[13] Similarly, Lysenkoists steadfastly refused to test their results by using proper experimental controls, and Lysenko even conspired to silence his scientific opposition by telling the Soviet government that it was composed of reactionaries seeking to sabotage agricultural progress.[14] Something more than just self-deception appears to be involved.

What probably happens is that proponents of grand pseudoscience are strongly committed to supporting a theory for which adequate evidence is unobtainable. They gather evidence which, interpreted very loosely, seems like it might support the theory. The proponents then decide that this evidence is adequate because they themselves believe the theory and are not willing to attribute their belief to anything other than the evidence. Having done this, they form a community with rules of inquiry which permit the loose interpretation of supporting evidence but do not permit arguments and information which cast doubt upon such interpretation. Proponents then view critics who refuse to follow these rules as biased, antiscientific polemicists who are unwilling to make the assumptions upon which scientific progress depends. The confrontation with critics becomes defined not as a scientific debate, but as a polemical dispute in which any kind of persuasive strategy is fair. They thus proceed to distort issues and evidence deliberately. Due to their own self-deception the distortion appears to them not as actual falsification, but merely as intentional simplification of matters for the sake of helping readers to see past the deliberate obscurantism and polemics of opponents. In other words, self-deception makes it easier to engage in deliberate distortion. At the same time this deliberate refusal to consider the opposition's strongest arguments shields the proponents from an awareness of the basic defects in their own arguments, and thus helps to perpetuate the self-deception.

4. Support by the Ruling Elite

The term *ruling elite* here refers generally to people who hold positions of authority in major social institutions and are thus able to make discretionary judgments which affect the institutions' course of development. It is axiomatic that grand pseudoscience requires such support. Otherwise it would lack the institutional basis needed to maintain a favorable reputation and disseminate findings widely.

The most important patrons of Lysenkoism were high-ranking agricultural officials and the Communist Party leadership. Lysenko received personal commendations and laudatory statements first from Stalin and later from Khrushchev. Higher education officials generally did not favor Lysenkoism, but their views carried less weight in party circles than did those of the agricultural leaders. As a result, the most distinguished Lysenkoists received numerous scientific honors and awards, as well as prestigious positions. Lysenko was rapidly promoted to head the Lenin Academy of Agricultural Sciences. His theories were consistently described as major scientific breakthroughs by the mass media and were presented as such in secondary schools. University faculties, by contrast, included more opponents than supporters, although most of the opposition was not outspoken.

After thirty years of repeated practical failures in agriculture, the top agricultural officials became disillusioned with Lysenko, and in 1964 were able to sway the party leadership toward similar disillusionment. Lysenkoism became one of the main issues involved in Khrushchev's ouster in 1964, after which Lysenkoism rapidly lost both official support and widespread influence.

It remains to be studied who have been the most important patrons of eugenics-psychometrics. Certainly some wealthy individuals, like Francis Galton and Mrs. E. H. Harriman, were instrumental in getting the enterprise started. Private foundations, like the Carnegie Institution and Commonwealth Fund, provided monetary support needed for large-scale expansion. Probably these are now less important then the federal education bureaucracy, from which the restorationists have derived most of their funds.[15] It is also likely that various university administrators have significantly aided the cause, as, for example, when the president of Stanford University promoted Lewis Terman out of the education department to become head of the psychology department.[16]

Elite support logically may be of either a positive or negative character. Patrons can allocate money and prestige to the proponents; they can also impose punitive sanctions upon the opposition. Lysenko's patrons clearly did both. There are numerous instances on record of scientists either losing their jobs or being sent to labor camps for publicly criticizing Lysenko and his theories.[17] This kind of interference was not continuously present but occurred primarily in the late 1930s and during the period 1948–1952. At other times some types of public criticism were allowed. As far as we know, elite support for eugenics-psychometrics has been entirely of a positive character. To the extent that sanctions have been imposed against critics, this has occurred locally, probably within academic departments. Further research may necessitate some revision of this conclusion.

5. Imaginary Solutions to Critical Social Problems

A defective paradigm is adopted because certain segments of the ruling elite have provided enough support for proponents of the paradigm to form a scientific community. The patrons do not see themselves as promoting pseudoscience, but as aiding the development of something which is already or will soon become a science. They themselves are fooled by the scientific "experts" whom they support and rely upon for advice about prospects and developments in science. At the same time, there are critics who expose fallacies and provide grounds for refusing to support the pseudoscience. What has to be explained is why the patrons choose to listen uncritically to the proponents and virtually ignore the critics.

This happens because the pseudoscience offers very attractive, but nevertheless imaginary, solutions to critical social problems. Lysenkoism developed in response to the Soviet Union's agricultural crisis of the 1930s, and promised to solve three important, interrelated problems. First, because harsh winters and political strife together had resulted in acute food shortages, new, frost-resistant varieties of wheat had to be developed quickly in order to prevent mass starvation. Mendelian plant breeders had suggested this could not be done in less than eight or ten years. Lysenko's neo-Lamarckian theory appeared to provide a way of doing this in two or three years, and for this reason the agricultural officials favored Lysenko over his opponents. Moreover, the Soviet government was ideologically committed to developing the most advanced, scientific farming system possible. But since investments were being channeled into the development of heavy industry, and later into military preparations, they could not afford the capital investment this would have required. Lysenkoism appeared to suggest ways in which a modern, efficient farming system could be developed without intensive capital investment. Finally, the traditional backwardness of Russian agriculture meant that most peasants and landholders were hostile to modern, scientific methods, and preferred the older, inefficient methods to which they were accustomed. Lysenkoist pseudoscience seemed to reduce the conflict between traditionalism and modernization by suggesting that many of the old customary procedures were in fact efficient, scientifically correct modes of farming.

Eugenics became popular around the turn of the century when it seemed to offer solutions to a variety of social problems—poverty, crime, drunkenness, slums, labor strife—which were then being perceived as acute crises. Believing that mental ability was inherited gave the new (propertyless) middle class an attractive solution to the perennial problem of transmitting middle-class status to their children.[18] Unable to bequeath the children farms or stores, they could at least endow them with superior genes which would guarantee their success in a competitive society. Similarly, believing that IQ tests measured general intelligence offered solutions to the major personnel problems of large organizations. By relying upon test scores employers could give everyone a job commensurate with his or her mental capacity, and thus be both maximally fair and maximally efficient.

6. Contributory Social Movements

The proponents engage in pseudoscience when they have a strong commitment to establishing ideas which cannot be established scientifically. A likely source of such commitment is participation in, or sympathy with, an ongoing social movement. Disseminating the basic creed of the movement becomes the principal object of false persuasion. Galtonian pseudoscience developed on a grand scale in the midst of the eugenics movement. Eugenicists played important roles in the early development of psychometrics, which they perceived as providing the key methodological advances needed to construct a science of eugenics.

Lysenkoism emerged in the wake of a movement aimed at reversing traditional status distinctions between practical workers and "ivory-tower" specialists. Prior to Lysenko's crusade there had been a conflict between agribiologists—practical agricultural workers led by Michurin—and academic scientists.[19] Lysenko sought to establish the supremacy of the practical over the theoretical by showing that untrained workers in the fields could devise better farming methods than ivory-tower scientists. His pseudoscience was intended to vindicate the Michurinist movement as well as solve pressing agricultural problems.

7. Opposition and Compromise

Scientists generally do not like polemics, and when conflict occurs they usually try to minimize its importance.[20] Accordingly, they are reluctant to attack grand pseudoscience unless it directly conflicts with their theories and work. Plant breeders in the Soviet Union for the most part managed to avoid a head-on confrontation with Lysenkoism. They gave the minimal approval necessary to protect them from reprisals. Geneticists, on the other hand, were more intractable, criticized Lysenko repeatedly, and thus suffered both repression against individuals and the banning of major genetical concepts. One writer, David Joravsky, explains this difference as a divergence in the structures of the two disciplines. Plant breeding was a "sprawling, highly empirical discipline," without any unifying theory. Specialists could pay lip service to Lysenko's achievements and then simply work in another area. Genetics was a "highly theoretical, formalistic discipline," the very existence of which was called into question by Lysenkoist pseudoscience.[21] So the geneticists could not afford to be eclectic as easily as the plant breeders. The latter had merely to slip in an occasional laudatory reference to Lysenko in their writings. Geneticists, however, could not coherently endorse both their own theory and Lysenko's. In some cases Mendelian genetics textbooks appeared encased in Lysenkoist introductions and conclusions. Others who wished to compromise wrote Lysenkoist texts and added technical appendices composed of Mendelian genetics.

The resilience of Galtonian pseudoscience may be attributed partly to the fact that its central claims have not directly conflicted with any established academic discipline. Reputable geneticists simply have chosen to work on other problems, where the methodological barriers are not as formidable. Eugenicists and restorationists have borrowed concepts and terms from genetics, but have been careful to avoid contradicting any of its major findings. Academic psychology has a structure similar to that of plant breeding. People working in one sub-area are likely to have very little in common with those working in another. Psychologists could, in this way, easily manage to endorse watered-down versions of Galton's theory without compromising the integrity or challenging the importance of their own work. They have simply demanded that learning be considered important in addition to heredity, a compromise which even the most extreme restorationists accept. American psychologists and Russian plant breeders have endorsed pseudoscience for different reasons—one has faced the direct threat of government reprisals, the other has felt a loyalty to colleagues and not wanted to stir up hostility—but in each case the decision to accommodate was facilitated by the disunified structure of the discipline.

Once a grand pseudoscience becomes established, specialists in adjacent disciplines are more likely to be concerned with containing it than with trying to abolish it altogether. As long as the pseudo-science does not contradict their own theories and writings they are content to adopt an attitude of laissez-faire. After all, the specialist's duty is to pursue truth in his own area, not everywhere it is lacking. Eventually an equilibrium is reached, specifying certain questions for the pseudoscience and others for the adjacent fields. As long as this equilibrium is maintained, controversy is kept to a minimum. Jensen's 1969 article shattered the entente in psychometrics by focusing on the race question, which previously had been relegated to anthropologists, and by professing a hereditarian theory to such an extent that it challenged the efficacy of compensatory education. Having impinged on the territory of other specialists, the article reawakened an old controversy. However, most of the ensuing criticism was directed toward reaffirming the equilibrium rather than rooting out Galtonian pseudoscience entirely. Consequently, critics did not dwell upon the inappropriate use of heritability, the faulty data base from which estimates were calculated, the limited validity of IQ tests, or even the illusion of culture-fair tests. Instead, they sought to revise heritability calculations downward from .8 to .6 or .4, to argue that racial differences in intelligence could not be computed from the data, and to defend the possible utility of compensatory education.[22] Similarly, most of the Russian scientists who criticized Lysenkoism did not say it was worthless. They praised Lysenko's practical achievements while attempting to argue that some of his theories were incorrect. Lysenko rejected their offers for an entente, and in 1948 had his opponents routed completely by government decree.

Because established grand pseudoscience is considered respectable and scientific, opponents face some compulsion to limit themselves to acceptable scholarly arguments and avoid unacceptable polemics. Writing is defined as polemical if it attempts to show malfeasance. So while specific criticisms of pseudoscience are allowed, arguments which cast doubt upon the proponents' competence and expertise are discouraged. The Soviet government allowed no public disagreement with any of Lysenko's work between 1948 and 1952; between 1953 and 1964 they agreed to tolerate limited criticism, but not polemics. Anything which saw Lysenkoism as entirely wrong, which doubted its practical utility, or which described how it gained acceptance was, of course, defined as polemical. Publication of the leading anti-

Lysenkoist journal was suspended in 1958 when the editors violated these rules. Scientific writing which was routine textbook material in the West was seen as polemical in the Soviet Union. Similarly, discussion of basic defects in the restorationists' arguments might logically be defined as elementary science, but in the context of an established grand pseudoscience, it is more likely to be viewed as polemical. This distinction helps to preserve congeniality among scientists, but it also prolongs the tenure of false beliefs.

A Note on the Relation Between Science and Pseudoscience

Because most people see science as good and pseudoscience as bad, they tend to imagine that the two are diametrically opposed. They assume that there is a natural hostility between the two, and that whatever facilitates one hinders the other. The case of Lysenkoism appears to vindicate this way of thinking. From it people generalize that pseudoscience will occur when investigators cease to respect rigorous thinking and experimentation, and that science thrives upon autonomy, while grand pseudoscience is the result of political interference in scientific affairs.[23]

Considering the case of eugenics-psychometrics forces us to amend these propositions. Unlike the proponents of Lysenkoism, eugenicists and restorationists have displayed great respect for rigorous thinking in the abstract. They have simply failed to apply it to their own work. Scientists' autonomy can never be absolute, since they depend ultimately upon patronage from sections of the ruling elite. They can have a sort of relative autonomy, which means freedom from direct interference in their affairs, but Galtonians have had this sort of autonomy and still have produced grand pseudoscience.

All that can be said generally about the relation between science and pseudoscience is that the rise of the former in public esteem has increased the temptation of proponents to engage in the latter, rather than seek some other means of disseminating their ideas. Dramatic advances in genetics around the turn of the century kindled interest in eugenics, and it is likely that the current wave of interest in the restorationists has been inspired partly by genuine discoveries made in biochemistry and neurophysiology during the last decade.[24] On the other hand, scientific progress certainly can undermine pseudoscience by gathering evidence which discredits it. The discovery of the structure of DNA helped to overthrow Lysenkoism, just as studies correlating IQ scores with creative accomplishments helped to discredit Terman's early claims.

Pseudoscience can inhibit scientific progress by leading investigators to ask the wrong questions, and by draining away resources which might otherwise have gone toward the advancement of science. Lysenkoism is an extreme instance of pseudoscience retarding the development of science. It is difficult to estimate the extent to which eugenics-psychometrics has done this, since it has not developed in opposition to any established science. In fact, eugenics-psychometrics has contributed positively to scientific advancement. At least in the area of statistical theory proponents made some genuine progress while professing Galtonian pseudoscience. It is likely that eugenics fostered the development of genetics by convincing patrons that such a science could solve important social problems. The false persuasion which has equated IQ score with general intelligence has also contributed significantly to quantitative studies of social stratification. To call studies "science" when they rely heavily upon pseudoscience is a dubious use of the term. Nevertheless, to the extent that such studies are acknowledged to have merit, it is worth remembering that pseudoscience contributed to the possibility of their being done in the first place. One may well retain the judgment that science is good and pseudoscience bad, but one should not expect to find in reality a consistently antagonistic relationship between the proponents of each. Nor should one assume that the progress of one will eradicate the other.

12. The Ideological Dimension

Understanding the dynamics of grand pseudoscience partially explains how false beliefs about mental ability have gained acceptance. But it does not account for the prominence of these particular ideas and the emergence of pseudoscience on their behalf. To do this we must consider the ideological dimension, since it is the IQ myth's political significance which has generated so much attention.

Nicholas Pastore has convincingly portrayed the nature-nurture debate as a thinly veiled expression of political sentiments. He studied the political attitudes of twenty-four scientists active in the debate and found that of the twelve hereditarians, eleven were conservatives; of the twelve environmentalists, only one was conservative and the rest were either liberal or radical.[1] Russell Marks has shown how the dominance of one side or the other in this debate has depended partly on the kind of social reforms being advocated by powerful interests at the time. When business leaders wanted to restrict immigration in the 1920s, hereditarian conclusions about innate racial inferiority were presented to the public. When school integration was favored after the Second World War, environmentalist conclusions about racial equality were put forward.[2] Given that the issue cannot be resolved empirically, it is reasonable to view the nature-nurture argument as politics expressed as science.

The basic political usage of IQ tests, however, depends less on the heredity-environment controversy than it does on the use of IQ scores as a measure of intelligence or mental capacity. Once this broad significance of the test scores is assumed, it becomes possible to equate test results with pure ability or all-around talent, and thus to see people with high IQ scores as deserving high-status, well-paying jobs. Since test scores correlate with social class, it is a short step to believing that the upper classes deserve their privileged positions and that the lower classes are capable of nothing more than unskilled work. This kind of justification for hierarchy and inequality is called *meritocratic ideology*.[3]

The general notion of meritocracy uses two related arguments to depict the class structure of western capitalist societies as natural and socially desirable. First, it pictures society as providing opportunity for all to rise in the occupational hierarchy. Inequalities of wealth, power, and status exist because people differ in how intelligent and industrious they are. Such differences are the cause of inequality, and since they themselves are products of nature, the inequalities which exist must also be natural. Secondly, it contends that society benefits by recruiting the most capable individuals into the most responsible jobs. These jobs must offer much greater prestige and salary than others as a way of attracting capable persons. Hence the existing inequalities perform the necessary function of conserving scarce talent and directing it to where it is most needed. Individuals employed in upper-class occupations deserve their wealth and privilege because their contribution to society is especially valuable. Conversely, the poor are poor because they are lazy and unintelligent. They merit nothing better than bare subsistence living because they contribute little to society, and it is in society's interest not to improve their position substantially.

Various forms of meritocratic ideology have been developed. Some have viewed the meritocracy as an existing reality; others have seen it as an ideal which society only approximates; still others have described it as a goal for the future requiring some important reform to bring it about. In the nineteenth century, theorists like Herbert Spencer claimed that economic competition was essentially meritocratic. Business success and failure were supposedly caused by individual differences in intelligence and industriousness. Now most writers see the school as the primary agency of stratification by merit. According to the twentieth-century version of meritocracy, schools separate students on the basis of ability, allowing the bright ones access to the advanced training which equips them for high-status jobs. The less intelligent students do poorly in school, receive less education, and are consigned to low-status employment. IQ scores, being the principal measure of general ability, predict academic performance as well as capacity for competence in professional and managerial occupations. By channeling students on the basis of their IQ scores and scholastic achievement, schools are helping to create a society where there is equality of opportunity and where position depends above all upon merit.

Whatever else one feels about this ideology one should not labor under the illusion that it is a product of empirical science. The idea of meritocracy in its general form preceded the development of IQ tests by at least a hundred years. The shift in locus of meritocratic competition from marketplace to school system has less to do with any test data than it does with changes in the economy and in patterns of social mobility. The eugenics paradigm was in essence an effort to verify scientifically an ideology already popular at the time, and it was the eugenicists' and intelligence testers' commitment to the ideology which led them to initiate much of the pseudoscience. As we have seen in Chapter 6, to depict American or British society as a meritocracy based upon IQ scores is false on two grounds: (a) the available evidence hardly justifies using IQ results as a measure of all-around talent or general ability, and (b) even if it were such, stratification appears to be based more upon social class background and amount of years in school than it does on IQ scores per se.

Criticism of meritocratic ideology should run deeper than merely pointing out that the significance of test scores has been exaggerated; it should challenge the basic premises of the ideology itself. This can be done in three ways: first, by tracing the development of the meritocracy conception; second, by analyzing those aspects of social reality which the ideology conceals or denies; and, finally, by examining recent projections of meritocracy in the future.

Historical Development of Meritocratic Ideology

The different versions of meritocratic ideology have become prominent for the most part because they have justified social class barriers and oppression. They have provided convenient apologies for middle- and upper-class privileges, and thus have been congenial to the outlook of most people in these groups. Being a versatile and persuasive component of political rhetoric, the image of meritocracy has appeared repeatedly, its forms and emphases shifting to mirror changes in the society and to point toward the necessity of social policies being advocated at the time. Over successive generations its format has been conditioned by the advancing scientism which has characterized the nineteenth and twentieth centuries—more and more the ideology has taken on the appearance of a scientific theory. The pseudoscience described previously represents an advanced stage of this process.

Since the French Revolution meritocratic ideology has been associated primarily with the industrial bourgeoisie, the capitalist class of urban merchants, financiers, and manufacturers.[4] Initially this class had to wage a two-front struggle—with remnants of the feudal aristocracy above it, and with the industrial working class below. The former monopolized positions in the church and civil service which were generally allocated by birthright. The bourgeoisie sought to gain access to these positions by demanding that they be given to all with talent, and that the special privileges of noble birth be abolished. The capitalists' opposition to the aristocracy led them to favor a formal equality represented by slogans like equality of opportunity and equality of all under the law. On the other hand, the capitalists' wealth was acquired through exploitation of the working class and foreign plunder. Their livelihood as capitalists depended upon the extreme substantive inequality which made available plentiful sources of cheap labor. Like the nobility, the bourgeoisie was a hereditary class—wealth and position were passed from fathers to sons by inheritance. Opposition from the proletariat compelled the capitalists to justify this inherited wealth, but their heritage of conflict with the feudal nobility constrained them from using any concept of birthright directly. They needed some mysterious notion of talent or virtue which theoretically anyone could possess, but which in practice usually coincided with possession of property and wealth. Concepts of intelligence and hereditary natural ability were devised and met this need. Meritocratic ideology emerged as a way of reconciling formal equality and substantive inequality.

The notion of meritocracy at first had both progressive and conservative implications. It called for destruction of the feudal system, but it simultaneously defended the bourgeoisie's hegemony over the working class. As the old aristocracy lost its power and the capitalists became unquestionably dominant, the progressive function of meritocratic ideology was accomplished, and the ideology became in effect more conservative. In the French Revolution one sees the image of meritocracy being used for radical ends, while in nineteenth-century England its major uses were distinctly reactionary. There the transition from aristocratic to bourgeois rule was accomplished more peacefully than in France by a gradual blending of the two classes.[5] Thus, in England meritocratic ideology was elaborated by a combination of aristocratic and bourgeois theorists who focused on the inferiority of the poor.

Throughout the nineteenth century meritocratic imagery was associated with the laissez-faire philosophy developed by Thomas Malthus and Herbert Spencer. This creed eschewed government intervention in the economy, except for protection of basic bourgeois property rights.[6] It justified maintaining an urban working class on the verge of starvation, a condition which clearly facilitated the rapid accumulation of capital. Malthus, an English clergyman writing in opposition to radical thinkers of the French Revolution, argued that there was a natural tendency for population to expand beyond what could be supported by the available means of subsistence. It had to be limited either by moral restraint and the voluntary curbing of sexuality or by the natural calamities of disease and starvation. Since the poor lacked the necessary morality, their numbers had to be curbed by the ravages of nature. All forms of relief for the poor were undesirable because they simply allowed a large class of paupers to exist. It was better for society to let nature take its toll.

Malthus' argument became popular in bourgeois circles because the elimination of poor relief in the countryside forced many laborers into the growing city where they could be exploited by industrialists. The argument contained important elements of meritocratic ideology. There was the clear implication that the lower classes deserved their fate, since their lack of morality was a principal cause of it. Also, the conditions of the poor were attributed to a natural law, the tendency of population to expand beyond its means.

Herbert Spencer, a middle-class bourgeois theorist, considerably broadened the philosophical basis of laissez-faire. He imagined a vast network of universal laws which converged on political conclusions roughly similar to those of Malthus. In other words, he greatly expanded the scientism which Malthus had initiated. Francis Galton, an aristocrat with some middle-class sympathies, went one step further by trying to gather empirical evidence for his laws. Spencer and Galton together revolutionized the prevailing conception of merit. In place of "moral restraint" which could account for poverty only indirectly through overpopulation, they presented the hereditary, biological traits of "intelligence" and "natural ability," whose variation allegedly could account for the entire system of social classes. Spencer focused on its role in determining the acquisition of wealth; Galton stressed that genetic superiority was responsible for eminence. Both saw in their biological reductionism the causes of racial domination as well as economic inequality. The extent to which they viewed nineteenth-century England as a meritocracy is neatly summarized by Galton's statement that "no man can achieve a very high reputation without being gifted with very high abilities; and . . . few who possess these very high abilities can fail in achieving eminence."[7]

Spencer's philosophy became popular largely because the upper classes favored its conservative implications. It provided the perfect answer to humanitarians and socialists favoring reforms to alleviate human misery. Whatever temporary benefits these might provide, Spencer argued, they could in the end undermine human progress by interfering with the processes of natural selection. There was, however, no necessary connection between Spencer's evolutionary approach and the laissez-faire conclusions he attached to it. Near the end of the nineteenth century the liberal social thinkers known as reform Darwinists rejected these conclusions and began using Spencer's laws and concepts to argue for increased government intervention.[8] Such was needed, they claimed, to control the evolutionary process intelligently. As this new perspective became dominant the prevailing conception of meritocracy shifted once again.

Lester Ward was the key transitional figure who redefined meritocracy, no longer viewing it as what society was, but as what society *could be,* if it instituted universal public education. Ward's theories were conditioned by his advocacy of this reform. He rejected the idea of innate upper-class superiority because it seemed to imply that the lower classes were not worth educating. Instead he claimed that "the average capacity for knowledge is equal for all classes of society."[9] In contrast to the biological determinism of Galton and Spencer, Ward became an environmentalist who insisted that intelligence could be developed by exposure to education. The existing society was not truly meritocratic, he argued, because the rich had unfair advantages over the poor. Only in schools was success a true indicator of talent and virtue, and only when society based its stratification upon performance in schools would it approximate the ideal of meritocracy. As Ward saw it,

> Every child born into the world should be looked upon by society as so much raw material to be manufactured. Its quality is to be tested. It is the business of society as an intelligent economist to make the very most of it. To do this its actual quality or capacity for usefulness must be definitely and accurately determined. The present process consists in throwing out as dross nine tenths of all the material obtained, with no other test than that this quantity comes from certain alleged ignoble sources rendered so by arbitrary decisions. The process of universal education is that of first assaying the whole and rejecting only so much as shall, after thorough testing, prove worthless.[10]

In other words, he conceived of schools as donors of opportunity on the one hand, and as proving grounds for talent on the other. His devotion to the idea of public education prevented him from imagining that the schools themselves might become instruments for reproducing society's class structure.

The same economic realities which underlay the emergence of compulsory public schooling insured that Ward's conception of meritocracy would predominate over Spencer's. Throughout the nineteenth century economic competition was producing the failure of numerous small businesses along with the growth of larger ones. Toward the end of the century the concentration of capital and the desire of capitalists to protect themselves from competition jointly led to the formation of mergers, corporations, and trusts. This transition from an economy composed of small, competitive enterprises to one with large corporations brought about a change in the character of the middle class. Having once been independent farmers, merchants, and artisans almost entirely, it came to include in ever greater proportions salaried employees who occupied positions in the middle and upper strata of organizational hierarchies. Middle-class status came to depend less upon ownership of capital and more upon having the kinds of certification which made one eligible for professional, technical, and managerial jobs. This in turn promoted the rapid expansion of public education.[11]

As opportunities for upward social mobility through education increased, other kinds of opportunities for upward mobility diminished, so the essential competition for middle-class positions came to be housed more and more within the school system.[12] The prevailing conception of meritocracy shifted because the situation and experience of most of the middle class was changing, and the new school-centered conception reflected the change.

When the testing movement reached full force after the First World War, universal public education was already a reality. This in itself meant that the idealized view of schooling which Ward had developed in a reformist context was now more conservative in its implications since it defended the new forms of inequality and social class which increasingly were administered through the school system. The early mental testers' image of meritocracy was conditioned by their advocacy of curricular differentiation and tracking within the schools. Most embraced Galton's hereditarianism; a minority favored Ward's environmentalism. Both groups assumed that adult mental capacity could be discerned from scores on tests taken at an early age. And both viewed the school as proving ground on the one hand and donor of opportunity on the other. It was assumed that simply being in school gave all children a fair chance for success, and that the responsibility for failure had to lie entirely with the child and his or her family. For the past fifty years there has been some oscillation in the relative importance of hereditarian and environmentalist versions of meritocratic ideology, but the basic format of the ideology has undergone no major change.

This brief review suggests that the image of meritocracy can be used either as a defense of the status quo or as part of a plea for reform. The scope of the reforms is, however, limited by the assumption that inequality and a hierarchical division of labor either are or can become natural, fair, and beneficial to society. Hence meritocratic ideology serves as a defense of the class structure even when it argues for increased mobility across class lines. Moreover, as the desired reforms become institutionalized, the ideology again becomes unequivocally conservative. In recent decades the meritocracy idea has been used to challenge overt forms of racial and sexual discrimination. But as these are replaced by covert forms, where the discrimination is mediated by performance on standardized tasks (such as culturally biased IQ tests), the concept of meritocracy comes to be used in opposition to the efforts of ethnic and racial minorities.

Meritocratic ideology originated in the bourgeoisie's quest for legitimization and political power. Its forms have evolved in response to changing social conditions. Its enduring popularity is partly the result of its versatility in having simultaneous appeal to conservatives and reformers. It has the appearance of a fundamental truth not because of any genuine verification, but because it has provided a convenient and effective way of arguing for political ends, and for this reason has appeared frequently in public discourse.

Schooling as a Stratification Process

All the different forms of meritocratic ideology have contained elements of truth. They have correctly identified certain aspects of reality. But they also have neglected to mention others. The omissions in every case are sufficiently important that the meritocracy conception winds up providing a limited and distorted view of the social processes it purports to describe. Galton and Spencer, for example, recognized that wealth and fame were frequently outcomes of competition, that social standing could be affected by occupational performance, and that children of wealthy or artistic parents tended disproportionately to become wealthy or artistic themselves. From these observations they derived the conclusion that social standing was an accurate index of personal merit and innate talent. Their reasoning, however, depended upon the key assumption that society gave every person a fair opportunity to become rich and famous. The obstacles to this kind of success had to be either unimportant and easily surmounted, or distributed equally throughout the population.

The reality was, of course, quite different. Wealth almost always accrued to property owners who could hire and exploit laborers. Workers, who possessed no capital, had very little chance of becoming rich. Occasionally individuals might rise from humble origins to become wealthy, but these were rare exceptions. In general, the more money one had, the greater one's opportunities to make money. Likewise, the chances for fame in science and the arts were distributed unevenly across classes. Children from lower-class families received little more than a token formal education and were quickly placed in grueling jobs. Moreover, within many occupations the chances for promotion and eminence depended largely upon family connections which were a by-product of upper-class status.

The nineteenth-century Social Darwinist meritocracy was a basically erroneous conception because its central underlying assumption—equality of opportunity for all people—was incorrect. What of the twentieth-century scholastic meritocracy?[13] On the surface it seems more plausible than its predecessor. Virtually all children attend elementary school and initially they are asked to perform similar tasks. They are graded objectively on standardized tests, and are tracked into different curricula on the basis of their performance. Hence the schools appear to be meritocratic institutions. However, this view also rests upon a crucial assumption. For scholastic achievement to be a valid indicator of personal capacity one of two things must be true: *either schools treat all children equally, or the differential treatment is not an important cause of unequal performance.*

The first is clearly not true. It is inherent in the process of classroom interaction that children who perform better are rewarded more, and children who learn slowly or misbehave receive a disproportionate share of scoldings and humiliation. This unequal treatment may often fall along class and racial lines—middle-class children receiving more positive feedback than working-class children; white children receiving more than black children. This could occur within a particular classroom, as well as across classrooms, where teachers' behavior was powerfully affected by the composition of the student body.[14]

Proponents of meritocratic ideology acknowledge that unequal treatment exists in schools, but they claim that differences in achievement stem almost entirely from variation in personal characteristics shaped by family background. They argue that the unequal treatment merely reflects differences in mental capacity which are shaped outside the school. However, another view is possible. Although unequal treatment in the classroom is not the *only* cause of unequal performance, it may well be a very significant cause. This would suggest that schools do not distribute opportunity evenly to all students, but unevenly according to how they are treated. Further, schools are not simply neutral proving grounds for individual talent and diligence; they are agencies which actively shape and expand differences between students. The conception of schools as a meritocracy is basically erroneous because it overlooks this aspect. Several observations support this view.

First, many studies have shown a relationship between teacher's expectations and pupils' achievement. Students are more likely to perform well when teachers expect them to do so. This effect shows up even when children selected at random are tagged as having high potential; provided the teacher believes the deception, the children's test scores rise. Available evidence suggests that this effect is easier to produce in the early grades than it is in the later ones, and it shows up more clearly on tests which closely relate to the content of classroom instruction than it does on general tests of scholastic ability.[15] In any case, the total effect of teacher's expectations on pupils' achievement occurring day after day throughout the school year is probably much greater than what can be produced by psychologists with a single deception.

Participant-observer accounts by elementary school teachers like John Holt point to an intimate relation between fear and failure in school.[16] Dull or slow-learning children are the ones who are most afraid. They pay less attention in class because trying to understand the teacher is aversive to them. They would rather daydream than attend to lessons and confront their own confusion and humiliation. In the early grades all children experience a great deal of fear. They are afraid to ask questions for fear of being considered "stupid." The bright children are the ones who surmount this fear and build up enough self-confidence to listen in class and concentrate on tests. The slower children cannot stand not knowing an answer, so they are unable to concentrate when given a problem to solve. They quickly grope for any answer, even a wrong answer, because bearing the shame of having been wrong is less unpleasant than enduring the tension of not knowing an answer and trying to figure it out.

Observers of ghetto schools report that children frequently display much greater ingenuity and ability to learn on topics outside the formal curriculum, such as sports, popular music, or interpersonal games, than they do in school. Their lack of interest in the curriculum coincides with the belief, shared by students and teachers alike, that children from ghetto backgrounds will not have much success in school and consequently must seek it elsewhere. Gerald Levy estimates that by the end of second grade four-fifths of the children have discovered they are "dumb."[17] Accordingly, their classroom behavior consists of a mixture of self-denigration, listless apathy, and hostility toward the teacher. By second grade,

> control rapidly becomes the primary issue. Most substitutes and floater teachers and one-third of the regular teachers cannot control their classes. In many of these classes children refuse to do any work, fight with each other, leave the room, run through the halls, and harrass the other classrooms.

> By the third grade, for many teachers the *only* issue is control. The children are hit, bribed, and manipulated in any way that will secure the class. By the end of the third year, in many classes, education has hardened into open class struggle between teachers and children.[18]

These accounts suggest that motivation is crucial for success in school, and that not all children are imbued with a strong positive drive to succeed. They also suggest that the kinds of motivation children develop—to block out unpleasant experience by inattention, to express hostility, to gain approval by performing tasks correctly—depend upon teachers' expectations, which are influenced by students' past performance, and upon students' self-images, which are influenced by the responses they receive from teachers. In other words, classroom interaction itself may be an important source of performance differences. By encouraging different sorts of children to develop various types of motivation, schools inadvertently train some students to be academically bright and others to be academically dull.

Children themselves report experiencing a considerable amount of boredom in school. How a child performs in school and how "intelligent" he or she becomes depend upon how the child chooses to cope with fear and boredom. Two main strategies are available: *reward-seeking* and *disengagement*. A child may solicit esteem from the teacher and classmates by volunteering answers in class and doing well on assignments. If he or she is rewarded frequently enough for doing so, school becomes less boring because the child can anticipate opportunities to solicit favorable responses from others. Paying attention becomes worthwhile. Being labeled bright enables the child to spend time working on problems because he or she can assume that there is enough time available to arrive at the correct answer. In general, doing well in school makes school less aversive, and making school less aversive makes it easier to do well in school.

Reward-seeking is not a viable strategy for all students. If a child initially performs poorly, the teacher may well not encourage the child for his or her efforts. If the child is viewed as stupid, performing before the teacher or other students may be cause for anxiety. To the extent that the child has expectations about school, they resemble dread more than enthusiasm. Disengagement is the strategy of the slower students. Given that school cannot be anything other than aversive, the object is to minimize aversiveness by minimizing one's involvement with school. They daydream in class. They do not concentrate on assignments. They pretend doing well in school is unimportant.

It is possible to imagine a downward cycle of fear and failure, and boredom and withdrawal, which grips the slower children and prevents them from learning or doing well in school. They don't pay attention in class, so they don't learn the subject matter. Having failed to learn the subjects they are tested on, they do poorly on tests, which in turn causes them to fear tests and to avoid concentrating on them, which lowers their performance even more. The teacher observes this poor performance and views the children as dumb, treats them as dumb, and encourages them to think of themselves as dumb. This then prevents them from developing the self-confidence which would relieve the aversiveness and allow them to pay attention in class and concentrate on tests.

One also can imagine an upward cycle of successful reward-seeking whereby bright students perform well, get teachers to view them as intelligent, and thus allow them to develop the self-confidence needed to perform school tasks effectively. They pay attention in class, volunteer answers to teachers' questions, and are rewarded for doing so. Anticipating a verbal reward makes it easier to pay attention, and to learn the subject matter. Knowing the subject matter enables them to feel confident about tests, and thus do well on them.

All students use the disengagement strategy to some extent. However, they vary greatly in their use of the reward-seeking strategy. Dullness in most cases results from an excessive reliance on disengagement. Children can afford to daydream and still be bright provided they maintain some involvement with their schoolwork. Students who find any degree of involvement painful or degrading are likely to be at first slow, and then increasingly backward as the years go by. By dispensing rewards and punishments in such a way as to make reward-seeking a losing proposition for some proportion of students, teachers inadvertently reinforce these students' excessive reliance on the disengagement strategy.

Brightness and dullness become reified by classroom experience as children become habituated to their degree of reliance on the reward-seeking and disengagement strategies. After one or two years of schooling, a child's position in the upward or downward cycle of motivation and accomplishment is not likely to change much. Hence IQ scores, reflecting rates of learning conditioned by one or the other cycle, remain roughly stable.[19]

This model is probably an improvement over the conception of schools as proving grounds, but it too fails to tell the entire story. Any verbal response's potency as a reward or punishment depends upon its meaning to the recipient, and this will vary according to the context. Teachers cannot automatically reward students simply by choosing to say encouraging things. Their statements must be credible and be perceived as sincere. Otherwise, they will be ineffectual as rewards. As Levy points out, in the ghetto school where teachers expect most of the students to fail, praise and exhortations to succeed are accurately perceived by children as a form of manipulation used to maintain control in the classroom.[20] Hence, teachers' ability to dispense verbal rewards depends upon their having genuine hopes for students' future progress. But where such hopes appear to have no basis in daily classroom interaction, and where expectations are low, the teacher's ability to provide incentive is greatly diminished. Since communications of failure are credible and those of success are not, children find evaluation by the teacher unpleasant, and they develop hostility against the teacher as a way of defending against this unpleasantness. This further diminishes the teacher's ability to dispense rewards, and it also generates a kind of peer-group pressure which provides incentives not to perform assigned tasks. In every classroom there is a finite amount of incentive which can be used to motivate learning.

It is always distributed unevenly, with the brightest children usually consuming the largest shares. The total amount available in a classroom may depend largely upon teacher's expectations about students' futures.

So far the model has made no mention of the home environment or family background.[21] These are indeed important factors, but the precise nature of their role in determining scholastic achievement has perhaps been misconceived. To view them as causes without making reference to the processes of unequal treatment in the classroom gives the impression that coming from a poor family or a minority subculture in and of itself impairs a child's ability to learn. This is the central message of most "cultural deprivation" and "culture of poverty" theorists, but it may be true only to a limited extent. Some of the disadvantages associated with being lower class could be disadvantages only because of cultural biases in the schools (and society). For example, attributes of physical appearance, such as skin color and quality of clothing, have no direct connection with learning ability, but result in impaired ability because they act as cues which trigger low expectations and in some cases hostility. Certain speech patterns may have a similar effect. Bilingualism, having a first language different from standard English—Spanish and black ghetto dialects are the most common in the United States—presents some obstacles to learning in schools, but their significance is greatly exacerbated by the school system's unwillingness to make serious efforts to surmount them. Instead of encouraging bilingual education, most schools view a lack of familiarity with standard English as evidence of mental inferiority. Likewise, a lack of familiarity with middle-class lifestyles and culture becomes a major disadvantage because the formal curriculum is heavily geared in that direction.[22]

Other disadvantages have a direct and inherent relationship with ability. For example, compared with middle-class parents, working-class ones are less likely to have done well in school, to have high expectations for their children, and to view school as an avenue by which personal goals can be achieved.[23] They are also less likely to help their children with homework. All these things tend to give middle-class children a natural lead in the classroom. But the ultimate significance of this lead could be greatly magnified by the school's tendency to encourage learning by faster students and discourage it by slower ones.

Relatively slight inequalities originating in the home environment become very important determinants of achievement when used as a basis for recruiting children into cycles of brightness training on the one hand and dullness training on the other.

To some extent, upward and downward cycles of motivation and accomplishment are a natural tendency. It is easy to give encouragement to students who are doing well, and very difficult to think highly of ones who are not. However, the strength and importance of this tendency will depend upon the kinds of policies schools adopt to promote or counter it. American public schools in general seem to have done more to assist than to curb it. They have maintained the myth that slowness indicates low mental capacity. Believing this has helped many teachers and administrators to stigmatize slower children. Racial and cultural biases in tests and curricula have been left without any fundamental alteration. Administrative regulations calling on teachers to cover a fixed amount of material in a given time are guaranteed to leave some proportion of students in a state of confusion.[24] The insistence on individual work and individual responsibility for performance also adds to the process. By contrast, an ethic of collective responsibility for the progress of all and classrooms organized around children helping one another might diminish the process somewhat.

The main reason why schools do not seriously attempt to undermine the process is that *the upward and downward cycles of brightness training and dullness training actually facilitate the schools' task of reproducing society's class structure.* School systems are not obliged to prevent mobility across class lines; in a minority of cases they actually encourage it. Their task is to produce in each age cohort a differentiated body of graduates who can be fit into existing occupational roles and statuses with a minimum of friction.[25] In this way, the basic structure of social classes is recreated even though particular families may rise or fall in the hierarchy from one generation to the next.

Schools are mandated to track students into different curricula which prepare them for entry at various levels in the occupational hierarchy. They are also supposed to insure that students with greater scholastic abilities are kept in school longer and directed toward middle- and upper-middle-class employment. They attempt to align students' self-conceptions with their eventual job prospects so those in lower-class occupations will feel they are capable of nothing better and will not feel cheated. All this can be accomplished more easily if students are quickly stratified into ability levels and trained in such a way that those in the higher levels learn more than those in the lower ones. An interactive process which has this effect may diminish the learning capacities of many students, but nevertheless be functional for reproducing the class structure.

Desirable jobs are the eventual fruits of academic success, and these exist in a limited quantity established by the economy and by actions of privileged interest groups.[26] Schools can afford to dispense only so many tokens of academic success; otherwise the tokens become devalued by increasing in number relative to the privileged positions they represent. For every student who is allowed to become successful, there must be other students who cannot. The class structure demands that the educational system produce a certain percentage of failures at every level. Since schools are expected to display no favoritism toward any particular group, they tend to recruit their failures from among the children who are initially hardest to teach; these being the ones who lack familiarity with middle class lifestyles and speech patterns. While schools theoretically allow for unrestricted upward mobility, in practice they provide only a limited exception to the rule of hereditary social class. Teachers' low expectations for disadvantaged children stem from and reflect the stratification process which allows these children very little chance of academic success. The true source of the downward cycle is not simply the pupil's slowness or the teacher's pessimism, but the economic realities which confront the school, and to which teachers and counselors must in some way conform.[27]

Meritocratic ideology views scholastic failure as a natural outcome of deficient heredity and/or home environment. By doing this it reconciles the school's contradictory purposes—to maximize educational opportunity on the one hand, and to reproduce society's class structure on the other.

The Emerging Future Meritocracy

Richard Herrnstein has suggested that the United States is in the process of becoming a hereditary meritocracy. Although not yet fully meritocratic, American society is becoming increasingly so because "the social barriers of the past—race, religion, nationality, title, inherited wealth—are under continuous assault, at least in principle."[28] This means that stratification is being based more and more on ability or merit, which to Herrnstein means, above all else, IQ scores. He believes that IQ scores are determined largely by heredity, so as a result of meritocratic selection the upper classes are coming to have clear genetic superiority over the lower. On the other hand, "the privileged classes of the past, based on religion, title, property, race, even physiognomy, were probably not much superior biologically to the downtrodden, which is why revolutions had a fair chance of success."[29] Increases in society's aggregate wealth further the process because "wherever the new wealth enriches people from the lower classes, it will recruit for the upper classes precisely those who have the edge in native ability."[30] Doing away with the social barriers of the past initially produces greater opportunities for social mobility. "However, the increase in mobility that we gain by eliminating arbitrary social barriers is self-limiting, perhaps even self-reversing," because after several generations of meritocratic selection, those left at the bottom are, biologically speaking, the dregs.[31] In this way, human society approaches "a virtual caste system, with families sustaining their position on the social ladder from generation to generation as parents and children grow more nearly alike in their essential features."[32] As automation eliminates many unskilled blue-collar jobs and replaces them with white-collar ones, the working class's lack of native intelligence will likely cause many of them to be incapable of holding jobs: "The tendency to be unemployed may run in the genes of a family as certainly as the I.Q. does now."[33]

This is the vision presented in the last chapter of Herrnstein's *I.Q. in the Meritocracy*. Most of the book is a popularization of the pseudoscience upon which the vision is based. The fact that the author relies so heavily upon pseudoscience to support his conclusions about the validity of IQ tests and the inheritance of IQ scores means that his notion of a future meritocracy cannot be taken seriously as a scientific forecast. This is not to say it is totally invalid; merely that it should be regarded as philosophy or ideology rather than science. Ideologies can be rejected simply by formulating alternatives and giving reasons for one's preferences. There are many grounds for rejecting Herrnstein's meritocracy theory, not the least of which is that it justifies oppression and exploitation. However, the most interesting thing to do with an unappealing ideology is to uncover the social reality behind it, since ideologies generally are distorted representations of actual phenomena. Herrnstein's emerging meritocracy is a mythical description of something else—but what?

We might begin by observing that the discussion of meritocracy is heavily laden with value judgments. Herrnstein repeatedly asserts the questionable premise that persons in upper class occupations contribute more to society than do persons beneath them in the hierarchy. But, as Noam Chomsky asks rather caustically:

> Is it obvious that an accountant helping a corporation to cut its tax bill is doing work of greater social value than a musician, riveter, baker, truck driver, or lumberjack? Is a lawyer who earns a $100,000 fee to keep a dangerous drug on the market worth more to society than a farm worker or a nurse? Is a surgeon who performs operations for the rich doing work of greater social value than a practitioner in the slums, who may work much harder for much less extrinsic reward?[34]

Similarly, it is assumed that the criteria of "merit" used for hiring and promotion are measures of talent, virtue, and capacity for achievement. But in almost every case a different view can be held. Consider the four most commonly used criteria: supervisor's ratings, academic grades, personality ratings (either quantified or informally registered in an interview), and IQ scores. The first two depend partly upon technical competence and intellectual proficiency, but they are also influenced by success in currying favor with the teacher or supervisor. So in any given case it is uncertain the extent to which marks reflect talent as opposed to conformity or obsequiousness. The failure of high school and college grades to predict performance outside of school must heighten our doubts about what they really measure. Personality ratings may be simply a disguised indicator of class background, servility, superficial likability, or some other combination of nonmeritorious traits. Scores on IQ tests measure a type of problem-solving proficiency, but how important that type of skill is for most occupations, or even high level occupations, is very uncertain. It is known that the tests contain a myriad of class and cultural biases, so it could be that when hiring and promotion are based upon IQ scores, they actually discriminate more on the basis of family background than on the basis of probable future performance.

Whether one sees indices of merit as just that or as something else in disguise will depend largely upon one's attitude toward the major social institutions. If one conceives of them as trying to maximize social utility by promoting progress and efficiency, then one will likely view their selection procedures as meritocratic. However, if they are viewed as primarily interested in maintaining a class structure and hierarchy at the expense of progress and efficiency, then the supposed meritocracy becomes only a veil covering procedures which are discriminatory. The former view is generally held by the upper classes, particularly by those directly involved in the running of institutions. The latter is espoused by disaffected minorities and by the lower classes when they act in opposition to those above them.

When society takes on the appearance of a meritocracy two things are happening. One is what Max Weber termed *rationalization*—society increasingly allocates positions on the basis of standardized, universally applied criteria of competence and achievement, rather than on the basis of personal favoritism.[35] However, rationalized hiring policies are not necessarily meritocratic. The standardized criteria may themselves be comprised of biases and favoritism. For policies to be seen as meritocratic, people must adopt attitudes traditionally espoused by the upper classes. Karl Marx called this practice *bourgeois ideological hegemony*. The bourgeoisie, by controlling the most important cultural institutions, is able to generate a consensus around ideas congenial to it.[36] The shared image of society as a meritocracy is part of that consensus. Since widespread rationalization is an undeniable fact in advanced industrial societies, the major requirement for the appearance of meritocracy is the hegemony of upper-class ideas. This occurs when the working class has weak political organization and is unable to assert itself against the prevailing bourgeois culture.

Herrnstein envisions a future in which social mobility and increasing wealth produce a society with sharply drawn hereditary class lines and no threat of revolution. His intervening variable consists of changes in the genetic characteristics of social classes. There is no good reason to believe that this variable exists in reality, but there are very good reasons to believe that bourgeois ideological hegemony, facilitated by social mobility and increasing wealth, can have the same effects. The problem is not that new sources of wealth siphon off the brighter workers leaving only the dregs, but rather that they enable *some* workers to develop middle-class lifestyles and to see themselves as superior to the rest of the working class. This promotes disunity, inhibits political organization, and thereby facilitates upper-class domination, ideological and otherwise. Opportunities for upward social mobility encourage workers to define their goals individualistically, and this discourages collective solidarity. Hence, it also promotes upper-class domination. Social mobility is eventually self-limiting, not because all the innately bright people will have risen, but because opportunities for mobility are largely a product of collective working-class struggles (for example, unionization), and as they diminish the class's readiness to carry on such struggles, they effectively bring about their own diminution. The division of the working class into relatively affluent and impoverished sectors, together with the continuous pressure of bourgeois hegemony, effects a change in the character of unions. They become less vehicles of class solidarity and more instruments for maintaining the privileges of some workers against the demands of less fortunate ones. Theories about unemployment being caused by defective genes appear because the same families and ethnic groups are kept perpetually at the bottom of the class structure, and because bourgeois ideology dictates that unemployment must be blamed on the unemployed, rather than on the capitalist system. Overall, as upper class hegemony undercuts proletarian class consciousness, and the privileged segments of the working class turn to defending their positions against other workers, the threat of revolution vanishes (for the time being) and society comes to be organized more like a hereditary caste system.

Social mobility, increasing wealth, the appearance of meritocracy, a quiescent working-class movement, and the emergence of a caste system based on race—all these constitute an integrated tendency which has been present in the United States and Western Europe during the last century.[37] Herrnstein attributes it to a biosocial mechanism of genetic selection and projects it forward indefinitely into the future. The mechanism is mythical, being a symbolic representation of upper-class domination. His projection is speculative. The tendency is the result of specific historical circumstances which may be expected to terminate in the near or distant future.

13. Revising the Image of Mental Ability

Orienting the study of mental ability around concepts like intelligence and general ability has served an important ideological function, enabling the proponents of meritocracy to equip their arguments with a facade of scientific verification. But it also has retarded progress toward a genuine understanding of intellectual and artistic achievement. The tremendous concern with IQ and related tests has facilitated tracking in the schools, but for perceiving the sources of notable accomplishments, it has meant that several generations of psychologists have been barking up the same wrong tree.

The very concept of intelligence levels is from the standpoint of science a foolish myth. All human beings possess intricately complex nervous systems, and collectively humans manifest a wide variety of talents and abilities, most of which involve thinking. To try to describe ability-in-general with a single measure condemns one to being vague and imprecise about what is really being measured, and after scores are tabulated one still knows less about a person's real abilities than one would by simply putting together a list of her or his specific achievements. Walter Lippman suggested that IQ tests were like an attempt to measure general athletic ability with a one-hour test of running, jumping, pulling, and throwing.[1] Such a test might give some clue to differences in athletic prowess, but would tell us much less than could be learned by examining performance in the different sports separately, forgetting about the notion of athletic ability in general.

Although intelligence testing never has had any real scientific justification, it has greatly influenced the public's image of mental ability. Lewis Terman's *Genetic Studies of Genius* established in the public mind that having the capacity for outstanding achievement was the same as having a very high IQ score. This link, fused by pseudoscience, has generated a number of popular misconceptions. If an IQ score above 140 really made one a genius, then it was reasonable to imagine all mental ability being basically like test-taking ability. Exceptional intellect was thus conceived of as a quick, efficient mind—a finely honed, rapidly functioning, answer-selection mechanism. Thinking that an IQ score was hereditary reinforced the already popular belief that genius was a biological anomaly which revealed itself early in life, and could not be developed by subsequent experience. The single continuum of IQ scores encouraged people to think of all ability as a single continuum. By implication this meant that the same attributes which enabled one to do well in school could allow one to become an outstanding artist or scientist. Hence, a genius was an exceptionally good student.

Ironically, *Genetic Studies of Genius* was an attempt to dispel popular illusions about exceptional creative ability. It wound up fostering a whole new batch of misconceptions, possibly even more erroneous than the original ones.[2] It is difficult to know how seriously these have been espoused, but it is worthwhile trying to correct them, because the image they form is fundamentally wrong.

One good way to approach the study of actual creative ability (rather than test-taking skills) is to look at descriptions of the experience and work habits of eminently creative people. Of course, this approach has certain pitfalls. It tells us only about people who have been publicly recognized as outstanding. It overlooks the multitudinous forms of creativity which exist throughout society in everyday life, and which are carried on without the benefit of public recognition. Thus, it tends to neglect instances of creativity where the contribution is to some group effort instead of to an individual product. Focusing on the experience of individual creators can generate the erroneous assumption that great writers, artists, and scientists work in near-total isolation. In reality, some sort of relationship with a supportive audience is almost always essential.[3] Personal descriptions are necessarily qualitative and subjective, so we cannot maintain any pretense of having the kind of precision which mental testers once claimed to have.

Nevertheless, this approach has the one great virtue of studying the phenomenon itself, instead of some fictitious representation of it. Also, the approach does yield some results. Eminent creative people appear to have much in common, even across disciplines. Outstanding painters, musicians, writers, and scientists all tend to have a tremendous emotional commitment to their work. They derive much satisfaction from it, persevere at it for long hours, and maintain a passionate involvement to the point of being obsessed. Rosamond Harding's *An Anatomy of Inspiration* recounts numerous instances of creative obsession in the lives of famous artists. Ann Roe's in-depth study of eminent American scientists concluded:

> The one thing that all of these sixty-four scientists have in common is their driving absorption in their work. They have worked long hours for many years, frequently with no vacations to speak of, because they would rather be doing their work than anything else.[4]

Galton had made a similar observation about eminent men in general some eighty years earlier:

> Such men, biographies show to be haunted and driven by an incessant instinctive craving for intellectual work. If forcibly withdrawn from the path that leads toward eminence, they will find their way back to it, as surely as a lover to his mistress. They do not work for the sake of eminence, but to satisfy a natural craving for brain work, just as athletes cannot endure repose on account of their muscular irritability which insists upon exercise.[5]

On the other hand, an efficient, rapid, problem-solving mind appears to characterize some highly talented persons but not others. One hears about two kinds of geniuses, illustrated by the contrast between Mozart and Beethoven.

> Mozart thought out symphonies, quartets, even scenes from operas, entirely in his head—often on a journey or perhaps while dealing with pressing problems—and then he transcribed them, in their completeness, onto paper. Beethoven wrote fragments of themes in

note books which he kept beside him, working on and developing them over the years. Often his first ideas were of a clumsiness which makes scholars marvel how he could, at the end, have developed from them such miraculous results.[6]

Mark Twain wrote quickly, averaging more than three thousand words a day on *The Innocents Abroad.* But the political economist Adam Smith declared after a lifetime of writing that he "composed as slowly and with as great difficulty as at first."[7] Such differences affect how prolific one may become—Mozart and Mark Twain produced more than Beethoven and Adam Smith—but they bear no necessary relationship to the quality of work which is ultimately achieved.

Where exceptional efficiency is displayed, it is likely to characterize the person only in relation to the particular creative activity. For example, a study of twelve internationally recognized chess masters revealed that they had extraordinary memories, but only for chess positions. They could quickly diagnose strategies by looking at a board, but apart from that they could not think any faster than the average person.[8] The poet and writer Stephen Spender has described poets as having a perfect memory for certain sense impressions, but lacking a good memory for things unrelated to their poetry.[9] When Donald MacKinnon and colleagues asked three groups of architects to describe themselves, the especially creative group placed this item very high on the list: "Reacts quickly to architectural problems; immediately generates a great number of ideas." The other two groups did not. But when statements about ability-in-general were presented, this difference failed to appear:

> "Grasps other people's ideas quickly."
>
> "Is flexible and adaptable in his thinking."
>
> "Has an active, efficient, well-organized mind."
>
> "Is intellectually gifted."
>
> "Has an exceptionally good memory."

All these descriptions either failed to differentiate among groups, or applied more to the uncreative ones. Similarly, scores on the Wechsler Adult Intelligence Scale showed no differences between groups.[10]

Reports of several investigators have converged on the finding that creativity requires heightened emotional arousal and gratification. Even among scientists the creative process does not simply involve calm, rational deliberation, but a sort of pleasurable excitement as well.

Rosner and Abt concluded interviews with twenty-three renowned, contemporary artists and scientists by saying there was general agreement that people worked best when they felt elated.[11] Even melancholy works required joy to produce them. As the composer Aaron Copland put it, "people create in moments when they are elated about expressing their depression."[12] This is not a new discovery; it merely echoes Wordsworth's dictum that the mind must be "in a state of enjoyment," when composing poetry.[13]

The emotional involvement required for creativity can also make working a source of deep frustration and torment. Notable artists do not always enjoy creating, although they must enjoy it some of the time to be able to do it at all. Having invested much emotional energy in the work, they are left vulnerable to dry periods of paralysis and depression.[14]

Creative breakthroughs usually occur during an experience of pleasurable excitement or inspiration. This experience is characterized by elation, rapid flow of thoughts, and a strong, inward, daydream-like concentration. Consider Tchaikovsky's description:

> It would be vain to try to put into words that immeasurable sense of bliss which comes over me directly when a new idea awakens in me and begins to assume a definite form. I forget everything and behave like a madman. Everything within me starts pulsing and quivering; hardly have I begun the sketch ere one thought follows another.[15]

Or Van Gogh's observation that there is "a terrible lucidity at moments, when nature is so glorious in those days I am hardly conscious of myself and the picture comes to me like in a dream."[16] Artistic products rarely assume their finished form during the initial inspiration. The same blissful excitement which encourages new discoveries also clouds critical judgment. So products are usually developed and refined while in a more sober emotional state; this process being known as secondary elaboration. The frequency and intensity of inspiration varies from one artist to the next. As psychoanalyst Ernst Kris points out, inspiration and elaboration "may be sharply demarcated from each other, may merge into each other, may follow each other in rapid or slow succession, or may be interwoven with each other in various ways." But wherever the quality of work reaches a certain level, inspiration is found to be present, since evaluations of art refer "less often to skill, i.e., perfection of elaboration, than to depth of meaning and expressive quality, of which inspiration is an essential ingredient."[17] Mastery of a craft is a prerequisite for exceptional achievement, but beyond a certain point, creative ability in the arts and sciences cannot be equated with degree of technical proficiency.

The importance of inspiration can be understood several ways. Creative discoveries are thought to originate as wishes, which are then transformed by craftsmanship into real products perceivable by others. Inspiration is an experience of relatively unrestrained wish-fulfillment, much akin to daydreams except that it furnishes material for future elaboration. The sensation of pleasure attending the first appearance of creative discoveries teaches the artist to value them and work on them further. The rapid flow of ideas allows her or him to develop them immediately into a form which can be retained in consciousness. Several thinkers report having a "feeling of absolute certainty" when creative breakthroughs are first made.[18] This estimate may be revised later, and the discovery be seen as false, worthless, or needing refinement. But the initial period of rapid gratification furnishes the material which careful scrutiny will later polish into something of value.

The fact that discoveries burst forth suddenly and effortlessly into consciousness, and usually cannot be summoned intentionally, leads many writers to conclude that the important analytical work comprising discoveries is first done preconsciously.[19] The heightened mental arousal of inspiration produces a temporary expansion of consciousness which allows the new insights to be recognized. Their initial appearance may be little more than a flash or sensation that something important is about to happen. They arise so rapidly that the person scarcely has time to write them down. If he or she attempts a deliberate, critical appraisal right away, the ideas may be lost altogether. So, Rosamond Harding concludes,

> the thinker must at first, at any rate, trust to his feeling, instinct, intuition or whatever it may be called, to guide him, however much he may revise or check afterward. Learning to trust to feeling or instinct and knowing when and how far to trust it is an important part of the creative thinker's technique.[20]

One of MacKinnon's most striking findings was that creative people in all fields consistently exhibited a preference for intuitive thinking:

> In contrast to an estimated 25% of the general population who are intuitive, 90% of the creative writers, 92% of the mathematicians, 93% of the research scientists, and 100% of the architects are intuitive as measured by [the Myers-Briggs Type Indicator].[21]

A final aspect of the creative process concerns the person's resistance to pressures for conformity. Whereas success in school requires at every level a thoroughgoing compliance with rules and assignments, and a readiness to internalize the wishes of a superior, exceptional ability demands at least a modest amount of independent thought. As Ann Roe notes about her sixty-four eminent scientists:

> It is of crucial importance that these men set their own problems and investigate what interests them. No one tells them what to think about, or when, or how. Here they have almost perfect freedom.[22]

Compared with their uncreative colleagues, the highly talented architects were much less likely to place responsibility to clients above all else. They were also less likely to make "a serious effort to keep up with current publications and the literature in architecture," and to consider responsibility to the profession above all else.[23]

Given the numerous studies which show no correlation between school grades and other kinds of achievement,[24] and the knowledge that an acquiescent, obsequious mentality may further academic success more than intellectual creativity, it is reasonable to suggest that scholastic aptitude and creative talent should be viewed as fundamentally different abilities, just as football and golfing abilities are viewed as fundamentally different. Admittedly certain kinds of strengths will facilitate both, but whether the kinds of training which promote one will also promote the other is at least open to question. Similarly, tests which accurately predict one cannot be assumed to say much about the other.

The preceding description of a general creative process is necessarily sketchy and incomplete.[25] It cannot begin to consider differences between disciplines or to rigorously test propositions. Nevertheless, it does suggest two conclusions. One, motivation and ability ought not to be conceived of as separate dimensions; it makes more sense to view ability as a product or expression of motivation. This does not mean that anyone can develop outstanding talent simply by having a strongly felt, conscious desire to do so, but rather that talent is developed by sustaining heightened motivation over time, and that many of the distinguishing features of genius are themselves produced by heightened motivation.

Two, creative talent is cultivated by involvement in a process. It results from a strong emotional commitment to a certain type of work and from the development of certain procedures in that work. When creative people are removed from their work and placed in a different context—say, a standardized test of some sort—the same motives and procedures may no longer obtain, and they may appear quite ordinary. Creative obsession when writing books or composing symphonies is no guarantee that the person will manifest a similarly strong desire to list many unusual words or perform arithmetic quickly and accurately when asked to do so by a psychometrician. When people describe their working procedures they directly recount the process which makes them creative; when they describe themselves generally in terms of traits or preferences, they reflect it indirectly; when they perform tasks not closely resembling their work, they most likely display a separate talent altogether, which may or may not have some weak connection with the original talent in question.

The most interesting thing to study about unusual ability is how it develops. By what kinds of personal evolution do individuals come to possess exceptional talent? Unfortunately, we know very little about this. The preponderance of studies have used as their criterion of mental ability, test scores rather than the actual creation of notable works. Hence, the type of mental ability most thoroughly understood is test-taking ability. Much more of interest could be learned by systematically studying the lives and experience of outstanding artists and scientists. However, the largest effort of this kind, the Cox study, gathered information on 300 geniuses, only to publish nothing but estimates of their IQ scores. The authors could have served the advancement of knowledge better if they had thrown away the final manuscript and published their research notes instead. To the extent that psychologists seek a genuine understanding of mental ability they will want to combine a rejection of past pseudoscience with a shift in methodological orientation. More attention should be paid to studying actual life achievements with interviews, questionnaires and biographical data; less should be directed toward designing and distributing standardized tests.

It is not hard to see how artistic creativity could originate. Intense imaginative activity is common among human beings, particularly when they are young. Inspiration is so much like a daydream that it is plausible to view the latter as a means by which the former can be learned and practiced. Oddly enough, Herbert Spencer reported in his *Autobiography* that as a boy he spent much time daydreaming, and that this led to the intense concentration he possessed in his later years.[26] While daydreams are purely fantasy, creativity involves the unification of work and fantasy. It merges imagination with conscious, directed activity. But this combination is by no means unusual or unnatural. It is what children do when they play. To quote Freud's analogy: "the writer does the same as a child at play; he creates a world of phantasy which he takes very seriously; that is, he invests it with a great deal of affect, while separating it sharply from reality."[27]

Highly creative people are exceptional in two respects. The normal pattern of adult maturation involves a renunciation of play, or at least its clear separation from work. Private fantasies and deliberate productive activity are kept apart. Creative talent stems from a merging of the two. Outstanding talent usually results from an extreme depth of involvement in the creative process; it is the fruit of exceptionally strong emotional commitment, coupled with an internalization of critical standards which comprise technical proficiency.

Mastering a craft involves internalizing the responses of others; it involves learning how to respond to constructions the way people who are already proficient would respond. The trick is to do this while continuing to value one's own work highly. Otherwise one would not be able to maintain favorable expectations, to continue rewarding oneself, and to sustain the heightened motivation. This combination of self-confidence and self-criticism is easily imaginable for those already doing good work. They gather recognition and support from others, or at least have considerable likelihood of getting it in the near future.[28] The problem is to explain how this combination arises in people not yet proficient. For example, does technical proficiency precede creative inventiveness, establishing a basis for the self-confidence which makes it possible? Or does inspiration come first, providing incentive for the development of competence? If the latter is true, how is the transition made from fantasy unrelated to work, to fantasy as a part of real achievement? What sorts of responses from others can aid the development of creative ability? Can they be harshly critical, fostering a determination to prove one's detractors wrong? Or must they be supportive, instilling an awareness of future potential beyond the limited achievements of the present? To what extent is self-deception a necessary part of the developmental process? Do people benefit from having an exaggerated sense of their own accomplishments before they attain the level of excellence? Or must they first learn to be critical and realistic, later coming to utilize flights of fancy? What sorts of experiences foster resistance to pressures for conformity? What sorts produce despair, and the abandonment of creative effort altogether?

Issues like these are the interesting ones to examine when studying mental ability. They focus on the question: How does one develop the positive feedback loop between motivation and accomplishment? For such a process must lie at the root of all types of creative ability. To understand the process better we must study its development over time, attempting to comprehend the inner experience of individuals, including the responses of others which crucially affect that experience. No laboratory simulation or performance test can substitute for an awareness of actual life occurrences. Although some uncertainty is inherent in relying upon individuals' memories, self-descriptions and interpretations, we will at least be studying the actual ability of interest, and not be taking some other phenomenon (test performance or whatever) and pretending that it is the same as the ability in question.

Concepts like learning and opportunity will have to be accorded meanings considerably broader than those common in everyday usage. We cannot conclude, as is frequently done, that a given behavior or ability has not been learned, merely because it was never explicitly taught. Learning occurs through self-directed activity as well as formal instruction; it can instill not only knowledge and technique, but also motivation and personal commitment. Opportunity means more than having the option to engage in an activity. Such a narrow definition of opportunity, although convenient for the presentation of meritocratic ideology, is worse than useless for understanding the development of ability. Opportunity exists in degrees, and refers not only to the availability of instruction, but also to the presence of environments conducive to maintaining heightened motivation. Its role cannot be understood unless we ask: Under what conditions and toward whom do significant people respond in ways which facilitate a strong emotional commitment to creative work?

Developmental and biographical studies can tell us much about the sources of ability, provided we are willing to settle for general patterns rather than rigid laws, and to tolerate the uncertainties which come from studying humans whose lives cannot be regulated thoroughly like those of laboratory animals. But it is not likely that these studies will do much to resolve the heredity-environment controversy. The more we examine the development of ability, the more we will become aware of types of learning which could plausibly be interpreted as the crucial sources of unusual talent. This will allow us to believe that geniuses are biologically ordinary people, whose unusual experience has expanded their mental capabilities far beyond the normal range. We may then abide by Coleridge's remark that human beings are caterpillars, very few of whom succeed in transmuting themselves into butterflies.

At the same time we will be left to consider why people respond differently to the same stimuli, and why some with seemingly less favorable environments accomplish more than others whose situation appears to be better. It may be that the crucial kinds of learning, once underway, are relatively impervious to external influences, and that this creates the appearance of "innate" ability, even though almost any genotype would suffice for those engaged in the right type of learning. On the other hand, it may well be that genetic differences *are* important determiners of ability. Certainly this is a possibility, but one which cannot be tested meaningfully until research in genetics has advanced to a stage where human genotypes can be mapped in detail, specific genes correlated with enzyme concentrations, and both genes and enzymes examined in relation to behavioral differences. Most likely this stage of development is a long way off; perhaps it will never be reached.

In the meantime, we have reason to doubt that the notion of genetically determined levels of mental capacity is a valid construct. Exceptional achievement appears to be the product of heightened motivation; people generally have the capacity to be highly motivated, but few are so consistently in their work. This suggests that people tend to function at levels far below the mind's biological capacity, and that whatever genetic differences in capacity may exist could be unimportant for this reason.

On the other hand, this is not to say that genetic differences are necessarily unimportant. They may well affect the probabilities of individuals embarking on the experiential processes which determine levels of ability. How much do they affect the probabilities? The answer is that we do not know, and we may expect to continue not knowing for many years to come.

The idea of genetically determined mental ability is best viewed as a popular myth which has little relation to science. It can be compared to another myth, popular centuries before, that creative ability resulted from spiritual possession. The word *genius* originally referred to a genie inside people, and was later applied to notable artists and thinkers because people believed their work to have been done by genies who emerged from inside.[29] Attributing ability to genes instead of genies uses the vocabulary of modern science and sounds plausible for this reason. But neither belief can be confirmed or disproved empirically, so in this sense the two are equally unscientific.

Existing evidence of heritability for IQ scores among Caucasians tells us virtually nothing about the likelihood of genetic determination of abilities. If better data were gathered more carefully and adequate attention were paid to the implicit uncertainties in the data, then it might be possible to derive new heritability estimates which were very approximate, but basically trustworthy. Probably these would be well below .50, and their main value would be in dispelling popular illusions created by the history of pseudoscience. Theoretically these estimates would establish some sort of upper bound for the conceivable extent of genetic determination of IQ scores in the populations tested. But they would not show whether the actual extent was closer to this upper bound or to zero.

Similarly, attempts to raise IQ scores by altering environments have little bearing on the nature-nurture question. If the attempts are successful, then they provide evidence only against an extreme form of genetic determinism. But then, very few people now believe in this extreme form anyway. If the attempts are unsuccessful, they provide no substantial evidence for genetic determination because the likelihood remains that investigators were unable to control the most pertinent aspects of environment. Either way the basic question is left unresolved.

Even if IQ scores were consistently found to have a heritability of zero, this result would apply only to the abilities measured by IQ tests. Other, more profound abilities could still require particular genotypes, despite the fact that a high IQ score did not.

Future research into the heritability of IQ scores should specify its limited objectives and make clear that a resolution of the basic heredity-environment question lies beyond its pale. When this is done investigators may then focus on the more interesting question of how variations in experience affect performance in school. Although IQ tests have some validity as measures of scholastic progress, probably some other kinds of tests could better serve this purpose. Comparing scores on parts of IQ tests can help diagnose brain damage, but here too, other tests will serve at least as well. On the one hand, IQ tests are thoroughly replaceable in all the positive functions they perform. On the other hand, they have been widely abused in serious ways—in the treatment of racial minorities, in raising needless anxieties about mental capacity, and in promoting public deception. Given this record, it would be no great loss if both the tests and the concept of IQ were eliminated. But more important than the elimination of any particular test is the realization of the limits of what can be accomplished by testing. Test scores can only describe performance; they do not explain it.[30] Understanding the sources of school success and failure cannot be done with tests alone. It requires close examination of the behavior, attitudes, and experiences of students, teachers, and parents. In particular, such research would benefit from serious attempts to trace the connections between structural requirements of the economy and daily interaction in the classroom.

Beyond the classroom, tests will probably continue to be used for purposes of selection in hiring. Such testing should be based upon modest assumptions. It should not maintain the pretense of measuring abilities like intelligence and creativity. Rather it should assume that abilities are specific to situations and activities, and should attempt to measure probable competence in a task by simulating the task as closely as possible.[31] The concept of intelligence should cease to be used as an explanation for patterns of social mobility. Researchers instead should focus on the relative importance of scholastic attainment and class background, as well as on the process by which jobs and promotions are distributed.

It is hoped that explicit recognition of past pseudoscience will help to curtail its future influence. Textbook writers should abandon the practice of taking refuge in ambiguous statements. They should openly confront the issues of what we really know about mental ability, as opposed to what many people erroneously have thought they knew. Conceptual clarity can help to free us from the legacy of the defective eugenics paradigm and all the mistaken notions it has inspired. The pernicious effects of many of these illusions makes their curtailment particularly important.

Appendix

Baron Von Zetnikoff's Plan to Resolve the Nature-Nurture Controversy

Probably the most controversial assertion in this book is that the nature-nurture, heredity-IQ question is inherently unresolvable within the confines of present-day empirical science. To say that further research is needed is certainly familiar and acceptable, but to say that further research will not answer the question is sometimes seen as heretical. "We just need better ways of controlling for the effects of environment," many social scientists will say.

But how can this be done? For reasons discussed in Chapters 7 and 9, no naturally occurring situation comes close to providing the necessary controls. Some more rigorous experimental procedure would be needed. But would we not in the process of administering the necessary controls create a situation so totally different from life as it is that our results would pertain only to the experimental situation and not to society generally? Nevertheless, it is worth trying to envision such an experiment, if only to see how difficult it would be to control for the effects of environment. The most significant attempt in this

Reprinted from the *Journal of Abnormal Sociology* 22, no. 3 (Fall 1972): 324–32.

direction has been made by the German baron, R. J. Von Zetnikoff, in "A Plan to Resolve the Nature-Nurture Controversy," excerpts from which follow below.

Baron Von Zetnikoff's interest in the nature-nurture controversy is a longstanding one, dating back to his days as a eugenicist in pre-Second World War Germany. With his emigration to the United States in 1945, this country received one of the world's foremost talents in the field of individual differences. The baron is noted for combining an interest in controversial issues with a methodological sophistication lacking in most of his colleagues. Unfortunately, his plan poses serious ethical difficulties, and he seems to be completely oblivious to most of these. This major drawback precludes an endorsement of his plan, although I share his curiosity about what the results would be. I will merely say that his plan represents a definite methodological advance over all previous efforts in the field. Whether it actually would resolve the nature-nurture controversy is left to the reader to decide.

Introduction

It is in the nature of the academic to retreat behind complexities. Nothing abhors controversy like a professor. When a matter is of interest to no one but a few scholars, the professor works painstakingly to develop an analysis, magnificent in its detail, and audacious in its length. However, when the academic is faced with an important question, his mind freezes up. He suddenly becomes overwhelmed by the complexities, and takes an equivocal position. He doubts everything, and says nothing original. His only firm commitment is to make the issue disappear—to bury it with complexities and equivocations. On important issues nothing can be certain enough to satisfy these cautionaries. They demand proof, and then proof that the proof is proof.

Such, unfortunately, has been the response of liberal academics to Arthur Jensen's recent work. To his well-reasoned argument they have responded with statements like, "The cumulation of effects is yet to be understood." The crux of their argument has been that it is not possible to estimate the heritability of IQ because existing studies do not adequately control for all the effects of environment. Raising children in different families does not control for the effects of the classroom environment. . . .

I, therefore, would like to propose a study which controls for all the effects of environment, and simultaneously utilizes clear measures of genetic superiority and inferiority. By contrasting children with superior heredity and inferior environment with children who have superior environment and inferior heredity, we can see clearly whether nature or nurture is more important.

In designing the environments we must control for three different kinds of effects: (1) *The environmental quality phenomenon.* For many years it has been known that upper class families provide their children with home environments which are culturally richer than the home environments of lower class children. Similarly, high quality schooling has advantages over low quality schooling. Environmental quality depends upon the intelligence of persons with whom the child comes in contact, the amount of personal attention a child receives, and the extent of the child's involvement in activities which foster cognitive development.

(2) *Operant conditioning effects.* During the last decade it has been contended that the dissemination of positive reinforcement and aversive conditioning in the classroom may affect children's performances. Reward makes it easier for children to pay attention in class and concentrate on tests; punishment has the opposite effect. A child need not be conscious of the positive or aversive conditioning for it to affect his performance.

(3) *Expectation effects* (sometimes known as the Pygmalion effect). Environmentalists frequently believe that a person's self-conception affects his mental capacity. Like William Blake, they contend that self-confidence is the key ingredient of talent. They also claim that others' expectations will affect how one performs. Specifically, they feel that teachers' expectations can dramatically affect pupils' IQ's. . . .

A truly rigorous study must control all three kinds of environmental effects. It has been argued that this is not possible because expectations, as well as rewards and punishments, depend upon performance. There is a positive feedback loop between how a child performs and how teachers act toward him. Thus, one cannot control for environment and measure performance because performance and environment are practically the same thing.

Perhaps this is so in most schools. My intention, however, is to design classroom environments where this is not the case. All three effects will be controlled in the schools, while environmental quality and expectation effects will be controlled in the home. Rigorous control of operant conditioning in the home is not feasible at this time.

Selection of Subjects

The study will utilize 400 subjects who will be placed in the experimental conditions shortly after birth, and will remain there until they have reached eighteen years of age. Two hundred will have a superior heredity, and 200 will be genetically inferior.

Genetically superior subjects will be obtained as follows: The editors of *Who's Who in America* will be asked to prepare lists of the 300 most talented men, and the 300 most talented women in the United States. As a rough guideline they will be instructed to choose about two-thirds from the arts and sciences while making the remainder statesmen, industrialists, military commanders, and distinguished hostesses. All persons with IQs below 120 will be eliminated from the sample, as will those whose racial heritage is in doubt. A further restriction is that all women must be under 40 years of age. With the remainder of the sample, we will pair men and women randomly with each other, thus generating well over 200 eugenic pairings. Each man will contribute an abundant supply of sperm to a sperm bank. Each woman will enter a convalescent home for one month, during which time she will be artificially impregnated twice a day for the duration. (Each will be given a pregnancy test upon entry, and any found pregnant will be promptly aborted. Women will not be allowed to leave during the month. Visitors may come only for thirty minutes each day, and they will be watched closely for the whole visit.)

The cooperation of reluctant subjects will be obtained by finding irregularities in their income tax returns, and having a judge inform them that they face the likelihood of prosecution and imprisonment. They will be encouraged to plea bargain, and will be offered the sentence of one year's probation, contingent upon participation in this experiment.

Undoubtedly there will be mishaps all along the way, so we start with a larger number of parental prospects, intending to reap a harvest of 200 genetically superior infants. Persistently uncooperative persons may be imprisoned; however, most parents will be freed from probation immediately upon successful delivery of the infant who immediately will be placed in the custody of our nursing staff. (Hopefully we will be able to give each parent a letter from the President commending him/her for having performed a valuable service for the country.)

Two hundred genetically inferior infants will be obtained by a similar process. Prospective infants will be selected from welfare rolls, and all will have IQ's below 70. They will be charged with vagrancy rather than income tax evasion, and will be offered similar conditions of probation.

All parental prospects in both groups will be white. Galton's hypothesis was that even within races nature was much more important than nurture for the development of ability. To use persons from any of the less well-endowed races would contaminate the effect we wish to study. . . .

Designing the Environments

For three months all infants will receive identical treatment in the New Jersey State Eugenical Fondling Home. At that age they will be placed for adoption. Half of each group will be assigned randomly to good and bad environments. Environments will be controlled until subjects are 18 years old. Subjects' performance and achievements will be recorded until the subjects reach 50. Thus we will have a four-celled longitudinal study with a total N of 400:

		Genetic Endowment	
		Superior	Inferior
Environment	Good	N = 100	N = 100
	Poor	N = 100	N = 100

Both home and school environments will be controlled.

Home Environment: Good

Adoptive parents must have IQ's above 120, and the father's occupation must place him in the upper ten percent of the population according to NORC prestige scales. Parents will be told upon receiving the infant, that this is the child of two very famous people who wish to remain anonymous. The child is expected to be very gifted, so a trust fund of $200,000 has been set aside, half of which will be used to pay for the child's education at a special private school to which he will be chauffered. The remaining half will be given to the parents to help cover household expenses. The money will be disbursed annually in equal amounts until the child is 18 and ready to attend college. Another $20,000 will then be provided for this purpose. In return the parents will be asked to commit themselves to remaining in the New York City metropolitan area until the child is 18.

Home Environment: Poor

Adoptive parents will be selected from among welfare applicants. Two hundred married couples with IQ's below 80 will be told that welfare aid is being given to persons like themselves *only* if they agree to provide a home for one of the state's unwanted babies. If they agree to care for the baby, they are obliged to support it until it reaches 18. Otherwise, they will face the risk of imprisonment for child abuse. Adoptive parents will be told that both of the child's biological parents were feeble-minded narcotics addicts, so not much good is to be expected from this child. No money will accompany the infant (other than the regular welfare stipend), but the state will provide for its education, bussing it to a special school for expected problem children. The child is legally obligated to attend this school until age 18, thus parents must remain in the metropolitan New York area until this time.

School Environment: Good

Each year students will be divided into classes of 15 each. They will begin school at age five, and from the beginning individual tutoring will be available in a wide range of subjects whenever the student or his parents request it. Tutors will be told that these children are exceptionally intelligent, and that they should never be made to feel ashamed of errors they have made. All tutors must have IQ's above 120 and be at least moderately accomplished in the field they are tutoring.

All grading will be done by machines which return percentile scores based upon national norms. However, the scores will be inflated according to the following schedule:

	%ile
Child's actual score	*Score child and teacher receive*
1–20	80–85
21–40	86–90
41–60	91–95
61–80	96–98
81–99	99

Children in general will have unusual curricular freedom and choice. Their time will be divided about evenly between individual work and learning as a group in the classroom. Each day there will be two group discussion periods, say from 11:00 to 12:30, and 2:00 to 3:30. There will be no regular lunch hour. However, food will be served continuously during the group discussion periods. Each time a child raises his hand and says anything relevant to the topic being discussed, the teacher will nod enthusiastically, and a waiter will serve the child an appetizing and nutritionally balanced hors d'oeuvre.

Once every month there will be an assembly of all 200 students and their teachers and tutors. At these six or seven students who have done something creative during that month will receive a special award. Every child will receive at least one award during his thirteen years in the school.

School Environment: Poor

Children will begin school at age five, and will be divided into classes of 40 each. There will be no tutors, although children will receive individual instruction from teaching machines. The teaching machines will be programmed to malfunction and deliver the child a moderately painful electric shock approximately once every fifth time he answers the machine. Shocks will be delivered according to a random interval schedule, and will occur two seconds after the child answers. If a child attempts to walk away from his machine without receiving permission, he will be punished physically by the teacher. If he sits at the machine but fails to respond, he will receive a series of moderately painful electric shocks. Any response will prevent the recurring shocks. It need not be correct.

Teachers will be retired prison wardens with an IQ below 100 in every case. They will spend most of class time lecturing students on juvenile delinquency, reckless driving, alcoholism, prison life, masturbation, venereal disease, and advantages of joining the army, and similar topics. The material on which students will be tested will be written on a special glare-reflecting blackboard. Frequently the material will be written illegibly, and staring at the blackboard for too long will give students headaches. Teachers will be instructed to allow orderly discussion in the classroom, but not to encourage it. When a child asks a question or states something the teacher will either look away or grimace, depending upon whether there is anything incorrect or offensive about what the child says.

All grading will be done by machines which return percentile scores based upon national norms. Children will be administered tests customarily given to an age-group three years older than them. Thus, the tests will seem difficult. Scores will be deflated according to the following schedule:

	%ile
Child's actual score	*Score child and teacher receive*
1–20	1–5
21–40	6–15
41–60	16–25
61–80	26–40
81–99	41–60

Interpreting the Results

IQ tests will be administered once every two years until the children reach age 18, so we will know how the differences in heredity and environment have affected intelligence. However, the truly interesting information will come many years later when the subjects' careers are rated at age 50. Five raters will rate each subject on a scale of one ("has done nothing whatever to merit either positive distinction or respect") to ten ("is one of the greatest geniuses of this century"). (Five is "is a solid, upper-middle class professional who is quite competent at almost everything he does.")

Few of us will be around for this happy occasion, but my prediction is that nature will prevail over nurture. I prophesize that the average of the ratings will look something like the following: Superior genes—good environment = 7; superior genes—bad environment = 5.5; inferior—good = 2.5; inferior—bad = 1.5. Not everyone agrees, however. Some sociologists at the RAND Corporation claim nurture will prevail over nature, although they admit that no genetically inferior subject will achieve a rating above seven. Finally there is the uncanny prediction of the eminent French statistician, F. C. Leerling. He predicts that there will be no statistically significant differences among any of the groups. This strikes me as ridiculous. But he, too, will have his chance to be borne out by the data. . . .

Notes

Notes to Chapter 1

1. "Science" may be conceived of broadly or narrowly. The broader conception, accepted by most European thinkers, sees it as any productive, factual investigation which has theoretical significance. The narrower conception, espoused by most Americans, identifies science with an experimental or quasi-experimental procedure in which general theories produce specific hypotheses to be tested against predictions made with reference to a set of quantitatively tabulated data. In this book the narrower conception will be used in order to differentiate pseudoscience from the wider category of ideology of which it is but one form.

2. Martin Gardner, *Fads and Fallacies in the Name of Science* (New York: Dover, 1957), p. 7.

3. Lee J. Cronbach, *Educational Psychology* (New York: Harcourt, Brace and World, 1963), p. 238.

4. Robert L. Isaacson, Max L. Hutt, and Milton L. Blum, *Psychology: The Science of Behavior* (New York: Harper and Row, 1965), p. 56.

5. Harry Harlow, J. McGaugh, and R. Thompson, *Psychology* (San Francisco: Albion, 1971), p. 354.

6. Richard J. Herrnstein, *IQ in the Meritocracy* (Boston: Little, Brown, 1973), p. 106.

7. O. D. Duncan, D. Featherman, and B. Duncan, *Socioeconomic Background and Achievement* (New York: Seminar Press, 1972), p. 79.

8. Ernest Hilgard, *Introduction to Psychology* (New York: Harcourt, Brace, 1962), p. 443. The most recent edition of this text (Hilgard, Atkinson, and Atkinson (New York: Harcourt, Brace, Jovanovich, 1971)) has eliminated all discussion of race differences in IQ scores.

9. John C. Loehlin, Gardner Lindzey, and J. N. Spuhler, *Race Differences in Intelligence* (San Francisco: W. H. Freeman, 1975), pp. 238–39.

10. Thomas Kuhn's *The Structure of Scientific Revolutions* (Chicago: University of Chicago Press, 1970) has explicated and popularized this conception of the term *paradigm*.

Notes to Chapter 2

1. Galton's work in eugenics actually began with two published articles in *MacMillan's Magazine* (1865). *Hereditary Genius* (London: Macmillan, 1869) was his first major work.

2. Galton, *Hereditary Genius,* p. B.

3. Ibid., p. 49.

4. Ibid., p. 357.

5. John Radford and Andrew Burton, "Changing Intelligence," in *Race and Intelligence,* ed. Ken Richardson and David Spears (Baltimore: Penguin, 1972), pp. 19–35, esp. p. 20.

6. Francis Galton, *Hereditary Genius* (Gloucester, Mass.: World Publishing Co., 1972), frontispiece.

7. C. D. Darlington, Introduction to ibid., pp. 9–21, esp. p. 20.

8. An informative discussion of Lester Ward's theories along with a reprint of one of his important articles can be found in *Shaping the American Educational State,* ed. Clarence Karier (New York: Macmillan, 1975), Ch. 4. See also Lester Ward, *Applied Sociology* (Boston: Ginn & Co., 1906), Chs. 8–10.

9. Charles H. Cooley, "Genius, Fame, and the Comparison of Races," in *Annals of the American Academy of Political and Social Science* (May 1897): 317–58.

10. The normal distribution refers to the familiar bell-shaped curve in which the greatest number of cases fall close to the mean score, and the numbers of cases diminish as scores move away from the

average in either direction. For a more complete discussion of the concept, see Frederick Mosteller, Robert Rourke, and George P. Thomas, *Probability with Statistical Applications* (Reading, Mass.: Addison-Wesley, 1961), pp. 230–40.

11. Galton, *Hereditary Genius* (1869), p. 49.
12. Galton, *Hereditary Genius* (1972), p. 79.
13. Herbert Spencer, *Principles of Psychology,* vol. 1 (New York: D. Appleton, 1897), p. 581.
14. Herbert Spencer, *The Study of Sociology* (Ann Arbor, Mich.: Ann Arbor Paperbacks, 1966).
15. Summary of Spencer's ideas quoted from Herman Schwendinger and Julia Schwendinger, *The Sociologists of the Chair* (New York: Basic Books, 1974), p. 43. This work provides very informative discussions of Spencer and other nineteenth-century thinkers, as does Marvin Harris, *The Rise of Anthropological Theory* (New York: Crowell, 1974).
16. Binet's results along these lines are described in Joseph Peterson, *Early Conceptions and Tests of Intelligence* (New York: World Book Co., 1925).

Notes to Chapter 3

1. Richard Hofstadter, *Social Darwinism in American Thought* (Boston: Beacon Press, 1955), p. 161.
2. Thomas Gossett, *Race: The History of an Idea in America* (New York: Schocken, 1965), p. 153.
3. Hofstadter, *Social Darwinism,* p. 32.
4. Nicholas Pastore, *The Nature-Nurture Controversy* (New York: King's Crown Press, 1949), introduction.
5. Donald Pickens, *Eugenics and the Progressives* (Nashville, Tenn.: Vanderbilt University Press, 1968).
6. Gossett, *Race,* p. 286.
7. Pickens, *Eugenics.*
8. Francis Galton, *Inquiries into the Human Faculty* (London: Macmillan, 1883), p. 200.
9. Hofstadter, *Social Darwinism,* pp. 162–63.
10. Ibid., p. 77.
11. Mark Haller, *Eugenics: Hereditarian Attitudes in American Thought* (New Brunswick, N.J.: Rutgers University Press, 1963), p. 20.
12. Quoted in Pickens, *Eugenics,* p. 45.
13. President's Research Committee on Social Trends, *Recent Social*

Trends in the United States (Washington, D.C., 1933), p. 428, quoted in John Higham, *Strangers in the Land* (New York, Antheum, 1967), p. 150.

14. *Encyclopedia Britannica,* vol. 9, 11th ed. (1910), p. 885.

15. Ibid., p. 428.

16. Kenneth Ludmerer, *Genetics and American Society* (Baltimore: Johns Hopkins University Press, 1972), p. 92.

17. Ibid., p. 16.

18. American Eugenics Society, *Report of the Committee on Formal Education* (1928), p. 5. Included in the survey were the heads of departments whic offered either eugenics or genetics courses— about 75 percent of all departments.

19. Clarence Karier, "Testing for Order and Control in the Corporate Liberal State," *Educational Theory* 22, no. 22 (1972): 154–83, esp. pp. 165–66.

20. Sequence of events is summarized in Haller, *Eugenics,* pp. 64–66.

21. Biometry or biometrics is the immediate predecessor of the current field of psychometry or psychometrics. Previously it was assumed that the qualities measured were biological. Now they are called psychological, and attempts are made to prove that they are biologically determined.

22. Francis Galton, c. 1905, quoted in C. P. Blacker, *Eugenics: Galton and After* (London: Duckworth, 1952), p. 104.

23. Karl Pearson, *The Life, Letters and Labour of Francis Galton* (Cambridge, England: Cambridge University Press, 1914–1930), 3A: 217–42, quoted in Higham, *Strangers,* p. 150.

24. Albert E. Wiggam, *The New Decalogue of Science* (Indianapolis, Ind.: Bobbs-Merrill, 1923), pp. 79, 99, quoted in Ludmerer, *Genetics,* p. 14.

Notes to Chapter 4

1. Edwin O. Boring, *History of Experimental Psychology* (New York: Appleton-Century-Crofts, 1950), p. 477.

2. Philip H. Dubois, *A History of Psychological Testing* (Boston: Allyn and Bacon, 1970), p. 23.

3. Boring, *Experimental Psychology,* p. 477.

4. Francis Galton, *Hereditary Genius* (Gloucester, Mass.: World Publishing Co., 1972), pp. 392–404.

5. The average black-white difference in IQ scores generally has been around fifteen points, or one standard deviation. The range of IQ scores, generally running from around 40 to about 160, comprises roughly eight standard deviations.

6. Galton, *Hereditary Genius,* pp. 373, 381.

7. Summary of Francis Galton's *Hereditary Genius,* presented in Morris Stein and Shirley Heinze, *Creativity and the Individual* (Glencoe, Ill.: Free Press, 1960).

8. Francis Constable in *Poverty and Hereditary Genius* (London: A. C. Fifield, 1905) pointed out that Galton selected his literary people only from the propertied classes, and that he included English judges and military leaders in the study even though their chances for eminence depended more on family connections than on actual ability.

9. Galton acknowledged this point explicitly in *Inquiries into the Human Faculty* (London: Macmillan, 1883), p. 217.

10. Francis Galton, *English Men of Science* (London: Macmillan, 1874), p. 192.

11. Galton, *Inquiries,* p. 235.

12. Simple correlation coefficients are the only statistic to be used extensively in this book. They are represented by the letter "r" and describe the degree of relationship between two quantified variables. Possible values of r range from -1.00 to $+1.00$, with zero being midway between. A correlation of zero signifies no relationship between the two variables; variation in one has no relevance to variation in the other. A correlation of $+1.00$ constitutes a perfect positive relationship between the two; any increase or decrease in one is accompanied by a corresponding increase or decrease in the other. -1.00 signifies a perfect inverse relationship. Generally when attributes of individuals are being correlated, correlations of .10 to .30 (or $-.10$ to $-.30$) are considered low; correlations of .40 to .60 are considered moderately strong; and any above .70 (or below $-.70$) are seen as definitely high.

13. Boring, *Experimental Psychology,* pp. 468, 471.

14. Karl Pearson, "On the Laws of Inheritance in Man," *Biometrika* 3 (1904): 131–90. The study is summarized in J. Fuller and W. Thompson, *Behavior Genetics* (New York: Wiley, 1960), p. 193, which also lists about ten of the replications and similar studies.

15. Charles Spearman, another eminent statistician and psychometrician, criticized the method of data collection in Pearson's 1910 study. See Spearman, "Correlation Calculated from Faulty Data," *British Journal of Psychology* 3 (1910): 271–95.

16. Fuller and Thompson, *Behavior Genetics,* p. 193.

17. Richard Hofstadter, *Social Darwinism in America* (Boston: Beacon Press, 1955), p. 164.

18. Karl Pearson, *The Fight Against Tuberculosis and the Death Rate from Phthisis* (1911) quoted in Nicholas Pastore, *The Nature-Nurture Controversy* (New York: King's Crown Press, 1949), pp. 31–32. Pearson's work did not significantly hinder the fight against tuberculosis. However, in the United States Charles Davenport's claim that pellagra was a hereditary disease managed to gain credence in prestigious medical circles several years after experiments had shown pellagra to be caused by malnutrition. Davenport's influence was one of the factors causing a twenty year delay in efforts to eradicate the disease by improving nutrition of poor persons. This delay adversely affected the health of millions of persons. See Allan Chase, *The Legacy of Malthus: The Social Costs of the New Scientific Racism and the Old* (New York: Knopf, 1975).

19. Karl Pearson, "Problem of Alien Immigration into Great Britain, Illustrated by an Examination of Russian and Polish Jewish Children," *Annals of Eugenics* 1 (1925): 5–127.

20. Kenneth Ludmerer, *Genetics and American Society* (Baltimore: Johns Hopkins University Press, 1972), pp. 50–51.

21. Charles B. Davenport, *Heredity in Relation to Eugenics* (New York: H. Holt and Co., 1911), p. 51.

22. Ibid., pp. 53–54.

23. Ibid., p. 31.

24. Ibid., pp. 24–25.

25. Quotation is R. C. Punnett's statement about C. C. Hurst, quoted in Ludmerer, *Genetics,* pp. 57–58.

26. Donald Pickens, *Eugenics and the Progressives* (Nashville, Tenn.: Vanderbilt University Press, 1968), p. 50.

27. David Heron, *Mendelism and the Problem of Mental Defect—A Criticism of Recent American Work* (London: University of London, publication of the Galton Laboratory, 1913), p. 61.

28. The majority of British geneticists at the time were Mendelians. Pearson's biometrical school was influential in England despite its opposition to the mainstream of English genetics.

29. Ludmerer, *Genetics,* pp. 76–77.

Notes to Chapter 5

1. Summarized in Joseph Peterson, *Early Conceptions and Tests of Intelligence* (New York: World Book Co., 1925).

2. Evelyn Sharp, *The IQ Cult* (New York: Coward, McCann and Geoghegan, 1972). Binet's search for measures is quickly summarized on p. 37.

3. Quotations to this effect are found in Leon Kamin, *The Science and Politics of IQ* (New York: Wiley, 1974), p. 5.

4. Kenneth Ludmerer, *Genetics and American Society* (Baltimore: Johns Hopkins University Press, 1972), p. 92.

5. Lewis Terman, quoted in Mark Haller, *Eugenics: Hereditarian Attitudes in American Thought* (New Brunswick, N.J.: Rutgers University Press, 1963), p. 165.

6. Because of the widespread use of the term *IQ* to mean *IQ score*, it will be retained in some places to correspond to that usage in extracts. Thus, although I have tried to use IQ score throughout, IQ and IQ score occasionally are used interchangeably. The term "intelligence" will refer to the hypothetical construct which tests attempt to measure.

7. Lewis Terman, "The Intelligence Quotient of Francis Galton in Childhood," *American Journal of Psychology* 28 (1917): 209–15.

8. *Biographical Dictionary of the American Psychological Association* (1973), pp. xxv–xxx.

9. Barbara Schieffelin and Gladys Schwesinger, *Mental Traits and Heredity* (New York: Galton, 1930), Part I, Ch. 2.

10. Lewis M. Terman, "Were We Born That Way?" in *Shaping the American Educational State,* ed. Clarence Karier (New York: Macmillan, 1975), p. 201.

11. Lewis M. Terman, "The Great Conspiracy, or the Impulse Impervious of Intelligence Testers, Psychoanalyzed and Exposed by Mr. Lippman," in *American Educational State,* ed. Karier, p. 311.

12. Lewis Terman, *The Intelligence of School Children* (New York: Houghton-Mifflin, 1919), pp. 13–14.

13. Lewis Terman, "The Conservation of Talent," in *American Educational State,* ed. Karier, pp. 188–89.

14. Terman, *The Intelligence of School Children,* p. 24.

15. Ibid., Chs. 4, 5 and 6.

16. Carl C. Brigham, *A Study of American Intelligence* (Princeton, N.J.: Princeton University Press, 1923). Brigham interpreted the data as clear evidence of the racial superiority of northern Europeans, a conclusion he subsequently repudiated. Eventually he came to head the College Entrance Examination Board.

17. Henry Goddard, "The Binet Tests in Relation to Immigration," *Journal of Psycho-asthenics* 18 (1913): 105–07.

18. Walter Lippman, "The Reliability of Intelligence Tests," in *American Educational State,* p. 291.

19. Sharp, *IQ Cult,* p. 43.

20. J. McV. Hunt, *Intelligence and Experience* (New York: Roland Press, 1961), pp. 21–25, summarizes results of several studies and discusses interpretations of them.

21. One of the earliest and most influential was H. M. Skeels and H. B. Dye, "A study of the effects of differential stimulation on mentally retarded children," in *Proceedings of the American Association of Mental Deficiency*, 44 (1939): 114–36.

22. Walter Lippman, "A Future for the Tests," in *American Educational State*, p. 303.

23. David K. Cohen and Marvin Lazerson, "Education and the Corporate Order," *Socialist Revolution* 2, no. 2 (8) (March–April 1972): p. 53.

24. William C. Bagley, *Determinism in Education* (Baltimore: Warwick and York, 1925). Nicholas Pastore, *The Nature-Nurture Controversy* (New York: King's Crown Press, 1949), pp. 43–47, includes a summary of the arguments surrounding Bagley's work.

25. Edward L. Thorndike, *Human Nature and the Social Order* (New York: Macmillan, 1940), pp. 320–21. A similar conclusion had been reached in 1930 using a much cruder process of estimation by Nathaniel Hirsch's *Twins* (Cambridge, Mass.: Harvard University Press, 1936).

26. Allan Chase, *The Legacy of Malthus* (New York: Knopf, 1977), pp. 342–53.

27. Quotation is from eugenics leader Paul Popenoe, "German Sterilization Law," p. 260, quoted in Ludmerer, *Genetics,* p. 117.

28. Mark Haller, *Eugenics,* p. 179.

29. Particularly noteworthy in this regard were two geneticists of Marxian persuasion, J. B. S. Haldane and Hermann Muller. Haldane's *Heredity and Politics* (New York: W. W. Norton and Co., 1938) stands as a classic refutation of early twentieth-century racial pseudoscience.

30. Franz Boas, *The Mind of Primitive Man* (New York: Macmillan, 1911).

31. The neobehaviorist critique of trait theory is ably presented in Walter Mischel, *Personality and Assessment* (New York: Wiley, 1968), Chs. 2 and 3.

32. This definition is presented by Sir Cyril Burt in "Mental Capacity and Its Critics," *Bulletin of British Psychological Society* 21, no. 70 (January 1968): 11–20. Between 1945 and 1968 Burt was the leading hereditarian psychometrician of either the United States or England.

Notes to Chapter 6

1. T. Anne Cleary, Lloyd G. Humphreys, S. A. Kendrick, and Alexander Wesman, "Educational Uses of Tests with Disadvantaged Students," *American Psychologist* 30, no. 1 (January 1975): 15–41. The full wording of this definition (p. 19) is: "Intelligence is defined as the entire repertoire of acquired skills, knowledge, learning sets, and generalization tendencies considered intellectual in nature that are available at any one period of time. An intelligence test contains items that sample such acquisitions. . . ." "The definition of intelligence proposed here would be circular as a function of the use of 'intellectual' if it were not for the fact that there is a consensus among psychologists as to the kinds of behaviors that are labeled intellectual. The Stanford-Binet and Wechsler tests both exemplify and define the consensus."

2. See, for example, Lewis Terman, *The Intelligence of School Children* (New York: Houghton-Mifflin, 1919).

3. For example, correlations between IQ scores and high school grade point average have ranged between .40 and .60. See Christopher Jencks et al., *Inequality: A Reassessment of the Effects of School and Family in America* (New York: Basic Books, 1972), Appendix 7. Similar figures are found for the correlation of IQ results and social status. See O. D. Duncan, D. Featherman, and B. Duncan, *Socioeconomic Background and Achievement* (New York: Seminar Press, 1972), Ch. 5.

4. Henry Goddard, "Mental Levels and Democracy," in *Shaping the American Educational State,* ed. Clarence Karier (New York: Macmillan, 1975), p. 169.

5. Lewis Terman, ed., *Genetic Studies of Genius,* vol. 1 (Stanford, Cal.: Stanford University Press, 1925), p. 66.

6. Ibid., p. 69.

7. NORC ratings are done by the National Opinion Research Corporation, based in Chicago. Duncan et al., *Socioeconomic Background,* p. 79.

8. Lewis Terman, ed., *Genetic Studies,* pp. 67–69.

9. Duncan et al., *Socioeconomic Background,* p. 79.

10. Catherine Cox, *The Early Mental Traits of Three Hundred Geniuses,* vol. 2 of Terman, ed., *Genetic Studies,* p. 84.

11. Ibid., p. 85.

12. Frederick Adams Woods, "Historiometry as an Exact Science," *Science* 33, no. 850 (14 April 1911): 568–74.

13. See Philip Aries, *Centuries of Childhood* (New York: Knopf, 1962) for documentation of this point and discussion.
14. A recent Gallup Poll shows a significant positive relationship between occupational status and use of alcoholic beverages. Divided by income groups, the results are as follows:

Income (annual)	Percentage who report using alcoholic beverages
Over $20,000	88
$15,000–19,999	78
$10,000–14,999	64
$5,000–9,999	58
Under $5,000	46

Reported in *San Francisco Chronicle,* 10 June 1974, p. 8.

15. This project was part of the *Genetic Studies of Genius* series. Results after thirty years are summarized in Lewis Terman, "The Discovery and Encouragement of Exceptional Talent," *American Psychologist* 9, no. 6 (1954): 221–30.
16. Ibid., p. 223.
17. Ibid., p. 224.
18. Donald P. Hoyt, "The Relationship Between College Grades and Adult Achievement: A Review of the Literature," ACT Research Report, no. 7 (September 1965).
19. Ibid., pp. 29–36.
20. Ibid., p. 36.
21. Several of the important studies are summarized in C. W. Taylor and F. Barron, eds., *Scientific Creativity: Its Recognition and Development* (New York: Wiley, 1966). For a summary of similar data with British scientists, see Liam Hudson, *Contrary Imaginations* (London: Methuen, 1966), pp. 113–14. For a much earlier study with the same conclusion, see Francis Galton, *English Men of Science* (London: Macmillan, 1874), p. 257.
22. Hoyt, "Relationship Between College Grades."
23. John L. Holland and James M. Richards, "Academic and Nonacademic Accomplishment: Correlated or Uncorrelated?" ACT Research Report, no. 2 (April 1965).
24. Statistical significance was tested at the .05 level of probability. Being significant at the .05 level means that the probability of this result being due to chance alone is less than one in twenty. Statistical significance at the .01 level means that the probability is less than one in a hundred.

25. John L. Holland and James M. Richards, "Academic and Non-academic Accomplishment in a Representative Sample Taken from a Population of 612,000," ACT Research Report, no. 12 (May 1966).

26. Michael A. Wallach, "Tests Tell Us Little About Talent," *American Scientist* 64, no. 1 (January–February 1976): 61.

27. The term "abilities" is used in the following sense: abilities of some sort are inferred to exist whenever recognizable achievements are produced with some regularity. This differs from the common usage that abilities are those things measured by tests; achievements result from those plus other factors, such as motivation, training, etc. The latter usage is rejected here because it does not allow us to ask about the extent to which abilities measured in test situations are specific to those and similar situations, as opposed to being general across all situations.

28. Six particularly relevant studies listed alphabetically are: (1) Samuel Bowles and Herbert Gintis, "IQ in the United States Class Structure," *Social Policy* 3, nos. 4 and 5 (November–December 1972 and January–February 1973), reprinted in *The New Assault on Equality*, ed. Alan Gartner, Colin Greer, and Frank Riessman (New York: Harper and Row, 1974), pp. 7–84.

    (2) Samuel Bowles and Valerie Nelson, "The 'Inheritance of IQ' and the Intergenerational Reproduction of Economic Inequality," *Review of Economics and Statistics* 56, no. 1 (Feburary 1974): 39–44.

    (3) J. Conlisk, "A Bit of Evidence on the Income-Education-Ability Interaction," *Journal of Human Resources* 6 (Summer 1971): 358–62.

    (4) Otis Dudley Duncan, "Ability and Achievement," *Eugenics Quarterly* 15 (March 1968): 1–11.

    (5) Z. Griliches and W. Mason, "Education, Income and Ability," *Journal of Political Economy*, vol. 80, no. 3, Part II, pp. S74–S103.

    (6) John C. Hause, "Earnings Profile: Ability and Schooling," *Journal of Political Economy* 80, no. 3, Part II, pp. S108–S138.

29. Samuel Bowles and Valerie Nelson, "The 'Inheritance of IQ,' " p. 44. If IQ is measured on children in the first or second grade before the scores have achieved their full reliability, then the predictive power of IQ is lower than if the measure is made on children who are older.

30. Bowles and Gintis have been criticized for augmenting their measure of social class by using a hypothetical combination of

occupational prestige and income. More importantly, it is felt that the statistical technique they use and elucidate in the article, multiple regression analysis, cannot adequately control for the effects of different variables when the degree of colinearity (intercorrelation of variables) is as substantial as it is in this case.

31. These data are summarized in Bernard Berelson and Gary Steiner, *Human Behavior* (New York: Harcourt, Brace and World, 1964), pp. 223–24.

32. Creative occupations less dependent upon formal schooling showed wider ranges of IQ: "artist" had a mean score of 115, and a range from 82 to 139; "musician" had a mean of 111, and a range of 56 to 147. Ibid.

33. Ann Roe, "A Psychological Study of Eminent Psychologists and Anthropologists and a Comparison with Biological and Physical Scientists," *Psychological Monographs* 67, no. 352 (1953): 52.

34. B. Meer and M. I. Stein, "Measures of Intelligence and Creativity," *Journal of Psychology* 39 (1955): 117–26.

35. L. R. Harmon, "The Development of a Criterion of Scientific Competence," in *Scientific Creativity*.

36. Donald W. MacKinnon, "The Nature and Nurture of Creative Talent," *American Psychologist* 17, no. 7 (July 1962): 487–88. Scores are summarized more completely in Frank Barron, *Creative Person and Creative Process* (New York: Holt, Rinehart and Winston, 1969), Ch. 4.

37. Ibid., p. 42. Both groups were administered the Wechsler Adult Intelligence Scale (WAIS) and both produced mean scores close to 130. Each group consisted of 40 persons. A third control group not matched for age also produced a mean score of around 130.

38. H. G. Gough, "Techniques for Identifying the Creative Research Scientist," in *The Creative Person*, IPAR, pp. III-1 to III-27 (1961).

39. Barron, *Creative Person*, p. III-34.

40. For example, a recent study of elementary school children reports that mental age on the Stanford-Binet IQ Test correlates .81 with overall score on the total battery of California Achievement Tests. Correlations of mental age with scores on the Wide Range Achievement Tests all are in the .70's. See Ernest D. Washington and James A. Teska, "Correlations Between the Wide Range Achievement Test, the California Achievement Tests, the Stanford-Binet and the Illinois Test of Psycholinguistic Abilities," *Psychological Reports* 26 (1970): 291–94.

41. Edwin E. Ghiselli, *The Validity of Occupational Aptitude Tests* (New York: Wiley, 1966), p. 121.

42. David McClelland, "Testing for Competence Rather than for 'Intelligence'," *American Psychologist* (January 1973), reprinted in *The New Assault on Equality.*
43. Ibid., pp. 3–4.
44. Quotation is from Irving Taylor, cited in *The New Assault on Equality*, p. 206.
45. Anne Anastasi, *Psychological Testing* (New York: Macmillan, 1968), p. 212. Anastasi and Lee J. Cronbach are generally considered the two foremost authorities on psychological testing. Cronbach's position on the validity of IQ tests is similar. In the most recent edition of his *Essentials of Psychological Testing* (New York: Harper and Row, 1970), he echoes this sentiment (pp. 290–91) and slants the evidence in favor of it. Harmon's, MacKinnon's and Gough's findings about the limited predictive validity of IQ tests all are ignored. Ghiselli's findings are reviewed, but in an unusual manner. Cronbach endorses Ghiselli's criterion that any correlation above +0.25 constitutes "high" predictive validity for IQ tests as predictors of job proficiency. Regarding the limited utility of school grades for predicting future accomplishments, Cronbach cites the Holland and Richards study, but ignores Hoyt's review of the literature and all the studies it summarizes.

Notes to Chapter 7

1. A fifth kind of evidence, the apparent inbreeding depression of IQ scores, is not mentioned here because the case for it is very weak and it has been criticized effectively elsewhere. See Leon Kamin, *The Science and Politics of IQ* (New York: Wiley, 1974), pp. 171–73.
2. Arthur Jensen, "How Much Can We Boost IQ and Scholastic Achievement?" in *Genetics and Education,* ed. Jensen (London, Methuen, 1972), pp. 105, 126–27.
3. One critique is found in the appendix of John Loehlin, Gardner Lindzey, and J. N. Spuhler, *Race Differences in Intelligence* (San Francisco, W. H. Freeman, 1975), pp. 292–99. The most comprehensive critique thus far available is D. W. Fulker, "Review of *The Science and Politics of IQ*," *American Journal of Psychology* 88, no. 3 (1975): 505–19.

    Both reviews attempt to discredit Kamin's work as much as possible, so that it can be dismissed. Hence the general derogatory conclusions should not be taken too seriously. The authors succeed in exposing Kamin's tendency to exaggerate the depth of certain ambiguities and the plausibility of some alternative hypotheses, and it is these specific criticisms which should be taken into account when reading Kamin.

4. For example, F. S. Fehr, "Critique of Hereditarian Accounts of 'Intelligence' and Contrary Findings: A Reply to Jensen," in Editors of the *Harvard Educational Review, Science, Heritability and IQ,* Summer 1969, esp. p. 41.

5. Kamin, *Science and Politics,* p. 97.

6. Ibid., p. 88.

7. Nicholas Wade, "IQ and Heredity: Suspicion of Fraud Beclouds Classic Experiment," *Science* 194 (November 26, 1976): 916–919.

8. Kamin, *Science and Politics,* pp. 85–95.

9. Ibid., pp. 175–76.

10. Ibid., p. 132.

11. For a persuasive argument that the significance of the confound is exaggerated, see Fulker, "Review of *The Science and Politics of IQ.*"

12. See the informative essay by Herbert G. Birch, "Boldness and Judgment in Behavior Genetics," in *Science and the Concept of Race,* eds. Margaret Mead, T. Dobzhansky, E. Tobach, and R. Light (New York: Columbia University Press, 1968), pp. 49–58.

13. R. J. Light and P. V. Smith, "Social Allocation Models of Intelligence," in *Harvard Educational Review, Science, Heritability and IQ* (Summer 1969): 1–27.

14. David Layzer, "Science or Superstition? (A Physical Scientist Looks at the IQ Controversy)," in *The Fallacy of IQ,* ed. Carl Senna (New York: Third Press, 1973), p. 125.

15. Criticism of the heritability concept usually is traced back as far as Jane Loevinger's article, "On the Proportional Contributions of Differences in Nature and Nurture to Differences in Intelligence," *Psychological Bulletin* 40 (1943): 725–56.

16. Arthur Jensen, *Educability and Group Differences* (London: Methuen, 1973), Ch. 2, and Richard Herrnstein, *IQ in the Meritocracy* (Boston: Little, Brown, 1973), p. 41.

17. For a quantitative description of the unequal distribution of rewards and punishments in a single classroom, see Ray C. Rist, "Student Social Class and Teacher Expectations: The Self-Fulfilling Prophesy in Ghetto Education," *Harvard Educational Review,* August 1970, pp. 411–51. The article also lists a number of studies showing the effects of teachers' expectations on student performance. See pp. 412–13 and bibliography.

18. This idea will be discussed in greater detail in chapter 13.
19. Arnold Gesell, "Maturation and Infant Behavior Pattern," in *Children with Learning Problems,* ed. Selma Sapir and Ann Nitzburg (New York: Brunner/Mazel, 1973), pp. 9–18.
20. The higher figure is from Arthur Jensen, "Boost IQ?" The lower one is from Christopher Jencks. Jencks's overall estimate was .45 plus or minus .20. When Jencks and associates applied Jensen's formula for calculating heritability to five types of comparisons based upon three different sets of data, they computed heritability coefficients ranging from .40 to .98. Christopher Jencks et al., *Inequality: A Reassessment of the Effect of Family and Schooling in America* (New York: Basic Books, 1972), p. 294.

Notes to Chapter 8

1. Arthur Jensen, *Genetics and Education* (London: Methuen, 1972), p. 161.
2. The term *qualitative* refers to the fact that all blacks were considered by their very nature inferior to all whites. A quantitative difference hold that blacks on the average are inferior to whites on the average, but that there is some overlap in the two distributions.
3. Thomas Gossett, *Race: The History of an Idea in America* (New York: Schocken, 1965), Chs. 1 and 4, especially. Also see John Higham, *Strangers in the Land* (New York: Antheum, 1967) and John Haller, *Outcasts from Evolution* (New Brunswick, N.J.: Rutgers University Press, 1963).
4. Leon Kamin, *The Science and Politics of IQ,* Ch. 2. See also Allan Chase, *The Legacy of Malthus* (New York: Knopf, 1977), Ch. 12.
5. See discussion in Russell Marks, "Race and Immigration: The Politics of Intelligence Testing," in *Shaping the American Educational State,* ed. Clarence Karier (New York: Macmillan, 1975), pp. 327–28. Brigham's repudiation is contained in C. C. Brigham, "Intelligence Tests of Immigrant Groups," *Psychological Review* (1930): 165. His original study had been entitled *A Study of American Intelligence* (Princeton, N.J.: Princeton University Press, 1923).
6. Evelyn Sharp, *The IQ Cult* (New York: Coward, McCann and Geoghegan, 1972), p. 78.
7. Anne Anastasi, *Psychological Testing* (New York: Macmillan, 1976), p. 224.
8. Lewis M. Terman, "Were We Born That Way?" in *Shaping the*

American Educational State, ed. Clarence Karier (New York: Macmillan, 1975), pp. 205–06.

9. Marks, "Race and Immigration," p. 330.

10. See Allison Davis, *Social Class Influences Upon Learning* (Cambridge, Mass.: Harvard University Press, 1948). Included on the inter-disciplinary committee were Robert Havighurst, Ralph W. Tyler, W. Lloyd Warner, Lee J. Cronbach, and others. Marks, "Race and Immigration," p. 333.

11. During the 1950s Terman privately expressed doubts about the validity of his earlier position. See Ernest R. Hilgard, "Lewis Madison Terman," *American Journal of Psychology* (1957).

12. The relation of testers' ideas to the larger social climate is discussed in Lee J. Cronbach's recent article, "Five Decades of Public Controversy over Mental Testing," *American Psychologist* 30, no. 1 (January 1975): 1–14.

13. This view is summarized in William Labov, "The Logic of Nonstandard English," in *The Politics of Literature: Dissenting Essays on the Teaching of English,* eds. Louis Kampf and Paul Lauter (New York: Vintage, 1972), p. 194.

14. Ibid.

15. Ibid., p. 238.

16. John J. Gumperz and Eduardo Hernandez-Chavez, "Bilingualism, Bidialecticism, and Classroom Interaction," in *Functions of Language in the Classroom,* eds. Courtney B. Cazden, Vera P. John, and Dell Hymes (New York: Teachers College Press, 1972), p. 100.

17. Average scores were 87 for blacks and 51 for whites when the test was administered to 100 subjects in each group, ranging in age from 16 to 18. George D. Jackson, "On the Report of the Ad Hoc Committee on Educational Uses of Tests with Disadvantaged Students: Another Psychological View from the Association of Black Psychologists," *American Psychologist* 30, no. 1 (January 1975): 89.

18. See, for example, T. Cleary, L. Humphreys, S. Kendrick, and A. Wesman, "Educational Uses of Tests with Disadvantaged Students," *American Psychologist* 30, no. 1 (January 1975): 15–41. This report was prepared at the request of the American Psychological Association's Board of Scientific Affairs.

19. This approach and several others are summarized in Nancy S. Cole, "Bias in Selection," *Journal of Educational Measurement* 10, no. 4 (Winter 1973): 237–55.

20. Arthur Jensen, *Educability and Group Differences* (London:

Methuen, 1973), pp. 301–02. The tests have been revised since their original publication, Raven's in 1947 and Cattell's in 1960. The other less popular approach to devising culture-fair tests has been to design ones which require fine discriminations in meaning among generally familiar word items.

21. John E. Milholland, "Review of Culture Fair Intelligence Test," in *Mental Measurement Yearbook,* ed. Oscar Buros, 6th ed. (1965) (Highland Park, N.J.: Gryphon Press, 1938–1972), no. 453, p. 719.

22. First is Abraham Tannenbaum, "Review of Culture Fair Intelligence Test," in *Mental Measurement Yearbook* (1965), no. 454. Second is Milholland, in *Mental Measurement Yearbook* (1965), no. 453, p. 720.

23. First is Martin Bortner, "Review of Progressive Matrices Test," in *Mental Measurement Yearbook* (1965), no. 490. Second is George Westby, "Review of Progressive Matrices Test," in *Mental Measurement Yearbook,* 4th ed. (1953), no. 314.

24. In Cattell's test manual the evidence for high g-factor loading appears to be deliberately exaggerated. Milholland writes, "One who tries to check these data [cited by the manual], however, is in for a frustrating experience. I was unable to locate a number of the references, and the ones I did find did not provide the information cited." "Review of Culture Fair," p. 719.

25. Anne Anastasi, quoted in Richard D. Arvey, "Some Comments on Culture Fair Tests," *Personnel Psychology* 25, no. 3 (1972): 433–48.

26. Tannenbaum, "Culture Fair Test," p. 722.

27. Westby, "Progressive Matrices Test."

28. Frank Riessman, "The Hidden IQ," in *The New Assault on Equality,* ed. Gartner, Greer, and Riessman, pp. 206–23. The theoretical problem of motivation and anxiety in test situations is examined and discussed in John W. Atkinson, Willy Lens, and P. M. O'Malley, "Motivation and Ability: Interactive Psychological Determinants of Intellective Performance, Educational Achievement, and Each Other," in *Schooling and Achievement in American Society,* ed. Hauser and Featherman (New York: Academic Press, 1976), pp. 29–59.

29. Ernest A. Haggard, "Social Status and Intelligence," in *Genetic Psychology Monographs* No. 49 (1954): pp. 141–86.

30. Raymond B. Cattell, *Abilities: Their Structure, Growth, and Action* (Boston: Houghton-Mifflin, 1971), pp. 80, 98.

31. Donald O. Hebb, "The Effect of Early and Late Brain Injury Upon

Test Scores," *Proceedings of the American Philosophical Society,* vol. 85 (November 1941–September 1942), p. 287. Hebb did much reputable work, but was not entirely immune to the persuasive effect of pseudoscience. See Donald Hebb, *The Organization of Behavior* (New York: Wiley, 1957), Ch. 11.

32. The selection of factors often involves considerable subjectivity on the part of the investigators, hence the method of factor analysis is readily subject to abuse. See J. Scott Armstrong and Peer Solberg, "On the Interpretation of Factor Analysis," *Psychological Bulletin* 70, no. 5 (1968): 361–64.

33. Cattell, *Abilities,* pp. 75–80.

34. Ibid., p. 80. Both the italics and the quotation marks around "clicked into place" are Cattell's.

35. Ibid., p. 428.

Notes to Chapter 9

1. The article was originally published in the *Harvard Educational Review* (Winter 1969) and has subsequently been reprinted in full in Arthur Jensen, *Genetics and Education* (London: Methuen, 1972).

2. Cyril Burt, "Mental Capacity and Its Critics," *Bulletin of the British Psychological Society* 21, no. 70 (January 1968): 18.

3. Jensen, *Genetics and Education,* p. 8.

4. Michael Katz, *The Irony of Early School Reform* (New York: Praeger, 1971), p. 208.

5. Hans Eysenck, *The IQ Argument* (New York: Library Press, 1971), and Richard Herrnstein, *IQ in the Meritocracy* (Boston: Little, Brown, 1973). Herrnstein's major contribution, apart from preparing an easy-to-read version of the basic hereditarian argument, has been to focus explicitly on the concept of meritocracy. His syllogisms about meritocracy will be considered briefly in Ch. 12 of this work, "The Ideological Dimension."

6. William Shockley is the most emphatic and explicit regarding eugenics. See his "Dysgenics—A Social-Problem Reality Evaded by the Illusion of Infinite Plasticity of Human Intelligence?" in *Shaping the American Educational State,* ed. Clarence Karier (New York: Macmillan, 1975), pp. 409–17. Karier briefly discusses Shockley's sterilization plan on page 408.

   The authors of *Race Differences in Intelligence* mention the possibility of dysgenic trends several times, but do not dwell upon the issue or propose a solution. Jensen writes in his book, *Educa-*

tional Differences (London: Methuen, 1973) (p. 352) that the worry about the nation's biological intelligence declining is "a possible serious social trend," about which there should not be "unwarranted complacency." Jensen expresses (p. 354) particular concern that the intelligence of American blacks may be declining.

7. Two companion volumes to Jensen's article in the *Harvard Educational Review* (Spring and Summer, 1969) bring out some of the errors. Many are listed in rapid succession in Jerry Hirsch's pungent critique, "Jensenism: The Bankruptcy of 'Science' Without Scholarship," *Educational Theory* 30, no. 1 (Winter 1975): 3–27. Leon Kamin's *The Science and Politics of IQ* (New York: Wiley, 1974) contains repeated critical references to both Jensen and Herrnstein.

8. Jensen, *Genetics and Education*, pp. 7–8.

9. Jensen, "How Much Can We Boost IQ and Scholastic Achievement?" in *Genetics and Education* p. 88.

10. Of the data cited in Ch. 6 of this book to evaluate the correctness of the meritocracy interpretation, Jensen cites only Ghiselli's correlations with trainability and performance. These he accepts at face value, not questioning the source of the correlations.

11. Jensen, "Boost IQ?" in *Genetics and Education,* p. 88.

12. Ibid., p. 202.

13. Arthur Jensen, *Educability and Group Differences* (London: Methuen, 1973), p. 75.

14. Ibid., p. 89.

15. John Loehlin, Gardner Lindzey, and J. N. Spuhler, *Race Differences in Intelligence* (San Francisco: W. H. Freeman, 1974), pp. 49–51.

16. Ibid., p. 246.

17. Jensen, *Group Differences,* pp. 291–320.

18. Loehlin, Lindzey, and Spuhler, *Race Differences,* pp. 64–65.

19. Ibid., p. 71.

20. The critique is directed toward an earlier and more limited version of Kamin's work, entitled "Heredity, Intelligence, Politics and Psychology." This essay is reprinted in *American Educational State,* pp. 367–93. Loehlin, Lindzey, and Spuhler point out that the material on separated twins and adopted children is similar in the two works, so criticisms of the essay would also apply to the book, but "would fall short of doing it full justice" (*Race Differences,* p. 299).

21. Loehlin, Lindzey, and Spuhler, *Race Differences,* p. 84.

22. Ibid., p. 294.
23. Ibid., p. 298.
24. Ibid., p. 299.
25. Burt generally maintained that for Caucasians in Britain IQ scores had a heritability of .87. But then his procedures are known to have been invalid, and actual fraud is suspected.
26. Jensen, *Group Differences,* p. 49.
27. Ibid.
28. Jensen, "Boost IQ?," pp. 111–14.
29. Covariance and correlation are related but not identical. Correlation is a measure of the extent to which two variables vary together. Covariance is the amount of variation in some third variable determined jointly by the first two. In general, the higher the correlation between two variables, the larger will be the effect of their covariance. The higher the correlation of genotype and environment, the greater will be the percentage of variation in IQ score determined by genotype-environment covariance.
30. Jensen, "Boost IQ?," p. 110.
31. Ibid., p. 111.
32. Loehlin, Lindzey, and Spuhler, *Race Differences,* p. 87.
33. Ibid., p. 88.
34. Ibid., p. 115.
35. Jensen, *Group Differences,* p. 363.
36. Loehlin, Lindzey, and Spuhler, *Race Differences,* pp. 238–39. Key parts of the definition are quoted on page 8 of this manuscript.
37. Ibid., p. 258.
38. The estimate is made by Richard C. Lewontin, "The Apportionment of Human Diversity," in *Evolutionary Biology,* ed. Th. Dobzhansky, M. Hecht, and W. Steere, vol. 6, pp. 381–98. Cited in Loehlin, Lindzey, and Spuhler, *Race Differences,* p. 37.
39. Loehlin, Lindzey, and Spuhler, *Race Differences,* pp. 120–33.
40. Ibid., p. 133.
41. Two writers presenting this typology are Hans Eysenck, *The IQ Argument,* and Raymond Cattell, *Abilities: Their Structure, Growth and Action* (Boston: Houghton Mifflin, 1971).

Notes to Chapter 10

1. Quoted in Philip E. Vernon, "Review of the Remote Associates Test" in *Mental Measurement Yearbook,* ed. Oscar Buros, 7th ed. (1972) (Highland Park, N.J.: Gryphon Press, 1938–1972), no. 445.
2. Quoted in George K. Bennett, "Review of the Remote Associates

Test," in *Mental Measurement Yearbook* (1972), no. 445.

3. Michael Wallach, "Review of the Torrance Tests of Creative Thinking," in *Mental Measurement Yearbook* (1972), no. 448.

4. Extensive evidence related to subtest intercorrelations and test-retest reliability is summarized in Michael Wallach, "Creativity," in *Carmichael's Manual of Child Psychology,* ed. Paul Mussen, 3rd ed., vol. 1 (New York: Wiley, 1970), pp. 1211–72. The Guilford tests were intended primarily for use with adults, and the Torrance tests for use with children.

5. Donald W. MacKinnon, "The Study of Creative Persons," in *Creativity and Learning,* ed. Jerome Kagan (Boston: Houghton Mifflin, 1967), p. 32.

6. John L. Holland, "Review of the Torrance Tests of Creative Thinking," in *Mental Measurement Yearbook* (1972), no. 448.

7. The RAT Manual lists correlations of .55 and .70 for 43 psychology and 20 architecture students respectively (1967).

8. Susan B. Crockenberg, "Creativity Tests: A Boon or Boondoggle for Education?" *Review of Educational Research,* vol. 42, no. 1, lists a number of studies which make this point. Particularly striking is John L. Holland, "Some Limitations of Teacher Ratings as Predictors of Creativity," *Journal of Educational Psychology* 50 (1959): 219–23.

9. These are listed in Leonard L. Baird, "Review of the Remote Associates Test," in *Mental Measurement Yearbook* (1972), no. 445.

10. For results with the Baron-Welsh Art Scale and measures of unusual word associations, see Donald W. MacKinnon, "The Nature and Nurture of Creative Talent," *American Psychologist* 17, no. 7 (July 1962).

11. See, for example, Frank Barron, *Creative Person and Creative Process* (New York: Holt, Rinehart and Winston, 1969), Ch. 6, for information about personality ratings, and Donald W. MacKinnon, "Creativity and Images of the Self," in *The Study of Lives,* ed. R. W. White, pp. 250–78, for self-descriptions. The significance of this evidence will be discussed in Ch. 13.

12. E. P. Torrance, "Curiosity of Gifted Children and Performance on Timed and Untimed Tests of Creativity," *Gifted Child Quarterly* 13, no. 3 (1969): 155–58.

13. H. Wallace, "Tests of Creative Thinking and Sales Performance in a Large Department Store," in *Creativity: 2nd Minnesota Conference on Gifted Children,* ed. E. P. Torrance (Minneapolis, Minn.: University of Minnesota Center for Continuing Study, 1960).

14. Lee J. Cronbach, *Essentials of Psychological Testing* (New York: Harper and Row, 1970), p. 395.
15. Robert L. Thorndike, "Review of the Torrance Tests of Creative Thinking," in *Mental Measurement Yearbook* (1972), no. 448.
16. See, for example, Paul Goodman's *Growing Up Absurd* (New York: Random House, 1956) and *Compulsory Miseducation* (New York: Vintage Books, 1966).
17. E. P. Torrance presented this argument very explicitly in *Guiding Creative Talent* (Englewood Cliffs, N.J.: Prentice-Hall, 1962).

Notes to Chapter 11

1. A notable instance is described in Ashley Schiff's *Fire and Water: Heresy in the Forest Service* (Cambridge, Mass.: Harvard University Press, 1962).
2. Nazi racist ideology developed on a large enough scale, but bore too little resemblance to scientific theory and hypothesis testing, and thus does not fully merit the designation of grand pseudo-science. The kind of sexual mythologizing described in Alex Comfort's *The Anxiety Makers* (New York: Dell, 1967) likewise seems to lack sufficient pretense of scientific verification.

   It is to be emphasized that not *all* of psychometrics or behavior genetics is pseudoscience. The latter has developed extensively within these fields, but it would be erroneous to call the fields themselves pseudosciences.
3. The three major books about Lysenkoism are, in order of importance, David Joravsky, *The Lysenko Affair* (Cambridge, Mass.: Harvard University Press, 1970); Zhores Medvedev, *The Rise and Fall of T. D. Lysenko* (New York: Columbia University Press, 1969); and Julian Huxley, *Heredity, East and West* (New York: H. Schuman, 1949).

   Only Joravsky's book makes a serious attempt to analyze the causes of Lysenkoism. Consequently it has been the most helpful for this chapter. The information about Lysenkoism in the chapter has been taken from these three sources. Only points which are particularly central or controversial will be footnoted.
4. Joravsky, *Lysenko Affair,* pp. 92–93, 126.
5. Ibid., p. 165.
6. Ibid., p. 126.
7. This analysis is put forward by Thomas Kuhn, *The Structure of Scientific Revolutions* (Chicago: University of Chicago Press, 1970). For several thoughtful discussions of Kuhn's work, see the

recent volume, *Criticism and the Growth of Knowledge,* ed. Imre Lakatos and Alan Musgrave (Cambridge, England: Cambridge University Press, 1970).

8. Medvedev, *T. D. Lysenko,* p. 170.

9. The biochemical discoveries which have made Lamarckian inheritance seem more conceivable are described briefly in the epilogue of Arthur Koestler's *The Case of the Midwife Toad* (New York: Vintage, 1971).

10. This passage is based upon the conventional assumption that Paul Kammerer did not succeed in his attempt to demonstrate Lamarckian inheritance in the laboratory. Koestler suggests that Kammerer's work may well have been valid, but even conceding that work's validity would not necessarily present a strong case for Lamarckian inheritance, since other explanations of the results are possible.

11. Joravsky, *Lysenko Affair,* p. 157, mentions that the hazelnut limb growing out of hornbeans appeared to be deliberate fraud, while the rye seeds mixed in with wheat plants most likely was the product of self-deception. Looking at the heritability data we may surmise that the reporting of Burt's adjusted figures as actual test scores was probably intentional distortion, whereas the failure to consider some of the statistical issues raised by Kamin probably involved unintentional errors.

12. My own personal experience attests to this for one major restorationist, Arthur Jensen.

13. Lee J. Cronbach points out that in Terman's response to Lippmann, some statements were defended vehemently even though Terman privately considered them only working hypotheses. He "apparently saw Lippmann as a presumptuous layman to be routed." Lee J. Cronbach, "Five Decades of Public Controversy Over Mental Testing," *American Psychologist* 30, no. 1 (January 1975): 10.

14. Since Stalin was primarily interested in imposing conformity to his bureaucratic rule in the arts and sciences, he was all too ready to oblige Lysenko's requests for repression of scientific opponents.

15. Loehlin, Lindzey, and Spuhler mention that they initially had difficulty getting their project funded, but that generous support eventually came from the U.S. Office of Child Development, the director of which—Professor Edward F. Zigler of Yale University— was sympathetic to the project. *Race Differences in Intelligence* (San Francisco: W. H. Freeman, 1975), p. ix.

16. Ernest Hilgard, "Lewis Madison Terman," *American Journal of Psychology*, 1957.
17. Joravsky's book has a lengthy appendix listing the names of repressed specialists.
18. For a discussion of the distinction between old and new middle classes see C. Wright Mills's *White Collar* (New York: Oxford University Press, 1950).
19. Joravsky, *Lysenko Affair*, p. 74.
20. This point is made by Warren Hagstrom, *The Scientific Community* (New York: Basic Books, 1965).
21. Joravsky, *Lysenko Affair*, p. 201.
22. The "ensuing criticism" referred to here is contained in the two companion volumes which followed Jensen's article in the *Harvard Educational Review*. See the Spring and Summer 1969 issues of that journal.
23. The latter point is made in all three books about Lysenkoism. Also see Michael Polanyi, *The Logic of Liberty* (Chicago: University of Chicago Press, 1951).
24. These recent discoveries bear no direct logical relation to the ideas disseminated by pseudoscience. It is simply that dramatic progress in biology and genetics tends to make people more excited about biological, genetic explanations in general.

Notes to Chapter 12

1. Nicholas Pastore, *The Nature-Nurture Controversy* (New York: King's Crown Press, 1949), esp. pp. 176–77.
2. Russell Marks, "Race and Immigration: The Politics of Intelligence Testing," in *Shaping the American Educational State*, ed. Clarence Karier (New York: Macmillan, 1975), pp. 316–42.
3. Bowles and Gintis use the phrase, "meritocratic ideology" in recent works, including their new book, *Schooling in Capitalist America* (New York: Basic Books, 1976). Schwendinger and Schwendinger use the terms, "meritarian argument" and "meritarian perspective" in *The Sociologists of the Chair* (New York: Basic Books, 1974). In any case, the meanings are similar.
4. Elements of meritocratic ideology appeared in the writings of some philosophers of classical antiquity. To speak of the ideology originating in the bourgeoisie's struggles for political power means that the modern versions can be traced to philosophical debates surrounding such struggles, and that the ideology's polemical value in

waging the struggles is largely responsible for the popularity it developed.

This chapter's discussion of the development of meritocratic ideology follows lines established by many thinkers, the first and most important of which was Karl Marx.

5. For a comparison of the processes of social change in the two countries, see Barrington Moore, *Social Origins of Dictatorship and Democracy* (Boston: Beacon, 1966), Chs. 1 and 2.

6. A succinct discussion of Malthus and Spencer can be found in Schwendinger and Schwendinger, *Sociologists,* pp. 29–57. Much in the next two paragraphs is taken from their discussion.

7. The statement is from Galton's *Hereditary Genius.* The quotation in full can be found on page 27 of this [*Pseudoscience and Mental Ability*] book.

8. Schwendinger and Schwendinger, *Sociologists,* p. 109.

9. Lester Ward, "Education," in *American Educational State,* p. 145.

10. Ibid., p. 151.

11. There were, of course, other reasons for the expansion as well. For discussions which consider the motive of social control, see two books by Michael Katz, *The Irony of Early School Reform* (Cambridge, Mass.: Harvard University Press, 1966), and *Class, Bureaucracy and Schools* (New York: Praeger, 1971). See also Bowles and Gintis, *Schooling in Capitalist America.*

12. J. H. Westergaard makes this point in "Sociology: The Myth of Classlessness," in *Ideology in Social Science,* ed. Robin Blackburn, p. 131.

13. The term *scholastic meritocracy* has two analytically separable meanings. The stronger meaning relates to Galton's vision of schools-as-proving grounds. It contends that schools provide all individuals with fair opportunities for success, and do not systematically bias the likelihood of success in favor of some individuals and against others. The weaker meaning merely contends that schools generally reward talent, and on the whole do not discriminate unfairly on the basis of social class, race, or other demographic variables. The two meanings are related. If the stronger were true, then the weaker would clearly be true as well. Theoretically the stronger could be false and the weaker true if the discrimination were distributed randomly across variables like race and class.

The discussion which follows questions the stronger meaning by piecing together evidence and reasoning which suggest that significant discrimination may be inherent in the process of unequal scholastic performance. The evidence is only suggestive, and further research is warranted on each of the points. Moreover, a serious evaluation of the weaker meaning of scholastic meritocracy would require attention to large-scale quantitative studies not mentioned. But a discussion of the stronger meaning provides the most direct way of illuminating the ideological nature of the scholastic meritocracy conception. The discussion certainly does not disprove the conception's weaker version. The only connection is this: to the extent that the stronger meaning is acknowledged to be false, the plausibility of the weaker meaning is reduced, because children from the lower classes and racial minority groups tend on the whole to perform poorly in school, and to the extent that there is unfair discrimination against poor students it is likely that they would receive a disproportionate share of it.

14. For a quantitative description of the unequal distribution of rewards and punishments in a single classroom, see Ray C. Rist, "Student Social Class and Teacher Expectations: The Self-Fulfilling Prophesy in Ghetto Education," *Harvard Educational Review,* August 1970, pp. 411–51. The article also lists a number of studies showing the effects of teacher's expectations on student performance. See pp. 412–13 and the bibliography.

    For a quantitative description of discrepancies across classrooms composed of different types of student bodies, see Eleanor Burke Leacock, *Teaching and Learning in City Schools* (New York: Basic Books, 1969). Leacock's results, while generally in line with this statement, suggest that characteristics of particular teachers will make a significant difference for the frequency of specific types of responses.

15. The most highly publicized study of effects of teachers' expectations is Rosenthal and Jacobson's *Pygmalion in the Classroom: Teacher Expectation and Pupils' Intellectual Development* (New York: Holt, Rinehart and Winston, 1965). This study has a number of methodological defects and has been strongly criticized. At most the authors were able to establish the effect on IQ test scores for the first two grades. However, both they and their critics point out that numerous studies have shown the effect clearly using other measures of scholastic achievement. These conclusions are drawn from J. Elashoff and R. Snow, *Pygmalion Reconsidered* (Worthington, Ohio: C. A. Jones Publishing Co., 1971); this work being the most extensive critique of the original Pygmalion experiment.

16. Many of the ideas in this paragraph are taken from John Holt, *How Children Fail* (New York: Pittman, 1964).

17. Gerald Levy, *Ghetto School* (New York: Pegasus, 1970), pp. 85–86. For additional first hand descriptions of interaction in ghetto schools, see Leacock, *City Schools*; William Ryan, *Blaming the Victim* (New York: Vintage Books, 1972); Jonathan Kozol, *Death at an Early Age* (Boston: Houghton-Mifflin, 1967); James Herndon, *The Way It Spozed To Be* (New York: Bantam Books, 1969); and Charles Silberman, *Crisis in the Classroom* (New York: Random House, 1970).

18. Levy, *Ghetto School*.

19. There are, however, numerous exceptions to both the stability of IQ scores and the stability of school performance. IQ scores on the average are somewhat more stable than school marks because the latter depends primarily upon recent learning whereas IQ scores are based extensively upon retesting of knowledge acquired several years before. If a child's motivation improves dramatically, the effect will be most apparent in comparisons of new knowledge with old; improvements in performance on tasks requiring old knowledge will be less dramatic.

20. Levy, *Ghetto School*.

21. The importance of home environment has been well documented. The importance of genetic differences remains a speculative issue, hence they are not mentioned here. To the extent that they are important, what is said would apply to them, too.

22. For informative discussions of the problem of cultural bias, see Leacock, *City Schools,* Ch. 3; also, Ryan, *Blaming,* Ch. 2, and Frank Riessman, *The Culturally Deprived Child* (New York: Harper, 1962). The opprobrium directed at most cultural deprivation theorists does not apply to Riessman. Also, note the article by Stephen and Joan Baratz, "Early Childhood Intervention: The Social Science Base of Institutional Racism," *Harvard Educational Review* 40, no. 1 (Winter 1970): 29–50.

23. Several informative studies are summarized in A. Morrison and D. McIntyre, *Schools and Socialization* (Harmondsworth, England: Penguin, 1971), esp. Ch. 1, "The Home Environment." There are some disadvantages, the inherency of which is difficult to assess. For example, Basil Bernstein's provocative distinction between restricted and elaborated linguistic codes (see Bernstein, "A Sociolinguistic Approach to Socialization; with Some Reference to Educability," in *Directions in Sociolinguistics,* ed. Gumperz and

Hymes, pp. 465–97) suggests that speech patterns in lower class homes leave children unprepared to think abstractly and profit from classroom interaction. It is difficult to know the extent to which this is true.

24. Sarason's discussion of programmatic and behavioral regularities is highly relevant to this point. See Seymour B. Sarason, *The Culture of the School and the Problem of Change* (Chicago: Allyn and Bacon, 1971), Ch. 6.

25. This is the central message of Bowles and Gintis, *Schooling in Capitalist America.*

26. "Established by the economy" does not mean that they are functionally designed to meet economic needs of the society, but rather, that they set by the decisions of the dominant economic units (i.e., corporations) regardless of overall effect on the society. The American Medical Association's regulation of admissions to medical school provides a good example of the number of desirable jobs being regulated by a privileged interest group.

27. The necessity of their conforming can be accounted for in different ways. An instrumentalist explanation would stress the importance of the capitalist class's political domination of the society enabling it to control school boards and thus appoint high-ranking administrators with values similar to their own. Thus the teacher faces a bureaucratic authority which demands compliance. A structuralist explanation would emphasize economic conditions confronting the school with an established situation which structures the interests of all parties, so the only rational thing to do is to prepare the mass of lower class children for lower class employment. To do otherwise would be to leave them poorly adapted for their probable life experiences. Either explanation points to the conclusion that conditions in school are not likely to change much outside of the context of a general political insurgency which challenges basic economic conditions as well.

28. Richard Herrnstein, *IQ in the Meritocracy* (Boston: Little, Brown, 1971), pp. 201–202.

29. Ibid., p. 221.

30. Ibid., pp. 208–09.

31. Ibid., p. 220.

32. Ibid.

33. Ibid., p. 211.

34. Noam Chomsky, "IQ Tests: Building Blocks for the New Class System," in *American Educational State,* p. 401.
35. See Max Weber, "Bureaucracy," pp. 196–244, in *From Max Weber,* ed. Hans Gerth and C. W. Mills (New York: Oxford, 1946).
36. For elaboration of this idea, see Karl Marx and Friedrich Engels, *The German Ideology* (New York: International Publishers, 1970), and Antonio Gramsci, *The Modern Prince and Other Writings* (New York: International Publishers, 1969).
37. This tendency has been especially strong in the United States and Great Britain, much less so in France and Italy, for example.

Notes to Chapter 13

1. Walter Lippman, "The Reliability of Intelligence Tests," in *Shaping the American Educational State,* ed. Clarence Karier (New York: Macmillan, 1975), pp. 290–91.
2. Terman particularly sought to dispel the notion that genius was frequently accompanied by insanity, and that highly creative persons tended to be physically weak and beset by health problems.
3. See Ernst Kris's discussion of the relationship between artist and public in *Psychoanalytic Explorations in Art* (New York: International Universities Press, 1952).
4. Ann Roe, *The Making of a Scientist* (New York: Dodd-Mead, 1952), final chapter.
5. Francis Galton, *Hereditary Genius* (London: Macmillan, 1869), p. 40.
6. Stephen Spender, "The Making of a Poem," in *The Creative Process,* ed. Brewster Ghiselin (Berkeley, Cal.: University of California Press, 1952).
7. Rosamond Harding, *An Anatomy of Inspiration* (Cambridge, England: W. Heffer, 1948), pp. 19–20, 41.
8. Edward Lasker, *New York Times Magazine,* 24 April 1949, p. 56.
9. Spender, "Making of a Poem," p. 121.
10. Donald W. MacKinnon, "Creativity and Images of the Self," in *The Study of Lives,* ed. R. W. White (New York: Atherton Press, 1963), pp. 250–78. Self-descriptions were administered by a Q-sort procedure, with fifty printed cards being arranged from 1 to 50 in order of the person's estimation of their applicability to himself. On the item relating specifically to architectural problems, the rankings were as follows:

	Creative Group	*Other Two Groups*
(1 = most applic.)	2.5	19; 21

Rankings for the other five mentioned were, respectively:

9	4; 6
16.5	17.5; 8.5
19	10; 12.5
21	14; 41.5
43	30; 32

For the source of data concerning their IQ scores, see Donald W. MacKinnon, "The Nature and Nurture of Creative Talent," *American Psychologist* 17, no. 7 (July 1962): 42.

11. Stanley Rosner and Lawrence Abt, *The Creative Experience* (New York: Dell, 1970), p. 385.
12. Aaron Copland, recorded in ibid., p. 274.
13. Quoted in Phyllis Bartlett, *Poems in Process* (New York: Oxford University Press, 1951), p. 19. Bartlett furnishes additional evidence for the idea on pages 19 and 20.
14. See Harding, *Inspiration,* for several descriptions.
15. Quoted in ibid., p. 9.
16. Quoted in ibid., p. 8.
17. Kris, *Psychoanalytic Explorations in Art,* pp. 59, 60. Max Weber makes a similar statement about the universality of inspiration in "Science as a Vocation," in *From Max Weber,* eds. Hans Gerth and C. W. Mills, p. 136. Harding, *Inspiration,* pp. 97–100, makes the point about scientists using several examples.
18. Quotation is from Henri Poincare, "Mathematical Creation," in *The Creative Process,* ed. Ghiselin. Spender, "Making of a Poem," develops the same point.
19. See Kris, *Psychoanalytic Explorations*; Poincare, "Mathematical Creation"; and Lawrence Kubie, *Neurotic Distortion of the Creative Process* (New York: Noonday Press, 1958).
20. Harding, *Inspiration,* p. 32. Harding uses the examples of Einstein, Edison, and Lord Kelvin to support her contention that intuition plays a major role in science.
21. MacKinnon, "The Nature and Nurture of Creative Talent," p. 489. "Intuitive" here means having an orientation toward internal thoughts rather than external things.
22. Ann Roe, "A Psychological Study of Eminent Psychologists and Anthropologists, and a Comparison with Biological and Physical Scientists," *Psychology Monographs* 67, no. 2: 49.

23. MacKinnon, "Creativity and the Self."
24. See the discussion in Ch. 6.
25. Those wishing to gather more detail should go to the sources from which examples have been drawn. Most highly recommended is Harding's *Inspiration,* then Ghiselin's anthology, *Creative Process,* Rosner and Abt's interviews in *Creative Experience,* and Ann Roe's several works on scientists cited earlier.
26. Quoted in Harding, *Inspiration,* p. 1.
27. Sigmund Freud, "The Relation of the Poet to Day-Dreaming," (1908), in Freud, *Character and Culture* (New York: Macmillan, 1963), p. 35.
28. Two writers who stress the importance of a receptive public are Kris, *Psychoanalytic Explorations,* esp. p. 60, and Paul Valery, "The Course in Poetics: First Lesson," in *The Creative Process.* The receptive audience need not include many persons, merely a few whom the artist defines as significant.
29. The *Oxford English Dictionary* traces this evolution of the word. See the entry under "genius."
30. This point is made repeatedly in Anne Anastasi, *Psychological Testing* (New York: Macmillan, 1968).
31. See David McClelland, "Testing for Competence Rather than for 'Intelligence,' " in *The New Assault on Equality,* eds. Gartner, Greer, and Riessman (New York: Harper and Row, 1974), pp. 163–97.

Index